DESTRUCTIVE
RELATIONSHIPS

DESTRUCTIVE
RELATIONSHIPS

A Guide to Changing the
Unhealthy Relationships in Your Life

DR. JILL MURRAY

JODERE
GROUP
SAN DIEGO, CALIFORNIA

JODERE GROUP, INC.
P.O. Box 910147
San Diego, CA 92191-0147
(800) 569-1002
www.jodere.com

Book design by Charles McStravick
Editorial supervision by Chad Edwards

The author of this book does not dispense medical advice or prescribe the use of any techniques as forms of treatment for physical or medical problems without the advice of a physician, either directly or indirectly. The intent of the author is only to offer information of a general nature to help you in your quest for emotional and spiritual well-being. In the event you use any of the information in this book for yourself, which is your constitutional right, the author and the publisher assumes no responsibility for your actions.

Library of Congress Cataloging-in-Publication Data

Murray, Jill, Dr.
    Destructive realtionships / Jill Murray.
        p. cm.
    Includes bibliographical references and index.
    ISBN 1-58872-026-8
        1.Abused women. 2. Abused women--Psychology. 3. Interpersonal relations.
    4. Self-help techniques. 5. self actualization (Psychology) I. Title.

HV6625 .M87 2002
362.82'92--dc21

                                                                                2002073026

ISBN 1-58872-026-8
04 03 02   4 3 2 1
First printing, September 2002

PRINTED IN THE UNITED STATES OF AMERICA

To Frank, who continuously
helps me understand the power
of true love, and Jennifer and
Michael, who help to create
what's pure and true in my life.

Contents

PART ONE

A Whole New Beginning

PART TWO

What Are the Patterns in Your Relationships?

Acknowledgments

THERE ARE SO MANY INCREDIBLE PEOPLE who have helped me on the journey to create this book. Without them, I couldn't have produced what you have here. All of them have nourished me creatively and spiritually, either personally or in my career. There is no true way to thank them in the way I would like because words are inadequate, however I'll give it my best shot.

To my publisher, Debbie Luican: Thank you for believing in my work and helping to create the vision of this book. You took a personal interest in me, and what we were able to accomplish together.

To my agents, Arielle Ford and Brian Hilliard: Thank you for all the rah-rah and enabling me to achieve what I have here. You are always my best advisors and greatest cheering section.

To Stephanie Gunning: I can't tell you how wonderful it is to work with you. You understand everything I am trying to say and reel me in when I get too far astray.

To my editor, Chad Edwards: I'm so happy that you worked on this book with me. You allowed me to keep my own voice and didn't try to change a single bit of who I am. I am so grateful to you.

To Myra Gordon: My sister and friend, you are part of everything I do. If it wasn't for your love and support, I wouldn't be doing any of it half as well.

To Dr. Paul Fick: Without your generosity and belief, I couldn't have achieved any of this. I owe so much to you and will remember it always.

To Judge Pamela Iles: What an inspiration and hero! Your commitment to eradicating abuse of all types has been your life's work. I only hope that one day—with your guidance—I will have even a portion of your courage, intelligence, and stamina. You change so many lives each day.

To Zohreh, Nicki, and Tina: My wonderful gal pals. Where would I be without all of your support, confidence, and trust? You make my world a better place.

To my husband, Dr. Frank Murray III: There are no words that can speak to the love and admiration I have for you. You teach me so much on a daily basis and the intensity of the unconditional love you have for me leaves me speechless. I love you more than I can tell you.

To my children, Jennifer and Michael: You are wonderful people. I am so proud to have been chosen to be your mother. Everything you do amazes me. I love you endlessly.

Foreword

Can You Change the
Abusive Patterns in Your Life?

H OW MANY TIMES HAVE YOU THOUGHT TO YOURSELF: "Why do people walk all over me? I'm a nice person. I try to be kind and helpful. Why am I constantly being treated like a doormat? I'm too smart to keep repeating these types of relationships over and over. Why can't my life change?"

Actually, most of us feel like that. A lot. The reason we are haunted by these questions is quite simple: We may be in destructive relationships.

I know that sounds dramatic, but I caution you against thinking of abuse as a black eye or a broken jaw. While physical violence is a threat for many, which this book briefly covers, it is at the far end of the spectrum. I encourage you to broaden your horizons and think about the many different types of destructive relationships—the subtler interactions that are increasingly common in your everyday life. You may know the ones I am referring to, where seemingly small situations with your boss, mate, friends, and even your children, parents, and siblings leave you feeling sad, angry, confused, and exhausted.

The author of this book, Dr. Jill Murray, writes about many common examples of what women tell themselves when they are in destructive relationships. See if you have any of these thoughts going on:

- "So, my boss is a little demanding. He's a genius and like all geniuses, he's just high-strung and a perfectionist."

- "Of course my husband has never hit me or anything like that. Don't be silly. He had a tough childhood and he is a little judgmental and controlling is all."

- "Okay, my friend and I can talk for an hour on the phone and she barely asks about me, but I'm her best friend and she needs me. Isn't being there for someone else what friendship is all about?"

- "My parents have been critical of me for as long as I can remember. They want me to be my best because they want what's best for me. It's tough, but they are getting on in years and there's no point in trying to change them now. I put up with their insults because it's just easier."

- "My son's a teenager. Sure he swears at me and treats me like dirt. What teenager doesn't have an attitude?"

We all know what it's like to let patterns go unchecked in relationships—as we watch situations that we cocreated run amuck with a life of their own. Maybe your boss has taken advantage of you to the point of making your relationship destructive. Maybe you helped him through a crisis at one time, rushing in to help, only to set a precedent that you were there to serve his life at the expense of your own. Now it's a year or two later and you realize that although aspects of your working together are still successful, your needs are consistently disregarded. This book explains that bending over backwards for someone who treats you badly isn't an example of "loyalty," as you might think, but rather a destructive relationship taking over—even when that someone is your own parent or child.

If these patterns are allowed to spiral, pretty soon you may find that most—if not all—of your relationships are frustrating, energy draining, and possibly even abusive. Your feelings aren't taken seriously, and your needs consistently go unmet. You lack self-confidence and feel worn down, putting yourself at risk for anxiety and even physical illness. As hard as you try to stay positive, you feel anxious and increasingly hopeless about your future.

Now, for the good news: You can change the dance once and for all, and the first step comes about by educating yourself. Your future relationships are under your control, and this book will help you to take charge of how you interact with others and how they interact with you. Instead of giving your pride and self-respect away to those who mistreat you, you will be able to stand for yourself without sacrificing the inherent goodness of who you are. Through this book you will embark on a journey toward authentic empowerment, while relying on the traits you admire most within yourself and others.

I know you're probably identifying with some of what I've just said, but it's likely that you're still not completely aware of how deeply these destructive patterns are affecting your life and the lives of everybody around you. Throughout my years as a journalist and as a media host,

I have met and interviewed countless people in nearly every type of destructive situation imaginable. It still surprises me how rampant destructive relationships are in our society—especially affecting women who appear to "have it all." I have often wondered why we women so easily slip into being taken advantage of without knowing it is happening, even when it's staring us in the face. I hoped to become more educated so that I could shed more light on these issues.

Meeting Dr. Jill Murray was a turning point in my quest to find out more. She was a guest on my talk show, *Leeza*, in 1999 to discuss her powerful work with women in abuse shelters. Her first book, *But I Love Him*, written for teenage girls and their parents, was soon to be released and Dr. Murray was quickly becoming a national expert on the subject of abusive relationships. I was struck by her complete understanding of the complications involved in all destructive relationships, including the lesser abuses that most of us will face in our lives, and trusted her guidance immediately. Soon, other media outlets including the *Oprah* show were backing her work, and it was obvious that she was, and is, enormously helpful at educating and encouraging us all to rise above all types of unhealthy situations.

Through this work, Dr. Murray reveals warning signs—what's common to experience in any relationship, and what's not. If you suspect that you are in a bad situation but aren't sure, it's helpful to know that it's normal to have doubts. You may sense that something is wrong, but be uncertain about how serious your situation really is. Maybe you trust that you're okay, but are getting pressure from people in your life to see what they think is "so obvious." This book will be a great support while you take the necessary steps toward your physical and emotional health, and the healthy development of your children, if you have them.

The chapters ahead will help you to understand the different forms of abuse: verbal, emotional, sexual, and physical, so that you can see what you have lived with and consequently denied and discounted. You will realize the ways in which you have participated in these patterns, including those that started with your parents. "People pleasing" will make the healthy transformation into pleasing yourself, which will ironically bring pleasure to the people in your life that really love you.

Some additional things you can look forward to through using this book are uprooting poor self-esteem issues so that you can reclaim your power; identifying your fears and banishing them through positive steps; naturally letting go of shame and guilt, thereby eliminating the need to keep secrets; establishing boundaries when dealing with an abusive *ex* during child visitations, holidays, and important decision-making times, and freeing yourself from no-win coping behaviors such as denial, minimizing, shopping, overeating, compulsive sex, or drug and alcohol use.

Through goal setting strategies, Dr. Murray will help you to create a beautiful future. She will help you to stay focused on the bigger picture by asking questions like, "Who do you want your children to become?" Your commitment to this work will enable you to model healthier ways of relating to yourself and to the world for your children. The importance of this cannot be stressed enough, because if they have witnessed your involvement in an abusive relationship with their father, your friends, your relatives, or your boss, you have unwittingly taught them poor ways of dealing with others. But now is your chance to rewrite those scripts.

I want to congratulate you for your willingness to stand up for yourself by picking up this book. Dr. Murray will explain that it's not normal to get so "comfortable" with endless demands, criticism or heartache, and it may seem that leaving or changing "the dance" appears as the bigger negative. It takes a lot of courage to look deeply into your life and make room for change. If you see yourself or someone you love in any of these words, I encourage you to continue reading on. You will be amazed by how quickly your thinking and external reality expands. Many people have used the words "magic" and "amazing" to describe their healing experience through this work.

In closing, Dr. Murray is a gift. She has taught me that destructive relationships catch up to the best of us; even the most strong, beautiful and successful women fall prey. But take heart: *it's never too late to break free*, and Dr. Murray's wisdom—gained through helping thousands in similar situations to yours—will show you how.

Many blessings to you for a joyous and healthy future!

— LEEZA GIBBONS
TV AND RADIO HOST, PRODUCER
HOST OF TV'S *EXTRA*

Introduction

YOU ARE ABOUT TO TAKE A FASCINATING JOURNEY. It is a journey that will take you from the beginning of your life to the present day. On this trip, we are going to examine the relationships in your life that have held you back, kept you down, and eroded your self-esteem.

Like many trips you have already taken, there will be moments of great joy, times that you wish you hadn't taken the trip at all and could just go home, and others when you are uncertain of your location or which road to take. Unlike those other trips, however, I can assure you that when you complete this journey, you will not return to the same house; that you will reside in a wonderful new home.

This journey, which you and I are going to travel together, has four distinct destinations. It will benefit you to take mental snapshots of each location along the way, so that you can remember where you were, because hopefully you will never go back there again.

The first stop on our itinerary is called "A Whole New Beginning." In this location, you will find that there is hope in your life, you will learn important concepts to take with you for the rest of the trip, and you will understand what you have experienced in your life up until this point.

The second stop is called "What are the Patterns in Your Relationships?" Here, you will examine the role your parents have played in your life, and learn about unhealthy work environments, unkind friends, and abusive family members.

The third stop on our journey will take you to a locale called "What Happened to Your Life?" It is here that you will begin to rebuild your home. The foundation will be in raising your self-esteem, looking at your emotional fears, dealing with feelings of shame, guilt, and the way you kept secrets, as well as improving your poor coping mechanisms, and looking at your personality types.

At our final stop, "Your Future Looks Great," you have a magnificent new home and here is where you furnish it. We will look at personal empowerment and goal setting strategies, ways to deal with the abusive people in your life and wondering if they can ever change, deciding what you really want for your children now and in the future, and finally, ways to build new and healthy relationships.

Does this sound like an impossibly long journey? Well, it's certainly more than a three-day weekend. You will need more than an overnight case or a duffel bag for this trip. But when you realize the difficult journey you were willing to travel to get to your present location, I think you will find this one much more exciting and rewarding. These are photos you are going to want to keep in a special album in your new home.

I am certain that you picked up this book because you were ready to look at your life and make improvements. I have listed some very important—and I believe, life changing—concepts that will help you steer your life course. I think that these ideas are so powerful, as soon as you "get" them, your life will instantly change in a more positive direction. As you begin practicing them, you will find that not only you, but also all of the relationships around you will transform.

Be kind to yourself while reading this book. A lot of "head garbage" will come up for you that may leave you feeling drained. Allowing those feelings to come up and pushing through them is important; you may have spent the better portion of your lifetime pushing them aside and refusing to deal with them. However, do not push yourself to the point that you are emotionally disabled for long periods of time. It is more important that you look at your life situations, and the ways they have affected you, examine them, deal with them, and go onto the next part. There will be ample time to look at all of these issues as a whole once you have made it to the end of each chapter.

Are your bags packed? Come on, then, let's go!

PART
ONE

A WHOLE NEW
BEGINNING

Introduction

A Whole New Beginning

WHEN WE SPEAK ABOUT DESTRUCTIVE RELATIONSHIPS, we really need to understand what destructive behavior is and the ways it may look in your own life. Being involved in unhealthy relationships is an emotionally and physically depleting experience. Don't you find that when you are in the middle of a confusing situation, it is difficult to see it for what it truly is? Many of us make excuses for our own behavior—and the behavior of others—as a way of life. It may help you get from one day to the next, but it also keeps you stuck. I think you'll be surprised at the many types of destructive behaviors you have been exposed to, often on a daily basis. Learning to recognize them is the first step in your journey to improvement.

Now, as we begin, let me ask you the same question I ask my own private practice patients before we engage in a therapeutic relationship: On a scale of one to ten—with one being not much at all and ten being the greatest you can think of—how important is it to you that you make significant changes in your life today? Be honest; no one is peeking into your brain. This number will help you understand your level of motivation. This number may change as you read this book, or it may change as situations in your life change. Now, let me ask you another question: On that same scale of one to ten—with one being terrible and ten being terrific—how do you emotionally feel today? I am asking because it may also help you to understand your level of commitment to your own growth as well as your level of stamina. Don't you find that when you feel sad or anxious for a long period of time, you also feel physically exhausted?

I'd like you to meet a few women who have already taken the voyage you are beginning. I believe you will gain so much by reading their stories and may feel a sisterhood with them. I usually think that most other women's stories are cleverer than my own and each time I think of the particular ladies you will read about, I learn something else I hadn't thought of previously. Reading their stories will help you identify your own abusive relationship and gain some insight on how to break free.

So, let me not keep you from that task one minute longer!

CHAPTER ONE

Yes, There Is Hope

WHEN A WOMAN IS IN A DESTRUCTIVE RELATIONSHIP, there are so many feelings: fear, shame, guilt, confusion, desperation, anger, humiliation, and longing. Often when she finally has the courage to end such a relationship, she assumes those feelings will magically disappear. When they don't, she is certain that all the times her abuser called her "crazy," "ridiculous," "stupid," "inadequate," or "demented" were all true. She may feel alone and that she made a poor decision. She may feel hopeless, frightened, and that she has traded one miserable existence for another. She can't imagine that her life will improve from this point onward.

I would like to introduce you to some women I know. They were all in a series of long-term abusive relationships in their families, at work, and with people they knew. Like you, they decided that they could no longer justify putting themselves, and in some cases their children, through the purgatory in which they lived. They came to the conclusion that they deserved to be happy and free. Were they as frightened as you are today? Absolutely. Did they make mistakes along the way to recovery? Most assuredly. Listen to their stories because they are you—spectacular in their courage and destined for personal success in all areas of their lives.

SANDY'S STORY

Sandy was a patient of mine who came to see me because she was unclear about her life's course. Although she had an executive level job, earned an impressive salary, boasted a fabulous wardrobe, and had great friends, she was unhappy. She was 39 years old, had never married, had no mate on the horizon, and her biological clock was ticking so loudly it kept her up at night.

After several sessions, Sandy began to speak about her childhood. She had never known her father, who died when she was two years old. Her mother had never remarried—or even dated, as Sandy recalled—and had ruled the household with an iron fist. Sandy didn't have any siblings and her ever-present feeling of loneliness was quite intense. When speaking of her mother, Sandy often started her descriptions with phrases such as: "She really had a tough childhood herself," "She couldn't help the way she was," "I really shouldn't say anything negative about her but," "I know she did the best she could," "I know I wasn't any piece of cake myself." There always seemed to be a disclaimer on her next thought about her mother.

As Sandy spoke of her childhood, it was very obvious that her mother had severely emotionally, and occasionally physically abused her. She was called "fat" and "repulsive" on a daily basis. If Sandy had a difficult day at school, her mother didn't want to hear about it. She blamed those difficulties on Sandy, that she must have done something wrong to deserve her maltreatment by a schoolmate or teacher. In fact, Sandy was very quiet and shy as a child. Although she earned straight As in each class all the way through high school graduation, that wasn't good enough for her mother. She just found other things to criticize. According to Sandy's mother she had lousy penmanship, she wore too much or too little makeup, her clothes didn't fit right, she wasn't athletic enough, and she spoke too quietly.

There were several instances in which Sandy recalled that her mother hit her with objects such as a cooking pot, utensils, and her fist. While she justified her mother's cruel behavior with excuses such as, "I'm sure it was difficult for her to raise me by herself," she slowly began to see that although she was now a grown woman, her mother continued to terrorize her life. Sandy still lived to please her critical mother and, of course, nothing she did was ever good enough, fast enough, or smart enough. Now, her mother's chief criticism was the fact that she couldn't even find a man that would have her.

Sandy's fear of disapproval and criticism as well as her mother's belief that she couldn't ever do anything right, kept her from taking the risks necessary to embark on a romantic relationship. Why even try when she was doomed to failure? Yet, she longed for the feeling of connection she had never experienced. While she could excel in the business world, her personal life was in shambles.

"How well do you think your mother ever knew you?" I asked Sandy at one session.

"What do you mean? She knew me better than anyone. She's my mother, for heaven's sake!" Sandy replied, quite incredulously.

"Okay," I said. "Maybe that was a silly question. Still, I was just wondering if she knew what your favorite musical group was when you were a teenager or what you dreamed of becoming when you grew up. Did she know what your favorite color was?"

Sandy stopped and thought for a while and then said quietly, "No, she didn't know any of that, I'm sure."

"What did you want to be when you grew up?" I asked.

"A vet and a mom," she laughed ruefully. "I guess I blew it on both of those dreams."

"Both of those areas include helping creatures that haven't any voice and are helpless without you."

"I never thought about that, but you're right," she said.

"I think it might be fair to say that your mother never really knew you and for whatever reason she might have concocted, she hasn't made any effort to know you now. Do you think that's right?"

"I think that's probably totally right," Sandy replied even more quietly than before.

"Do you think that we could also say, then, that whatever she said about you and whatever labels she put on you were totally false, and maybe even a projection of how she felt about herself?"

"They might have been."

"Sandy, I am not your mother and I am not going to judge anything you say or be critical of any of your feelings. You are allowed to disagree with me without consequence. I am looking for you to be definitive in your statements here."

"Okay, but what does that say about me if everything you've just said about her is true?" Sandy began crying. "Does that mean my whole life has been a lie?"

"No, not at all. The parts about you getting good grades, being a kind and helpful person, and trying to please a woman who could not be pleased are all true. The untrue parts were that you were unattractive, stupid, slow, and unworthy of love and affection."

"But my mother told me . . .," Sandy cried.

"Sandy, if a stranger on the street told you those horrible things about you, would you believe them?" I asked.

"Well, of course not. They don't know anything about me."

"And neither did your mother. At least a stranger might be able to look at you and see that you are an attractive, intelligent woman without putting any of her own judgments on it. Your mother put all her own unresolved junk with her own life onto you and made you believe it was true," I explained.

"What do I do now? How can I make her see who I am?"

"You probably can't," I said. "You cannot change her. You can only change the way in which you relate to her and how much of yourself you give to her to trample."

After that session, Sandy and I worked on controlling her own reactions to her abusive mother, a woman who so completely dominated her wonderful daughter that Sandy's life decisions were based upon her mother's notion that she would never amount to anything.

Sandy is now 42 years old, and while she hasn't married yet, she has been able to establish some meaningful relationships with men. Today, she is seriously involved with a 45-year-old man who has custody of his three children. She adores the man and his kids and they feel the same about her.

Sandy's decision to begin thinking differently about herself in relation to her mother freed her of a lot of her pain and self-doubt. She is able to express her feelings and wishes and be a whole woman and companion.

MELANIE'S STORY

When I first met Melanie, she was out of her seven-year abusive marriage for exactly two weeks. She was certain, without a doubt, that she had made a huge mistake, and wanted my advice as to how she could beg and plead with her husband to take her back without being physically injured. This lovely 38-year-old woman had dark circles under her eyes, tapped her foot constantly, and absent-mindedly twirled her long brown hair around her fingers for the entire hour we spoke. Clearly, she was highly agitated.

"I just want to get back to him. I made a ridiculous mistake. I listened to my mother and sisters. They have been telling me since we got married that I should leave him, and finally I did. I thought I couldn't take it anymore, but now I know I can and I just want to go home," she said and began to cry. "It really wasn't that bad. A lot of the time he was really sweet, you know? He'd bring me flowers sometimes and we'd go out to dinner. Sometimes, we'd curl up on the couch together and watch an old movie. Those times were so wonderful. I know I could make it work this time."

Melanie had developed what I call "nostalgia amnesia." She had conveniently forgotten the abuse and only remembered the kind and loving times. No abuser is 100 percent evil, and even he may have his nice moments. Obviously, she preferred to recall only those times because it justified her reason to return to him. Her mother and sisters remembered the entire mess.

"Well okay, Melanie, we could certainly work out a plan for you to return. I can't guarantee your safety, of course, but if that's what you want to do, you have free will and can make your own decisions," I said. "What I'm curious about first are the reasons why your family thought you should leave your husband."

"I don't know," she said, almost a little too reflexively for my comfort.

"Well, if you did know, what would the answer be?" Since she looked bewildered by the question, I said, "I find that when people say, 'I don't know,' it really means

'I don't want to know' or 'I'm too lazy to find out.' Which one of those applies to you?"

Melanie looked a little embarrassed and then said, "I guess I don't want to know."

"Thank you for your honesty. I really respect that quality in you," I told her. "Do you think it's possible that you have lived quite a while not wanting to know how you feel or see things as they are?"

She laughed nervously and said, "That's probably true. I tend to see only the good sides of people. I trust very easily and wear my heart on my sleeve. Mark, my husband, always told me I was an idiot for acting that way and believing that all people were good. He told me that everyone's just out for themselves and could care less about me."

"Including him?" I asked. "In my business, we call that *projection*, which is when someone feels a certain way and so thinks all people feel that way. Or they feel something, but can't own it, so they say that perhaps you feel that way."

"Oh yeah. He did that all the time. He'd say that I must have been having sex with any guy that I saw, when actually he was having all these affairs. Or he'd say that I was so fat when really he could stand to lose about 50 pounds."

"Or he called you an 'idiot' when he actually felt that way about himself," I interjected.

"Well, probably he did," she said sadly. "He came from a really horrible family and he told me that when he was growing up, his father always called him a *horse's ass* or a *dufus*. He couldn't help the way he treated me. He was just reacting to the way he was treated."

"How old is Mark? In his thirties?" Melanie nodded. "Is there any reason that he should be cruel to you because he was emotionally abused 20 years ago? I mean there is no excuse for his father treating him that way, to be sure. I'm just wondering why you feel that it's acceptable for him to take that anger out on you? Do you deserve that?"

So began our first of 26 therapy sessions that lasted seven months. Melanie came to understand that she was frightened of making it on her own. She had a succession of abusive partners since she was 16, two of whom she had married before this third marriage to Mark. She felt like a complete failure and that she probably never was going to find anyone who was better than him.

She never counted on finding herself—and that person was so much more magnificent than any man could be. She could actually take care of herself better than anyone else. She'd never considered that possibility.

How did Melanie start out as a woman who wanted a plan for reuniting with her abuser to a confident woman—with occasional doubts—who went on to get her real estate license in seven short months? It wasn't easy.

Melanie didn't take a magic pill and I didn't wave pixie dust over her head. She didn't go to sleep feeling like a failure and wake up feeling like a winner. For the first three sessions, I listened to her rhapsodize about her husband's exemplary qualities and every reason in the book why she should return to him. During each session, I assured her that if she really wanted to go back to him, she could. But perhaps another session of talking might be worthwhile? Giving her "permission" to go back and being willing to listen to her short list of "wonderful things about Mark" let her relax and be open to learning more about herself.

During Melanie's relationship—and perhaps in yours—everyone in her family and all of her friends kept pounding into her head that she had no other recourse but to "leave the creep." What they were unwittingly doing was replacing one controlling person for a whole heap of other controlling people. Instead of Mark telling her what to do, the other loving people in her life were telling her what to do. Melanie's challenge was finding what her spirit wanted her to do. She was so accustomed to letting others make decisions for her, and saying, "I don't know" to any question that was posed to her, she really didn't have her own voice.

Melanie needed to find something that was hers alone, something she liked to do, a comfortable place in her own skin. We worked on the empowerment activities you will find throughout this book. She went to a women's focus group. After taking a series of occupational and aptitude tests, she discovered that she had a real flair for real estate sales. She laughed, remembering how much she enjoyed drifting through "open houses" in her area when Mark wasn't home (he thought it was ridiculous and frivolous) and imagining what it would feel like to live in these homes. Although she was afraid of failure, she studied for her real estate license and even found that she was a good student and intelligent woman, not the "idiot" that Mark constantly told her she was. She passed her exam on the first try.

At the end of our work together, Melanie had just received her first commission check. She Xeroxed it and framed it. Five months into her recovery process, she joined a divorce support group at her local women's center, and shortly thereafter decided to pursue a legal end to her relationship. She began developing female friendships, which had been denied her while she was with Mark. She found great comfort in the sisterhood with these women. She joined a YMCA and began attending exercise classes, discovering that it was enjoyable to flex her physical as well as her mental muscles again.

Are you getting the impression that Melanie was a fearless champ all along the way, or even at the end of our sessions? Oh, no. At the beginning of almost every therapy appointment, she said, "I don't think I can do this anymore. Maybe I made a mistake. Maybe I was foolish in thinking that I could really be on my own. It's just too hard!"

After a while, this became a running joke with us. She'd sit down on my couch, put her hands to her head, and wait for me to say, "Waiter, please, start the session with a fine whine." She said this statement in a plaintive wail, and then got down to work. Again, she just needed permission to feel the fear and know that it was completely normal.

It took Melanie another year to start feeling fully confident that she had a future without her husband. Even after her divorce was final, she had many moments of doubt and remorse. Many times, Mark's words of disgust echoed in her ears, which didn't bring her back to square one, but maybe square three! She wrote to me many times and let me know of her progress. In her last letter, which came to me 16 months after the conclusion of our therapy—a full two years after our first appointment—she confided that she actually liked the woman that she was and decided to see if another man would like that woman as well. She was very hesitant, but allowed one of her new gal pals to arrange an introduction to one of her male friends. She thought the evening went well—they went for coffee—and he asked if he could call her again.

"Dr. Murray, I feel like a teenager again," she wrote. "All the insecurities, so many butterflies. But I remind myself that I'm not a girl, I'm a strong and independent woman who can make good decisions. I have a lot to offer a man and he'd be lucky to have dinner with me!"

I didn't hear from Melanie again, but I have seen her real estate signs at several houses around town. I have complete confidence that she has developed—and will continue to develop—the life she wants for herself. She earned it.

CATHERINE'S STORY

Catherine was a recent patient of mine who came in because of anxiety symptoms. She frequently had heart palpitations, headaches, a nervous stomach, and a general feeling of fear and dread. After her physician performed a number of tests—all of which came out fine—he gently suggested that she might want to talk with a therapist.

She laughed nervously. "My doctor thinks all of this is in my head."

"Well, I don't think he believes that. He knows you definitely have physical symptoms that are bothering you. Since he can't find the medical cause, he thought you might be having some life difficulties that are affecting your health. There is a definite mind-body connection, you know?" I explained.

As Catherine began telling me about her life, it became apparent that she was working very long hours for a tyrant of a boss.

"Why are you working ten to twelve hours a day during the week and most Saturdays as well?" I asked.

"Well, that's just the way he does things. He is a very focused man and is very successful. When I took the job as his administrative assistant I was warned that the hours would be long and that he liked things a certain way." She laughed again. "He had a slew of assistants who didn't last long. I've been with him for seven months, which is a record, I think."

"Does everyone who works for him work as many hours as you?" I asked.

"No, just me. He likes me to do everything for him. I guess he's happy with the way I do it. Everyone else pretty much works from nine to five."

"Do you get out for lunch or breaks?"

"Oh, not usually. He works through lunch, so I do too. I bring my lunch to work every day and try to grab a few bites here and there."

"Wow, you're such a dedicated worker. He must really appreciate all that you do for him," I said, knowing that he didn't, but wanting her to say it.

"Well, you'd think so, wouldn't you?" she laughed once again. "No, I don't think I've ever heard him thank me, though I'm sure he must be grateful for all that I do. All my bosses have been like that, but you know men . . .," she trailed off.

"Maybe not," I said. "Tell me about them."

"I just mean that they expect a lot from you and don't know how to say thank you. It's a guy thing. They must be embarrassed about expressing their emotions."

"All men?" I asked.

"Well, sure as shootin' every man I've ever known," she laughed again. "Don't you find that to be true?"

"I've certainly met some men—and women—like that, but I don't let myself get taken advantage of by them. If their demands are outrageous, I tell them. I also make sure I don't hang around with people who can't say thank you," I stated.

"I don't mean to make him sound horrible," Catherine said quickly. "My boss is a genius. He built that company from the ground up and he's so successful. If he wants things done a certain way, that's part of my job."

Catherine and I went on to discuss her boss' unreasonable demands on her time and attention, the way she waited fruitlessly for any crumb of approval or attention, which she never received, and the connection between her anxiety symptoms and her work stress.

Not surprisingly, Catherine's father was very much like her present and previous bosses: unable to be pleased with anything she did, stingy with affection and compliments, making her work overtime for recognition. Once Catherine began seeing the ways in which she was recreating her childhood experience with her father, we started focusing on listening to her inner voice and body, which were wise and quick to let her know when something didn't feel right.

We worked on assertiveness training skills and honoring her efforts. She attempted to speak with her boss about her unfair working conditions, to which he replied, "If you don't like it, there's the door. Don't think I can't replace you in a second."

Needless to say, this led to her leaving her job. However, she was able to translate her organizational and hard working skills into her own decorative basket business. As her own boss, she was able to pursue what she liked, worked the hours she felt were necessary for success, and saw the fruits of her own efforts. She is also going forward with a harassment suit against her former employer.

Catherine also began making better choices in men after she confronted her father on the ways in which he treated her unfairly. Although he didn't apologize, she did see a definite difference in the way he began to treat her: with the respect and kindness she—and every woman—deserves.

MING'S STORY

Ming was a beautiful Asian woman I counseled while at Laura's House, a domestic violence shelter in California. When she and her 13-year-old son came to us early one morning, she had a black eye, a swollen lower lip, and bruises on her upper arms and breasts. She had lost the hearing in her right ear and only had partial hearing in her left ear. Her son was shivering, even though it was July and reasonably warm for 5 A.M. He was hunched over and didn't look any of us in the eyes. When our shelter director tried to put her arm around him in comfort, he flinched and moved away.

Ming had been married to the same man for 26 years and also had a 25-year-old son who lived in San Francisco with his wife and infant daughter. Ming's husband was also Asian, raised in his native country until he was in his teens, as was Ming. They met while attending the same church with their families.

Ming had always been very submissive to her husband, as he told her that was her obligation. Since she was raised in the same kind of household, she saw nothing wrong with it. His obligation was to provide for his wife and sons, which he did very well. Ming's role was to look after the children, care for their home, cook, and not ever to bother her husband.

Ming's husband was cruel to her from the beginning of their marriage, although she hadn't seen it that way. If he didn't like what she had prepared for dinner, he would throw his plate against the kitchen wall, ordering her to clean it up and fix another meal that was more to his liking. If the boys had been outside playing with friends just before their father arrived home, and weren't bathed and in their pajamas, he would curse her and insult her as a mother.

Sex was his prerogative at any time he wanted and she was to accommodate his wishes, even as his desires became more perverse, painful, and demeaning. She knew that he had relations with other women, but since he was the man in the family, she was forbidden to complain about it. Once, as a young bride, she had sought her mother's understanding of this situation.

"What are you thinking, Ming?" her mother had chided her. "He is a man. All men are the same. He is no worse than your own father or any other man. Why do you complain so? He gives you a beautiful home, food on your table, and has gifted you with two sons. You should know your place and be quiet. Don't ever let me hear you talk like that about your husband again."

Ming was alone in her misery. Her husband began pushing her around, choking her, and grabbing her by the hair. Sometimes, he wouldn't physically assault her, but put his mouth against one of her ears and screamed at her. She began losing her hearing. If her older son spoke up and told his father to stop harming his mother, he would be thrown across the room amid a barrage of insults. The younger son crawled into his room on his stomach, like a soldier in combat, and hid in his closet when the frequent violence occurred.

When she arrived at the shelter, she was in shock and still wasn't sure what had prompted her to leave on this specific occasion or how she ended up at our doorstep. Since her son couldn't or wouldn't speak, he couldn't supply any details either. She did recall that her husband hadn't come home the night before, but that was often the case when he spent the night with another woman.

As you can see thus far in Ming's story, she was involved in a highly abusive relationship, which was also complicated by the protocol of her culture and the lack of family support. In fact, her family was just as abusive to Ming as her husband in another way. Since she had nowhere to turn, or even any idea that she deserved any better than she had, it was truly a miracle that she left before she was killed.

Ming walked around in a fog for three days. Her son did not speak at all and avoided eye contact with the other 17 residents of the shelter. Sometimes he sat in the corner of his bedroom and rocked. We were very concerned about him. We had filed a child abuse report with Children's Protective Services, as we did with all children who came to us. Our strong feeling was that even if children aren't physically abused, they have experienced severe emotional abuse by being witness to their mother's abuse, or even by being exposed to the devastation that occurred in the home. Unfortunately, this young man was not able to give a statement to the investigator who came out to talk with him. Ming's thoughts were fragmented at the time and she cried for hours when asked to discuss incidents in her home. While the investigator was able to write statements such as, "appears to be severely traumatized" on her report, it certainly wasn't enough to hang a legal case against the abuser.

On day five, Ming came to the conclusion that her older son should send for his brother and her, and they would live with him. The shelter workers thought this was a very odd concept until we remembered that in an Asian family it is the oldest son's obligation to take over for the father. In the absence of the father, he is now the patriarch. We could understand why this would be a logical next step for her.

However, while her culture would certainly condone—or perhaps even encourage—Ming going to her older son to be taken care of, we wanted to encourage her to try and make her own way in the world. Wouldn't she be going from one caretaker to another and from a submissive role in one home to the same in another? If her son had married an Asian woman, she might have understood that her mother-in-law was to be looked upon as the matriarch of the household. But he had married a very strong and independent American. We foresaw further strife and ill feelings ahead for Ming and her son.

We asked Ming to stay at the shelter for the designated 45 days and try out a new way of life. If she felt too uncomfortable, she always had the option of calling her son. Ming agreed to that. Of course, it was her pattern to agree with almost anyone, as she felt she had no right to a differing opinion.

As Ming stayed and was exposed to different women and their ideas, as well as being part of the twice daily educational and support groups, we began to see a change in not only her, but her teenage son. They felt safe, they were accepted, and had options in their lives. Since, sadly, most of the children in our shelter were under the age of eight, the young man was looked up to by the little ones. They followed him around and wanted to sit where he sat, eat what he ate, and eventually hung on his every word.

At the end of 30 days, Ming told us she wanted us to help her find a job. It seems that despite what her husband had told her about her cooking, she was a fine chef. Each of the women at the shelter is required to make dinner a different night for all the people in the household and everyone eagerly looked forward to Ming's night. As a matter of fact, several women told her they would do her chores if she would take their night of cooking. In the beginning, she quickly agreed, not wanting to displease anyone. However by the fourth week, she had grown tired of fixing dinner almost every night for so many people. She actually began using her new assertiveness-training skills, saying that she'd rather not that particular evening. To her surprise, no one became angry with her at her denial of their request, they simply said they were disappointed because they enjoyed her cooking so much.

We were able to help Ming prepare for an interview at an Asian restaurant. While she had hoped to get a chef position, they told her that she would be an assistant for a few weeks until she proved herself. She was delighted nonetheless. It was Ming's first job and she proudly pranced around the shelter with her first paycheck. They asked if her son would like to clear tables, and he, too, was thrilled with his job.

Ming was the most surprising woman I ever saw at the shelter. The entire staff was sure that she would crumble in

DESTRUCTIVE RELATIONSHIPS

a matter of days after arriving there and quickly return to her abusive husband, probably to be killed by him eventually for daring to leave him. Ming had a different concept. Even though she had never seen the world other than as a submissive, mistreated, sheltered woman, she discovered her newfound freedom to be intoxicating and was more grateful than any other woman I had seen come through our doors.

She and her son took up residence with a young waitress at the restaurant who was looking for a roommate in her small apartment. Although they had come from an extravagant home, they loved their cramped apartment. They were safe and secure. They decided what to do, what to eat, what to wear, and never had to worry again about being hurt physically or emotionally.

When the young waitress heard Ming's story, she became enraged at the husband and tried to convince Ming to "take all his money" in a divorce. Ming laughed at the thought. "What could I possibly buy that I don't have right now?" she asked. "I was married to a man with so much money and yet I lived in a prison. Now, I am in a castle and every day brings so much happiness."

TERRI'S STORY

Terri was a wonderful woman I met at a fund-raising walk for breast cancer a few years ago. Since it was a 10K walk, we had lots of time to chat. She was very friendly. After bragging about our children, we started talking about husbands, friends, and all the other relationship stuff women so easily discuss.

"When I get home from this walk, I have to bake seven dozen cupcakes for a school party tomorrow," she said.

"That's 84 cupcakes," I said. "I've heard of overcrowded classrooms, but that's ridiculous."

Terri laughed. "It's not just my daughter's class, but the two other fourth grade classes as well. They are having a joint springtime celebration party."

"Wow, that's a lot of cupcakes for one person to make. Didn't the other classes have room moms who would bake for their own kids?" I asked.

"Oh, they probably did. But I'm always the one everyone calls when they need something done. I'm pretty reliable that way. I really like being involved in the classroom, so whenever they need art supplies, cookies, or a chaperone for a field trip, I'm always volunteered."

While making small talk, Terri also told me that her male and female friends treat her the same way: imposing on her to pick up their kids from soccer practice because they can't get there in time, inviting their children over to her house so they can run a few errands child-free then not picking them up until after dinner, and betraying confidences she's shared with them.

Her story started me thinking about all the other women I have known who were "doormats" for their friends. They were afraid to say "no" or didn't think they had a right to do so. They were taken advantaged of because of their "disease to please." Let me just say here that I would have definitely put myself in the same category at one time.

Lo and behold, Terri gave me a call a week later, as we had traded phone numbers. We decided to meet for coffee a few days later—at a spot that was halfway between us—and she offered to pick me up even though I lived 35 minutes from her home.

"Terri, the thought behind meeting halfway was so that it was only 15 minutes away from each of us, remember?" I asked.

"Oh, I know, but I just thought if you'd rather go together, I don't have a problem picking you up," she said easily.

Jeepers, I thought, this gal volunteers for that kind of treatment. After we met and chatted for a bit, I asked her if she thought that overextending herself was a pattern in her life.

"No, I don't think so," she said cheerfully. "Why do you ask? Have I offended you in some way? If I have, it wasn't intentional and I really apologize."

"Terri, you're a terrific person. You don't have to do anything special for me. I'm happy just to know you," I assured her.

Terri had a hard time sitting still. Whenever I wiped my mouth on a napkin, she'd jump up and get me a new one. When I was halfway through my cup of tea, she grabbed it from me and asked for a refill.

"Terri, you need to stop doing all this. You're making me nervous. Why don't you just relax and enjoy our time together?"

We eventually left the coffee house and parted ways. Neither of us ever called the other again. I think we both felt very uncomfortable together, she, because I wouldn't let her behave in the usual way she thought she needed to with a friend, and me, because I didn't want to be her "therapist" and continuously confront her actions.

I'm sure you know women like Terri, or maybe you are a Terri yourself. If so, I would ask you to consider what kind of effect it is having on your life. Do you feel tired all the time? Do you feel used or resentful? Do you get the respect you deserve from your friends? Do you wonder why they don't take you seriously?

We will discuss this pattern of being a "doormat" in your friendships later in this book and start making an effort to change your thinking about it.

MARIA'S STORY

Maria was another wonderful and courageous woman I met at the shelter. She was 24 years old, had a two-year-old daughter named Susie, and had recently suffered a miscarriage at the hands of her abusive husband. When we admitted Maria, she very strongly stated that she had left her husband because "he killed my unborn child and would kill Susie and me if we stayed with him." I'm sure that was true.

Maria quickly adapted to life among a large group of people. She had been one of nine children growing up and so she didn't mind the constant chaos and noise that was ever-present in the shelter. It felt comfortable to her, like she was at home again—except we soon learned that home hadn't been so great either. Her father was an abusive alcoholic who raged when he was drunk. He was partial to his sons and treated his daughters and wife like slaves.

Maria was getting along nicely until she contacted one of her sisters who told her that their priest was very upset with her for leaving her husband. It seems that he had gone to see the priest and told him that she was having an affair, took their daughter, and ran off with this man. Maria's sister told her that the priest wanted to see her at once.

Maria was so upset by the situation that she decided to go back to her husband so as not to upset the Church. We tried to explain to her that her husband had lied to the priest and she could call the priest and explain the true facts. She said that wouldn't solve anything and that her church did not condone divorce for any reason. It was her sin and the only way she could make it right was to go back and ask for forgiveness and hope that her husband would be gracious.

We tried to convince her that she had nothing to be apologetic about. Didn't she remember what her husband had done to her? Surely, she could make her priest understand. We talked and talked with Maria about the situation. Her fear was not so much retaliation by her husband, but what her choice to leave him meant for her in her religious community and the way she perceived God would judge her.

Sadly, Maria left the next morning and went home to her husband. Both the staff and women at the shelter were unbearably sad and frightened for Maria. Almost every woman who leaves her abuser entertains the idea of returning home when the realization of life without him sets in.

Four months later, Maria came back to us. Her gorgeous baby daughter had a clump of hair missing on one side of her head. It seems her husband became so enraged at the child for watching *Sesame Street* while he was trying to sleep off a hangover that he picked her up by her hair and shook her violently. Maria grabbed her daughter and ran out of the house to the bus station, and eventually came to our shelter. She looked frightened and sheepish, thinking we wouldn't take her back, which of course we did most gratefully.

The next day, we helped Maria call her priest and arrange for a meeting at a location other than the church, as her husband might go there trying to gain information about her. When the man saw the little girl, he began to cry.

"I couldn't imagine that what your husband was saying about you was true," he told her in Spanish. "I have known you since you were a baby yourself. I wish you had come to me before any of this happened."

When Maria questioned him about the sin of leaving her marriage and whether God would be able to forgive her, the priest put his arms around her. "It is not your sin. Look at your child and what your husband did to her and you and your hearts."

Maria was overwhelmed with relief and gratitude. She went to the police department and filed criminal charges against her husband. He was charged with spousal abuse and child abuse and sentenced to three years in prison. This gave Maria ample time to start her life over as a free woman.

During her 45 days at the shelter, she blossomed into a confident young woman. Her husband sent letters to her family, begging them to encourage her to visit him in jail. His letters were pathetic and Maria saw that. He wasn't the big, mean man he pretended to be. He had used his power and control to cover up his own insecurities and deep fears. Maria eventually saw that she was the one in charge all along, but because he was such a dangerous bully, she gave up that power to him.

Maria has moved on to a happier life with her daughter. They moved in with one of her sisters and her family. She began volunteering at her church where she was such an efficient and dependable worker that they hired her as the priest's assistant.

Before she left the shelter, she told me, "It is my duty to forgive my husband, but I will never forget what he did to Susie and me. I will never allow him or any other cruel man to be part of our lives again."

TANYA'S STORY

Tanya was a patient of mine in my private practice. She was definitely one of the most strikingly beautiful women I had ever seen in person. She looked like a cover girl. Tall and slim with long, honey colored hair and piercing blue eyes, she always wore very fashionable and expensive clothing with the perfect purse, shoes, and jewelry to match each outfit. She had two equally beautiful children: a three-year-old daughter and a one-year-old son. I could imagine that their father must be very handsome and what a lovely family they must have made . . . *in photographs.* In fact, she did show me their recent Christmas photo taken at the beach, all of them in matching blue jeans, white shirts, and bare feet. They all had big, toothy grins, except the baby, who proudly showed off his gums.

"What happened to this family?" I asked her looking at the picture.

"What family?" she replied taking the photo back and stuffing it angrily into her purse. "That wasn't a real family. That was an illusion that I created because I wanted it so badly. I guess I thought that if we looked like the perfect family, it would just happen. For a while, I thought maybe it had. We were the envy of all our friends. Our pictures were in newspaper columns when we went to the latest charity fund-raiser or had a large party in our home. We really looked great, didn't we?"

I am often reminded that abuse knows no religion, education, economic class, or race. Sitting in front of me with a cast on her arm was the valedictorian of her college class, a Caucasian woman who was married to a man who earned more than $400,000 per year. She had a fabulous home in the best part of town, wonderful jewelry, great car, and expensive clothes. She had a live-in housekeeper and an au pair to help her care for her children. Still, she was also one of the saddest women I had ever met.

I asked Tanya when the abuse began and she told me of the incident that led her to call the police recently and sent her husband to jail for three days. She pointed to the cast on her arm. "He grabbed my arm while I was trying to get away from him and pulled it behind my back, twisting and twisting as I screamed."

"That was when the abuse began?" I asked skeptically. "I asked you about the first incident of abuse, not the most recent one."

I purposely reminded her of my question because I have found that the level of denial in women who have been in long-term abusive relationships is so strong that they frequently have trouble seeing that the horror has gone on far longer than they had thought.

"Tell me the first time you knew something was creepy," I said.

Tanya looked down and was quiet for several minutes and began to cry.

"Our honeymoon," she said so softly I almost couldn't hear her. "We were in Las Vegas, visiting Hoover Dam. In the middle of the tour, he decided it was too boring and wanted to go. I was enjoying it and told him so. He told me he was leaving and I could go with him or not. I thought he must be joking and when he left the group, I thought he was going to the bathroom. He didn't; he actually left me at Hoover Dam, which was a long distance from our hotel with no way to get back. I was stuck there. I hadn't even brought my purse because I didn't see any reason to lug it around, so I didn't have taxi fare. I just sat on the front steps and cried. When a stranger asked if they could help me, I told them that I was fine and was waiting for my husband. Almost two hours later, he drove up and just stared at me. I got in the car without saying a word.

"I looked at his face as he drove back to the hotel. It was so cold and hard; it really frightened me. I remember thinking, 'Oh no, what have I done? Can I have the marriage annulled?' Then I thought about the wedding and party my parents paid for only three days before, and the large table piled high with gifts for us. I couldn't back out of it now. I decided not to make him mad anymore and we would be fine. How ridiculous is that? We never spoke about that time in Las Vegas, but he has left me high and dry in other places with and without the kids."

Tanya then went on to recount tales of her husband's road rage when he would drive so recklessly she would be frightened for her life. She told me of the many times he withdrew and punished her by not speaking to her for several days at a time. He pretended she didn't even exist. He choked her on many occasions and had rough sex with her. He'd push her against walls and pull her hair. He told her many times that she embarrassed him in public and all his friends told him to leave her on several occasions.

As Tanya told me these stories over a few sessions, she was getting angrier and angrier. "I hate him," she said. "I really hate him. Look what he's done to our lives."

"Who are you angry at, Tanya?" I asked her during one of these sessions.

"What do you mean? I'm incredibly angry at him!"

"Who else are you angry at?" I asked again.

She looked at me as if I was speaking a foreign language. I didn't come to her rescue, but let her think about the question a bit longer.

"Me," she said quietly after several moments and began to sob heavily. "How could I have let this go on? How could I have brought children into this mess? Justin is only a year old. His father wasn't just being emotionally cruel to me when I decided to get pregnant. He was actually hitting me and leaving bruises all over my body. When he was being cold and withholding, blaming me for everything that went wrong in his life, I believed that if I just did better, he would stop. In the beginning, I thought that if we had a child, it would calm him down and he would see how important family is and treasure it. That's when I conceived Daniella. But I shouldn't have been so stupid. I was an idiot."

"Stupid," "idiot," and "ridiculous" were names I know he called her and I told her how important it was that she start treating herself more kindly. I did want her to identify the anger she had at herself because I believed it was a first step in her healing process. There was nothing she could do about what had happened in the past, and it seemed that each time she brought it up she became increasingly angry. That type of anger would get her nowhere and would only grow with her frustration over it. She could learn a lot from her anger at herself and start taking steps to understand her motivations and begin forgiving herself.

This is not a popular concept in the therapy profession, I can assure you. Women in abusive relationships are routinely referred to as "victims," however I don't buy into that philosophy. The fact is, I can't think of any successful victim in history. I can think of a lot of courageous women who took a stand despite all the obstacles in their way. I'm sure they were frightened and had many moments of doubt, but they worked through those fears and stuck to their guns.

That is the woman I wanted Tanya to become, and exactly the woman I want you to become.

Today, Tanya is divorced from her husband and has joint custody of her children. This has been a terrible difficulty for her to overcome because she doesn't feel her children are safe with their father and furthermore doesn't think he deserves them. He is an abuser, after all. Why does he get all the rights and privileges of any other divorced dad? That is a very legitimate feeling and you may be going through that struggle as well. I have devoted an entire chapter to the subject of dealing with your past abusers later in this book.

Tanya is a fairly contented woman now. My therapeutic plan for her was to focus on empowerment so that she could see how much true power and control she had in her life, especially as she went through her divorce process with her husband trying to take the house, her car, all their joint savings and investments. She felt very helpless and she was back in the old place of submission and thinking that if she was just a nice girl, he would see how nice she was and play fair. That didn't happen. Tanya's lifestyle was taken from her and now she and her children live in a small condominium. But they live there safely and without fear.

It was a difficult adjustment for Tanya. She has had many, many days of anger and bitterness. However, she keeps putting one foot in front of the other, using the techniques I will describe to you throughout this book. She still has a way to go and has decided that she never wants to marry again. We'll see. In the meantime, she has seen how much true power and insight she has and uses it well on most days. She feels happier than she has in a long time.

I hope that you were able to identify with some of the pain and struggles Sandy, Melanie, Catherine, Ming, Terri, Maria, and Tanya have gone through. I want you to see that what you are feeling is normal and to be expected. Other women have gone through these difficulties as well. On the whole, their recovery from their abusive relationships has not been easy or quick. It required introspection, accountability, very hard work, and a great willingness to do what was necessary, even on days when they didn't feel like it. It also required trying on new and perhaps uncomfortable ideas and working through fears rather than giving in to them.

Do you feel ready to do the same? Then let's get started!

I am going to offer you the opportunity to do some very significant soul and life changing work throughout this book. Every chapter will include at least one "assignment" for personal discovery and growth. These are not difficult tasks, although they may be emotionally difficult.

Go out and buy yourself a beautiful journal. You deserve it. You can write the assignments in your book and reflect on your progress as the days go by and marvel at your amazing success.

Here is the first task:

ACTIVITY
What Is Your Story?

You have just read the stories of several women's destructive relationships and the insights they gained. Take a few moments now and journal about the story or stories that led you to this book. When you saw the title of this book, *Destructive Relationships*, something rang true in your own life and you related to it. Who does your story involve? What have they done to you? How many instances of wrongdoing have you experienced with this person or persons? Be as detailed as you like and then review what you wrote, letting it sink in.

CHAPTER
TWO

Important Concepts to Understand

WHAT MAKES YOU SO QUALIFIED TO WRITE THIS BOOK?

IN PROMOTING MY FIRST BOOK, *But I Love Him*, I was asked *What makes you so qualified to write this book?* many times. Hey, it's a legitimate question. What makes me think I've got all the answers? Why should I write this book instead of you? Well, aside from a few initials tagged onto the end of my name and some varied experiences in the field of abuse, maybe nothing. Let me tell you who I am and some very important concepts I have come to learn as truths.

While I worked as a therapist in a domestic violence shelter for a few years, I learned so much from the 250 or so women whom I counseled. What incredible courage and fortitude! I have said quite often—and I still believe it to be true—that there aren't any more courageous women in history books than the women in that shelter.

Among the truths I learned was that when a woman is in an abusive relationship, usually she is in several abusive relationships and does not realize it. Certain predictable patterns emerged as the women I counseled spoke of their childhoods and their present relationships with their parents, children, bosses, coworkers, and male and female friends. They were "doormats" for most of the significant people in their lives. They were used, taken advantage of, and not respected, treated unfairly, or dishonored. It was heartbreaking for those of us who cared about them. These women also didn't know how to get themselves out of this pattern and go on to live healthy lives.

After working at the shelter, I also led groups for court-mandated male abusers and child abuse offenders. I learned a lot about the use of power and control to intimidate partners, employees, children, and the like. Many of those in my groups were professionals in the community and other well-respected folks. Not only did I find that survivors of abuse can be of any economic, social, racial, or educational class, but abusers can be as well. Sadly, I also learned that while the success rate for survivors of abuse can be fairly high, it is very difficult to change the thinking and behavior of abusers.

I was also married for 19 years to my high school sweetheart and we had two incredible children—twins who are now 20 years old. Would I consider the relationship with my first husband abusive? No, I really wouldn't. But it was definitely unhealthy for me and probably for him, too. We married far too young, straight out of college, and hadn't really dated others before we met. Like all young people, we thought we were pretty brilliant and had all the answers when actually neither of us had been shown wonderful models of marriage. How were we to know?

Living with someone and feeling more alone than if you were truly alone is possibly one of the worst places to be on Earth. When my husband and I finally divorced, it was the saddest thing I've ever had to do. I felt incredible shame and disappointment. I could hardly look my children in the eyes. I took total blame, which of course, was ridiculous.

I went back to school—graduate school, a step that I had put on hold for 19 years in order to support my husband in his career and raise my children. It was there that I met my current husband, Frank, who is now the driving force of my success and stability, and object of my deep love and friendship. Who knew that would happen?

When I was in school, I recall reading a quote from a psychologist named Virginia Satir that I think is very profound and to which I continue to relate: *Most people prefer the certainty of misery to the misery of uncertainty.* Is that as true of your life as it was of mine? Think about it for a moment. Most of us drag on day-to-day fairly miserable, but at least it's our misery. We own it and we can claim it. We're miserable, but you know, there's a certain comfort in that misery, isn't there?

Taking a risk to change your life—the misery of uncertainty—is really scary! It's like jumping off a cliff and hoping you'll land safely. However, it's not until you are ready to take that jump—having done all the planning to make sure you actually will land safely—that your life can change. Then, you will be the creator of your own destiny.

Are you ready to try? Great. Then let me tell you a little about those truths I mentioned at the start of this chapter.

TRUTH #1

Love Is a Behavior

We were all raised to believe that love is a feeling, but where has that idea led you? We've all been told, "Listen to your heart. Your heart will never lead you wrong." That is total garbage. Your heart will always lead you wrong! Why? Because it's your heart's job to pump blood throughout your body. It's your brain's job to make decisions for you. Listen to your brain. Your brain will never lead you wrong.

I would also add that you should listen to your body's cues because the mind-body connection is so strong that you can know that something's up when your stomach is in knots, you have a three-day headache, or you have a chronically sore throat or backache. It is your body knocking on your head saying, "Hello? Anyone in there? Wake up. I'm trying to tell you something here." Do you know why you have that queasy, nervous stomach? Because you can't stomach what's going on in your life. That headache is telling you that you can't stand to think about this problem anymore. The sore throat means there are words caught in your throat, things you want to say but are preventing yourself from doing so. That backache is trying to tell you to get a spine already!

Listen to your body instead of making excuses, because it, too, is trying to tell you that love is a behavior.

When we begin to look at people's behavior rather than their words, our lives instantly become clearer. When we look at their actual behavior rather than what we decide their intent must be, our lives become easier. When we look at behavior rather than making excuses for it, pushing it away, saying we must have misunderstood or it must be our fault, we are living more authentically and seeing people for who they are, rather than what they wish they would be.

Love—and I'm not just speaking of romantic love, but also love between friends, parents, children, siblings and respect you share with your boss and coworkers—is all about how you are treated and how you treat others.

For the next three days, practice looking only at the behavior of every person in your life. You will be amazed, shocked, and, most likely, a little dismayed.

TRUTH #2
You Only Have Control Over Three Things in Your Life

Wait a minute. That doesn't sound right. You thought you had control over everyone and everything you survey. Uh-uh. Just three things, my friends:

- Your own thoughts
- Your own behaviors
- Your own reactions

That's pretty much it. But what a tremendous amount of control that really gives you when you use it and refuse to give it away to others.

Think about the following scenario for a minute. How many times have you been frustrated or upset because someone in your life wouldn't change to see your point of view, treat you better, etc? Many, I'll bet. I know of what I speak, let me tell you. Here's the problem: Everyone has control over the same three things you do, which means that your control begins and ends with you and no one else.

Let's look at those three items you can control in more detail.

- *Your own thoughts:* Sometimes it seems like you are going crazy, right? You feel like your mind is racing in 12 different directions and none of your thoughts are things you would like to think about. Your mind seems to have a mind of it's own! That's because you haven't taken control of it. However, you absolutely can take complete control of your thoughts and the ways in which you think about them. You—and you alone—get to decide.

- *Your own behaviors:* One thing I have learned for certain: *All abuse is intentional and is learned behavior.* When you have been the object of abusive behavior, it was a plan. It was not accidental. It was a choice made by people who had complete control over their behaviors. So do you, which means that any old time you choose a different path in your life, you can do so.

- *Your own reactions:* You get to choose the way in which you respond to those around you and to situations that present themselves. Your reactions aren't automatic; you choose them. Here's a very simple example that doesn't involve other people. You don't have control of the weather. It may rain cats and dogs today. You have 100 percent control over your reaction to that weather. Will you say, "I can't believe my bad luck." "Why is it always raining when I have important things to take care of?" Or will you say, "It's raining cats and dogs. I hope I don't step in a poodle!"

See? The first reaction makes you a helpless little "victim" to the weather, while the second sets you up to have a positive day with a sense of humor and fun despite the lousy weather.

TRUTH #3
We All Have Free Will

Okay, we've agreed that we don't have control of the weather, other people's behaviors, thoughts, or reactions. But if we do have control of most everything in our lives, we can decide what to do about it. We can actually make clear choices.

You aren't programmed to act in a certain way. Yes, I will admit that due to your childhood and family background, you are predisposed to behave in a certain way. But, hey, you're an adult now. You get to call the shots. Isn't that refreshing?

TRUTH #4
You Are Not a Victim

Here's where I may lose some of you, I'm sure, but please stay with me for just a minute more. If we agree that you have total control over the three most powerful things in your life and also that you have free will, you cannot see yourself as a victim. You have made choices in your life. Some of them have been poor choices, but you made them nonetheless.

Can I tell you how many times I have wished I was a victim of circumstance, that someone else "made" me do it, that I didn't have any other choice, or that my childhood "drove" me to do some of the things I've done? Well, a lot, let me assure you. But it's simply not the truth. When I realized that and started taking responsibility for my own life and decisions, I was able to change my life in a most dramatic way and create true and lasting personal success.

Take a moment and consider this question: Can you think of any successful "victims" in history? Neither can I. When we think of our personal heroes—mine is Rosa Parks—they may have been men or women who others saw as victims, but it was because they refused to see themselves as victims that they became victorious.

There are true victims in the world. Children who have been abused are victims. Citizens of foreign countries whose land has been overtaken are victims. I could go on, but you get my drift. There are victims, but they aren't you. Victims are people who truly did not have a shred of a choice in what was done to them. How does a three-year-old push a sexual molester off of her? How were the Jews supposed to fight off hordes of Nazis that invaded their neighborhoods and loaded them onto cattle cars going to a concentration camp?

The very moment you refuse to see yourself as a victim and see yourself as a strong, capable woman, your attitude—and therefore your life—will instantly change, as if by magic. I promise.

TRUTH #5

All Abuse Is Intentional and Is a Learned Behavior

Here's another piece of truth many of you may not care to hear, because if you buy my idea you have to come to the painful truth that the people you care about—your abusers—knew what they were doing when they hurt you. In addition, you also have to believe that if abuse is learned behavior, they must have practiced it somewhere in order to get good enough at it to cause you pain. Ouch!

If all this is true—and it is, I assure you—then what do you do with your excuses? "He didn't mean to shove me; it was just an accident." "She's just having a bad day." "Oh, you know how kids are—they're all mouthy." "He doesn't usually say things like that."

If we all have 100 percent control of our own thoughts, behaviors, and reactions and we also have free will, then we automatically know that a mouth doesn't open on it's own and call you a "bitch." A hand doesn't come out of a pocket by itself and push you against a wall. A tongue doesn't form the words, "You really look fat in that dress," without the brain being attached. This is all planned behavior. Perhaps it is planned only a few seconds beforehand. Nonetheless it is intentional.

It is also true that abuse is learned somewhere. For example, it may have been taught in the childhood home from parents or out in the world as a means of protection. Don't use this as a reason to make another excuse for abusive behavior, however. Don't use the logic that his father was abusive, so now he's abusive. Don't think: His parents fought all the time so that's the only way he knows how to act. Don't say, "She was abused as a child, so now she has a lot of anger."

True, these are all reasons why one becomes abusive. The good news about abuse as a learned behavior is that it can also be unlearned. So, while an abusive home or trauma in childhood may have taught someone to be an abuser, he is now an adult and can choose new nonabusive behaviors if he wishes. It is also a fact that there is no logic in the reasoning that because someone was abused as a child he should now inflict all of that on you.

ACTIVITY
What Choices Have I Had?

Think back as far as you would care to, maybe to when you were ten years old or perhaps just as recently as three months ago. It's your choice. Now, structure your journal paper like this:

I felt like a "victim" when ...	Who was involved?	What I could have done differently?

These may be very long lists! That's okay. You are about to change your patterns of abusive relationships, so won't it feel powerful to look back on this assignment in a few weeks?

When you fill in the third column, remember the five truths listed above. Even though you may think for the moment that you couldn't have done anything differently, now you know that you could. Think of any answer. It will help your brain practice different and more creative thinking processes, which are essential if you are to get yourself out of your rut and make true change.

For example, let's say you have a terribly demanding, ungrateful, and abusive boss. You feel victimized on a daily basis (you fill in your boss's nasty behaviors). You may be thinking, "I couldn't do anything differently. I can't just up and quit. I have two kids to support. I'd lose my house or apartment. I couldn't pay the bills. I don't have any choice but to stay there and take it and hope that my boss will change and see the wonderful person I truly am!"

That's not likely to happen, so let's think of some alternatives. Maybe you could quit and you could live with your parents during the time it takes to find a new and more rewarding job. I know, I know, your parents are so critical of everything you do and they would think you were a complete failure if you moved in with them temporarily. True, but if you had to, you could live with them. You could sign on at a temp agency before you quit so that you had some income. It might be fun and interesting, and if you didn't like the people you were working for, at least you'd know it's not permanent. Then you could even ask for a different assignment.

Do you see the idea? You may not see these as perfect solutions, yet the activity lets you know that you always have a choice.

After you finish this activity, take a look at it clearly. Do you see certain patterns? Do you most often feel like a "victim" when you try to please others? When you don't speak up? When you are frightened or fear some sort of loss? Who are the people in your life who make you feel this way most often? Do you see that you have chosen the same sort of dead-end solutions over and over again?

Take heart! Now that you can clearly see the ways in which you have given your control over to others and allowed yourself to be blinded by words instead of behaviors, you have taken a crucial first step in change! Good for you!

CHAPTER
THREE

What Did You Experience?
Verbal, Emotional, Sexual, and Physical Abuse

WHEN MOST OF US THINK OF AN ABUSED WOMAN, our mind immediately conjures up a vision of a small, weak, defenseless female covered in bruises. Perhaps she is bleeding or has broken bones. That's not me, we think, full of superiority. That could never happen to me. If any guy raised his hand to me, I'd kick him to the curb and get outta there.

Well, maybe you would. But then again, there are two things wrong with your argument: 1) Not every abused woman is physically abused. In fact, the vast majority of abuse is not physical. 2) By the time your relationship became physically abusive, you would hardly notice it. It would have become an ordinary occurrence in your life because there would have been a long history of verbal, emotional, and sexual abuse that preceded it.

I can imagine that you're having a hard time accepting my proposal, so let me explain what these levels of abuse entail and why virtually every one of us has already experienced them in many life situations.

VERBAL AND EMOTIONAL ABUSE

It is often very difficult to distinguish between these two types of abuse because they frequently go hand in hand, occurring simultaneously. For example, calling a woman demeaning names, such as "bitch," "whore," "fat," "lazy," "stupid," "demented," and so on are verbally abusive. If you have ever been referred to by those names or others, think of your emotional response. What did it do to your feelings about yourself? How did it affect the rest of your day? Did it change the ways in which you interacted with that person or others?

All types of abuse have these same common denominators: power and control. In my opinion, verbal and emotional abuses are perhaps the most devastating types of power and control techniques. When you think about it, a broken bone will heal and bruises will fade, but when a soul is degraded and destroyed, how does that heal and how long does it take? As many of you can attest, that is the most difficult process and it affects everything we do in life from our work relationships, personal relationships, to our relationships with ourselves.

The verbal and emotional abuser systematically degrades your feelings of self-worth. He may blame you for his own shortcomings, humiliate you, call you names, tell you that you're crazy for feeling a certain way, and use menacing or intimidating looks.

Let's take a look at some common verbally or emotionally abusive behaviors. How many have you experienced with one or more people in your life?

IGNORING YOUR FEELINGS

> *I remember that so often when I was growing up, I would have a fight with a female friend, or I felt insulted by a teacher, or any of the other type of stuff like that that kids feel. I would run home to my mother and try to explain how I felt. She would say, "Oh, that's nonsense. You shouldn't feel that way. It's just ridiculous. Now, go wash your face and stop behaving like such a baby." That was devastating to me. I felt so alone and that I must be crazy. After a while, I stopped expressing my feelings at all to her and then to anyone else. I became emotionally numb.*
>
> — NANCY, 48

Nancy brings up an important aspect of habitually having your feelings ignored: pretty soon you forget how to have them. They are either too dangerous to feel, because there may be rejection involved in feeling them, or pointless, because who cares about them anyway?

How many people in your life have ignored your feelings of pain, loneliness, fear, rejection, sadness, insecurity, or emptiness?

NAME-CALLING

> *"You're so stupid and slow, you'll never find anyone who treats you like I do," Jim would say to me. I know it was a threat to get me to stay, but after a while I started thinking to myself, "Gee, I sure hope not."*
>
> — TRACY, 28

When I worked in the domestic violence shelter, I'd ask the women to list the names they were called by their mates. They could have been reading from a script, for they had all heard the same litany of garbage. In addition, they were told that: "No one would ever want you," "You're damaged goods," "You're just completely worthless," "No man is going to look at you twice with ___ [number of] kids," etc.

The list goes on and on, but I think you get the idea. Let me just say that if you heard those or similar words or statements from your abuser, I am terribly sorry. I would like you to consider the psychological concept of "projection," which essentially means that when people can't own up to their shortcomings they toss them out onto you and say that you possess those qualities.

If you have been called degrading names or cute little endearments such as "bubble butt," or "moo-moo wearin' mama" (my own personal favorite for originality in a low-class category), I hope you can take a moment here to wonder whether you were told those lies about yourself when they actually were really about your abuser.

Perhaps you just said to yourself, "Oh no, my _____ [husband, boss, friend, mother, etc.] would never refer to himself in that way. He thinks way too much of himself."

Well, maybe others think the same of you from the outside. But consider an idea. Imagine that you had those or other names hurled at you and in response you actually told your abuser, "Well, if I'm really all of those things, why do you keep me around? What does that say about you?" Hmmm.

WITHHOLDING APPROVAL, AFFECTION, OR APPRECIATION

Would it be so terrible if my boss said, "Thank you," "Great job," "I really appreciate how hard you work," even once?

— ANN-MARIE, 32

Many of you completely understand that statement. You either work for someone—man or woman—who doesn't appreciate your efforts, you live with a mate or children who just expect for you to do, do, do for them, or whatever you do for your friends or parents is never enough. You may feel that you constantly have to "top" the last great thing you do for them. Aren't you exhausted already?

When my husband was upset with me, he would go off in a pout. He didn't slam doors or curse at me; he just gave me the long, silent treatment. He acted like he was so wounded and that I was so horrible he couldn't bear to share the same air space as me.

— Lynn, 41

Can you relate to Lynn's feelings? This goes to the point of power and control in a nonphysical manner. Lynn's husband had total power and control without saying a word or lifting a hand. In doing so, she felt damaged and like she herself was a bully or someone so completely without worth that he couldn't bring himself to talk with her or be in the same room.

INTIMIDATING LOOKS

He never had to say a word. He could give me that look with his head slightly down and his eyebrows raised and it was all over for me.

— Claire, 29

You may know what Claire is talking about. If you grew up in a family that was angry, violent, or included substance abuse, you became very adept at reading expressions on your parent's faces. You may have spent a lot of time looking out for their bad moods before you brought up a

51

subject. You could anticipate their behavior as soon as they looked at you. You had to; it's the way you survived. You then used this neat, little trick with every significant person in your life. Be aware that you are extra sensitive to others' feelings and behaviors; an abusive person will use that to their full advantage.

MONOPOLIZING YOUR TIME

My boss thinks that I live to meet his needs. It doesn't matter if it's an hour past my lunchtime; he still has more petty things for me to do for him. My kids feel like I have nothing to do in life except drive them to their friends' houses, pick up three teammates for soccer practice, or bake two dozen cookies for class at ten o'clock at night.

— FRANCIE, 40

Many women tell me they feel like the people in their lives are smothering them. In the beginning, it feels nice to be needed. It makes them feel important—invaluable really. Soon, however, others' needs are dictating their lives and their own needs are being squashed down.

ISOLATION

I was very social before I married Steve. I had lots of girlfriends that I'd known forever. They didn't like him and warned me not to marry him. One of them was divorced, two had been in bad relationships, and another one hadn't had a boyfriend for a long time. I was pretty certain that they had become bitter about men and were a little envious of my happiness. I tried to excuse their behavior because of that and also because we had always been there for each other during the bad times. After we got married, Steve started making little comments about them, which eventually became bigger. It started becoming a hassle to see them because he would make such a fuss about it when I did. He said they were "dykes" who couldn't stand men and that kind of trash. Pretty soon, one by one they stopped calling because I always had an excuse as to why I couldn't go out.

When I made the mistake of telling Steve that a guy at work had innocently flirted with me, he went to the office and slugged him. My boss was very upset about it and suggested I leave or the guy would press charges against my husband. Steve said I didn't need to work anyway because he made good money and could take care of us. It just started that way—the isolation, I mean—and continued until there was no one in my life except him.

— Sue, 32

Women involved with abusive mates are frequently isolated from the rest of the world. Very often, women who have been raised by abusive parents speak of a type of isolation in childhood as well. Keeping a woman or child away from any emotional supports or outside influences is necessary in order to create the proper atmosphere for the "brainwashing" to take place, and to create a dependency and a willingness to obey.

Partners and parents do this in much the same way: being very critical of a woman or girl's friends, restricting telephone access, insulting her friends in front of her so that they voluntarily stay away from her or she feels so embarrassed that she cuts off contact with them to avoid further pain. After a time, she may become too depressed and weak to fight back.

HUMILIATION

*My supervisor always had some sort of smart com-
ment about me at staff meetings. She'd say things like,
"Jeannie's a house frau; let's see if she knows how to fix the
coffee maker in the lounge," or, "What do you think of that
idea, Jeannie? Do you have an opinion today or is your
brain in neutral because you were up with your baby all
night again?"*

— JEANNIE, 29

Jeannie makes an interesting point about humiliation:
Abusers can degrade you with a smile on their face and
also in the guise of a joke. Perhaps comments like those of
her boss were meant to make her cry or leave the room so
that she would then be labeled "too sensitive" or one who
"can't take a joke."

*When I was a kid, my parents would do things like say
to their friends, right in front of me, "If we had stock in the
Clearasil Company, we could retire by now." Or if we were
at a pharmacy, my mother might yell to me down the
aisle, "Oh here's a new type of diet pill. Do you want to try
these?" They still do it to this day; making snide little comments or embarrassing remarks in the guise of trying to
be helpful. I've asked them to stop. They can't understand
how hurtful it is to me.*

— BECKY, 34

MAKING THREATS

*I'd get so frustrated with Don that I'd tell him, "This is
it. I can't take another day of this." He'd start to cry and tell
me, "I'll kill myself if you leave me," or "I couldn't go on if*

*you ever left." What was I supposed to do? I'd feel respon-
sible for the rest of my life if he did anything to himself
after that.*

— MEG, 28

Usually, when we think of threats or threatening
behavior, the first thing that pops into our heads is a person brandishing a weapon or saying, "I'll kill you," not,
"I'll kill myself." While the first statement is certainly
extremely threatening and can happen, it is the latter
statement that is most manipulative. As Meg stated, it is
not only a direct threat, it also makes the woman feel
responsible for her partner's actions. If he does something
to harm himself, it would be her fault, not his.

*He'd get right in my face and say in a real low voice,
"I could kill you with my bare hands right now if I wanted
to, but I'm not ready to go to jail over you yet. But, mark my
words; there will be a day not far off where it won't matter
anymore."*

— MELISSA, 31

This type of scenario not only creates fear in the
woman out of threat of harm, it also keeps her on edge,
not knowing when he might carry out the threat on a
whim. Her life becomes an effort not to enrage him to that
point.

MAKING TRIVIAL DEMANDS

*I worked at a company where you could wear nice
sandals on "casual Fridays." My boss decided one day that
we could not wear any shade of pink toenail polish on*

those days. I couldn't tell you why, but she would really get on you if you did.

— AMY, 30

My husband decided that when he came home from work at 6:30, dinner should be on the table, the boys should have already had their baths and be in their pajamas to greet him. At first, I thought this was something out of a 1950s sitcom and told him so. His answer was, "I make the money around here, and your only responsibility is to see to the house and the kids. I think I deserve this much after a long day, don't you?" It made me feel ungrateful, but I still didn't see the need to have boys, ages four and six, bathed, and in PJs when it was still light outside and their friends were still playing. I told him how difficult it was and his reply was, "Okay then, make sure they are bathed and in their pajamas at 6:00." Huh?

— CATHY, 35

You may be wondering why those demands were made to begin with. So am I, and as you can see so are Amy and Cathy. When trivial demands are made, the abuser arbitrarily sets them and there are consequences to not following through. We could surmise that perhaps Amy's boss didn't personally care for pink nail polish and so didn't want to see it around the workplace. But notice that it was only on Fridays and only on the toes, not the fingernails, that day or any other day of the week.

Cathy's husband may have been brought up in a household in which he had to be bathed and in his pajamas very early in the evening. He may have come from a very traditional, male dominated home in which his dad made the rules. I'll bet he didn't like some of the rules his father set down and neither did his mother, so why would he want to make the same rules in his own home? Also, did you follow his "logic" that since Cathy argued about the difficulty she'd have in following his original demand, he upped the ante?

A couple of important concepts to remember about trivial demands is that not only are they petty and non-sensical, with consequences to follow if not met, but because they are trivial, they could—and usually do—change at any time. And then there are new rules to follow. They also have the effect of keeping a woman in a topsy-turvy world in which few things make sense and parts of reality are obliterated. You can't figure out why the rules are there, you just know that you have to follow them or else.

MAKING YOU FEEL LIKE YOU'RE "CRAZY"

> *My boyfriend will say something like "I'll call you at six tonight." When he doesn't call, I'll ask him about it the next day and he'll swear he never said that. This type of thing goes on in different ways and then when I bring up something important he's done that upsets me, he'll say, "I never did that. You're making up stories again. You know you can't get anything straight."*
>
> — TINA, 47

Tina describes a type of "crazy-making" that has the effect of causing her to doubt her own judgment. She starts to feel stupid and psychologically off-balance. As her boyfriend convinces her—in subtle ways—that her psyche is becoming more and more impaired, she feels hopeless and more dependent on him to take care of her.

CHECKING UP ON YOU

At first, I considered it very flattering that Craig called me five or six times a day at work, when I was out with my friends, or at the market on my cell phone. He really seemed to care and told me so. At night, if I was going home from his place, I'd be coming in the door and hear the phone ringing. He might say, "I've been calling you for five minutes. What took you so long to get home? I was worried about you." I thought it was really sweet that he was always so concerned.

— KELLI, 25

Checking behaviors are very insidious because they are usually veiled in concern . . . in the beginning. As Kelli mentioned, she felt flattered that her boyfriend needed to make sure she was all right no matter where she was, even working behind a receptionist's desk or buying eggs. What he was really doing, however, was making sure he knew where she was, what she was doing, and most importantly, that she wasn't with another man.

To this day, my father calls every day so that I can give him a full report about where I was that day, who I was with, and what I was doing. If I don't give him complete details, he acts hurt and accuses me of not caring about him. He tells me I should be lucky to have a parent that's interested.

— BETH, 32

I can't be out of the house for ten minutes before one of my kids calls me on my cell phone and asks what I'm doing and what time I'll be home. Their father does the same thing. Aren't I allowed to have even a little time to myself?

— CARLY, 39

BETRAYAL OF CONFIDENCES

Why do I always end up with friends I can't trust?

— PATTY, 41

I'll tell my best friend something private and three days later I'm quizzed about it from four other people.

— ADRIENNE, 36

I told a coworker something that was upsetting me about our boss one day at lunch. The day after that, he calls me into his office and starts talking to me about it in a real defensive, accusatory way. I was caught completely off-guard. I didn't say anything to her, but she had the nerve to bring it up later, saying she told him because she could see that it was really upsetting me and she didn't think I'd tell him on my own.

— SUE, 38

You may have revealed yourself to people in your life only to find out that they've abused your trust. Make no mistake: This is a form of emotional abuse. They are deliberately exposing you at your core or making decisions for you without your consent.

SEXUAL ABUSE

For the purposes of this section, I am not including sexual harassment in this category. That topic will be covered fully in Chapter Six.

Many of you may have been sexually abused as a child or young girl. Therefore sexually inappropriate behaviors could now seem normal or the right of the abuser, while your feelings and thoughts on the matter seem insignificant. Another group of you may not have been able to develop your own strong voice in your family's home and don't think you have the right to speak up when something feels sexually creepy. Some of you may not know what is or isn't "allowed" in sexual situations.

Let me give you my thoughts on what I believe to be sexually abusive behaviors. How many of these can you relate to?

My husband needed to have sex every night. Sometimes twice a day. It didn't matter if I had the flu, was eight months pregnant, was nursing a baby at the time, was tired, or had just gotten my period that day and was feeling achy and non-sexual. He would call me a "frigid bitch" and then stomp off into another room to pout. Sometimes, he told me that if I didn't give it to him, he'd find some other woman who would. He never treated me gently in bed or thought of satisfying me.

— GRACE, 43

The sex kept getting weirder and weirder. He started asking me to do things I think he must have seen in porn videos or magazines. I felt like a whore.

— TRISH, 31

What Did You Experience?

When we were out with his friends, he'd grab my butt or stick his hands down my blouse and quickly fondle my breasts. Sometimes he'd give a kind of playful bite to my nipples through whatever I was wearing. It was embarrassing and the women in the group would look at me like I was nuts.

— GAYLE, 29

Grace, Trish, and Gayle all describe instances of sexual abuse. Traditionally, men have been raised to believe that sex anytime, anywhere, and in any form was their right. Likewise, women have been raised to believe that the woman's job is to acquiesce to her man's demands and that she should always be available to him. Perhaps you were raised in that way to a certain extent, either by outright teaching or by example.

Most women I have spoken with do not believe that marital rape exists. They are very forthright in their belief that rape only exists outside of a committed relationship or that rape must involve a stranger. I must state emphatically that those beliefs are incorrect. Just because you are living with a man—marriage certificate or not—he is not entitled to force sex on you in any way. That is called rape. It is not his right, his prerogative, or his whim. If sex is not completely consensual, it is rape.

Any unwanted touching or kissing is also sexual abuse. You have the right to say where and when. He cannot take it whenever he feels like it.

If you have ever had sex because you were afraid not to, or because you knew your partner would harass you until you did, it was forced sex. He doesn't have to tie you down or verbally threaten you in order for you to understand that it was against your will.

PHYSICAL ABUSE

As I mentioned in the beginning of this chapter, when many of us think of abuse, physical abuse is what immediately comes to mind. In fact, that is society's concept as well. As you have already seen, there are other types of abuse that are more common and I'm sure you have related to many of them.

If you have ever been hit, pushed, slapped, kicked, bitten, choked, slugged with an object, or had one thrown at you, you can more easily define your physical abuse. Other forms of this abuse are subtler.

> I was afraid to drive with him and even more afraid if our daughter was in the car with us. He was usually in a bad mood when he drove. Who knows why? There didn't have to be a reason. The least little thing could set him off. Anyway, when he drove, it was way too fast and very recklessly. He would cut people off on the freeway and tailgate other cars. I was scared to death, but if I said something, he'd slam on his brakes and tell me to get out.
>
> — DARCY, 39

> Once, my boss was really berating me. He was telling me everything I did wrong that week and he had quite a list. I felt like I was going to cry and didn't want to let him see me doing that. It would have been so unprofessional and make me look weak. Not to mention, it would give him something else to yell at me about. I said I understood what he was saying, I was sorry, and that I needed to leave. He grabbed me by the arm and wouldn't let me go. He said, "I haven't finished yet." I felt like a prisoner.
>
> — FRANCIE, 50

*We were on our way home from a party in an un-
familiar part of the city and got lost. I kept telling him that
he was going the wrong way and we ended up in a dangerous area. I was really scared but I felt intuitively like
I knew where we should go. Instead of taking my advice or
finding a gas station to stop at and ask directions, he
pulled over to the side of the road and said, "Get out."
I couldn't believe it. I told him it was dangerous and that
I was sorry if it seemed like I didn't trust his driving. He said,
"You're so smart; I'm sure you'll figure out a way to get
home." Then he drove off and just left me standing on the
sidewalk after midnight in this section of town. I could
have been killed.*

— DENISE, 37

*He threw a plate at my head and would hurl the TV
remote at my legs. When I told him that he could have hurt
me, he said, "It didn't hit you, did it?" I think he was trying to
tell me that the objects missed me and so I shouldn't accuse
him of physical abuse, but I just think he had bad aim.*

— LINDA, 42

What these women describe is physical abuse. Did
their abusers leave any marks? Not on their bodies, but
plenty on their souls.

It is very important to understand that physical abuse
always escalates. If you have accepted being pushed or
shoved onto a bed or against a wall telling yourself that it
didn't hurt or that it was just an accident, your abuser has
no doubt interpreted that as permission to do it again or
something more harmful.

I am often asked if one push is physical abuse. My
answer is that each person has to decide for herself how
much is too much. Why would one incident be acceptable? Do you believe that he didn't have any other way of

expressing his feelings than by putting his hands on you in a cruel fashion?

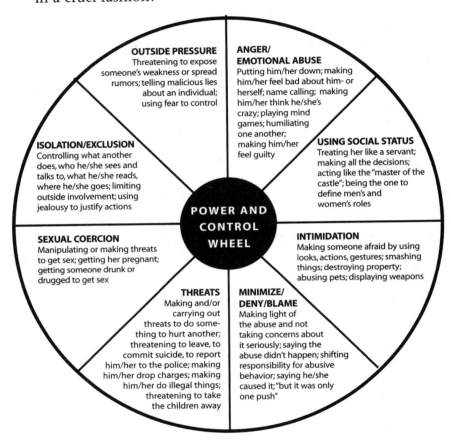

Take a good look at the Power and Control Wheel above. It is important for you to know that if you are in a relationship in which any one of these behaviors is happening, you are in an unhealthy, destructive, abusive relationship. As a matter of fact, I am not talking about all of the items inside one piece of the pie, but one item inside one piece of pie. That news may be shocking to you as you look at these behaviors and identify various people in your life to which these apply. Granted, some of these items apply exclusively to romantic relationships, but most of them do not. Take a few minutes and truly study this wheel. It makes it very simple to see abusive relationships in the light of day.

ACTIVITY
How Have I Handled Past Abuses?

Now that you have seen all the different components of verbal and emotional abuse, sexual abuse, and physical abuse, I would like you to make an inventory of all the people in your life who have done these sorts of things to you. It may be quite long. Get out your journal and structure it this way:

Name of person	Abusive act	How I felt	What I did about it, or excuse I gave

Try to rack your mind and think back as far as you can permit yourself. Do you see a pattern? How many emotionally or verbally abusive acts have you accepted?

Can you see how you generally felt? Did it cause you to feel worthless, sad, or hopeless? Did you stay silent? Why? Maybe it was easier that way or you felt powerless to help those people see your view.

What excuses did you give yourself or others about the abuse? You may have thought or said, "He's just that way." "I can't change her. It's not my place."; " If I say anything, I'll get fired."; "She's just having a bad day."; "It was my fault. I shouldn't have egged him on."; "I deserved it.";

"She has PMS."; "Everyone's entitled to one (or two, or nine, or twelve) mistakes."; " I'm not perfect, either."

Keep this list handy. We will refer to it throughout the rest of the book. Right now, you will need to sit with this list, and, as difficult as it is, really let the reality of your abuse sink in. Do not push it away. Do not deny it or tell yourself that it wasn't that bad. Each of those incidents was that bad. I'm sorry it happened to you.

WHAT ARE THE PATTERNS IN YOUR RELATIONSHIPS?

Introduction

What Are the Patterns in Your Relationships?

You want me to list all my abusers? Okay, should I start
with my father and brothers, or just the present day stuff?

— CHRIS, 33

IN DOING THE ACTIVITIES OF THE PREVIOUS THREE CHAPTERS, you have probably seen some patterns revealed. These represent the unhealthy ways that you have allowed others to relate to you and what you have or haven't done about it. Below are some of the possible patterns. Please put a check mark next to the statements that apply to you. You may find that you mark every category.

- ❑ My mate (or former mates) has abused me
- ❑ My parents have abused me
- ❑ My children have abused me
- ❑ I have been abused at my place of work
- ❑ My friends have abused me
- ❑ I have been verbally abused
- ❑ I have been emotionally abused

❑ I have been sexually abused
❑ I have been physically abused

Let's take a moment and look at the list above. Now you've identified those who have treated you unfairly and the ways that they have treated you. So what are the patterns in your abusive relationships? Do people of authority treat you in a disrespectful way? Are your abusers primarily men or women? Do you find that you can't say "no" to a request from virtually anyone? Do you have trouble with rude children? Have you experienced a string of bad romantic relationships? Are you still acting like a child with your parents? The next step is to determine what effect these patterns of abuse have had on your life.

> *When I really think about it, everyone in my life treats me like crap!*
>
> — DONNA, 23

WHAT I HAVE DONE ABOUT ABUSIVE BEHAVIOR

As women, we are often taught—whether directly or indirectly—to look inward when we are being treated in an abusive manner. That is often a good idea and indeed largely what I am asking you to do in this book. However, when we are told that we must take total responsibility for another person's behavior and, what's more, *we* need to fix it—that is an unhealthy attitude.

You may have had a variety of reactions in response to abusive behavior directed at you. Take a look at the lists below and see how many of the comments or attitudes to which you relate. Again, you may find that you have experienced several or all of these at different times in your life.

- I have chosen to remain silent when abused.

- I have denied that the abuse occurred.

- The excuses I have made to myself, or others, were:

  - *He was tired.*
  - *She probably has PMS.*
  - *I'm sure I heard him incorrectly.*
  - *I must have deserved it.*
  - *He didn't mean it the way it sounded.*
  - *He had a bad day at work.*
  - *I should be more understanding.*
  - *If I hadn't done _____, it never would have happened.*
  - *I'm probably being too sensitive.*
  - *He must have been drunk.*
  - *I should be more patient.*
  - *Maybe I'm just going crazy.*
  - *She's my best friend, so I forgive her again.*
  - *She's the boss, so I just have to take it.*
  - *That's just the way he is.*
  - *They're my parents and it would be wrong to speak up.*
  - *It would cause more problems to be confrontational.*
  - *It really doesn't bother me that much.*
  - *I'm probably making too big a deal of it.*

- I don't confront my abuser, but overeat when I get home.

- I have become very depressed.

- I know that I overspend or compulsively shop to deal with my bad feelings.

- I drink or use drugs on a regular basis.

- I get unreasonably angry with people other than my abuser(s).

- I feel frightened a good deal of the time.

- I have difficulty sleeping.

- I feel worried about the future.

Are these some of the ways that you've dealt with your abuse?

I make excuses for everyone in my life except myself.
— AMY, 30

This may have been the first time you really took a good look at the patterns of abuse in your life. Until now, you may not have known why you are so frequently depressed, have physical ailments more often than you should, or why you may have felt stuck, powerless, or doomed. Do you have the same type of excuses for all of your abusers (e.g., you take the blame or think you are being overly dramatic)? The way you feel about yourself and your world critically affects every part of your life, including your health, interpersonal relationships, and ability to function. Acknowledging these patterns is a crucial first step in demolishing them. It is important to keep these patterns in mind as you go through the rest of this book.

How did these patterns begin? Well, like almost everything else, in childhood. Now that you recognize your patterns, let's see where they came from.

CHAPTER
FOUR

The Role Your Parents Played in Your Destructive Relationships

WE LEARN SO MUCH in the homes in which we are raised. Hopefully, we learn that we are wonderful, precious, and valued members of our family. When a child knows she is loved and accepted, she can weather almost any calamity with her self-worth intact, knowing that while she is presently experiencing difficulties, she will be clear-minded and think her way out of her situation, thriving in the process. Even women with good self-esteem are prey to abusive relationships. But it's a bit harder to convince ourselves that we should maintain them.

In this chapter, I'll discuss how your parents may have inadvertently set you up to be part of an abusive relationship or several. While we'd like to think that our parents did the best they could for us, in many cases their best hasn't been good enough. That may sound harsh, but I believe that every child has a birthright to be treasured and told that she or he is perfect exactly as she is. We can all think of historical or entertainment figures who grew up dirt poor, discriminated against, and with a myriad of other reasons they should not succeed, yet they did, either because of or in spite of their bad luck. When asked how they managed to make their dreams come true, rather than ending up drug addicts or criminals, they all talk about the love they experienced in their homes.

Let's take a look at some ways in which children's hearts and souls are often disrespected. Perhaps you can relate on one or many levels.

WHEN A CHILD'S BASIC EMOTIONAL NEEDS ARE UNMET

In her wonderful book, *Facing Codependence*, Pia Mellody describes some of the natural characteristics of a child that can become difficulties for her later in life if squashed or not cherished by her family:

- A feeling of not being valuable can create difficulty in experiencing appropriate levels of self-esteem.

- Not being allowed to be vulnerable may foster difficulty setting functional boundaries.

- Not being allowed to be imperfect may result in an adult woman's difficulty owning and expressing her own reality and imperfections.

- Feeling naturally dependent—that is, needy and wanting—can create an adult who has difficulty taking care of her adult needs and wants.

- A child who isn't allowed to be immature at the correct time of immaturity can have difficulty experiencing and moderately expressing her reality in her adult life. She may act chaotic or controlling.

I know this may sound crazy, but I remember so clearly my father saying to me, "Stop being such a baby," when I was no more than four years old. What did he think I was? A grown woman? How was I supposed to act?

— MARY, 38

You may have been raised in a home in which you were told that your view of reality was ridiculous. You may have been told that you shouldn't feel the feelings that you felt. I remember so many times in my childhood—and even womanhood—when my mother said to me, "Oh, that's just silly. You shouldn't feel that way." It not only hurt my feelings, it made me feel very alone and that I couldn't trust my own emotions. Have you ever had the same experience?

ACTIVITY
My Unmet Emotional Needs

In this exercise, I would like you to begin examining the needs that Pia Mellody articulated from the list above. On a sheet in your journal, write these words:

- Valuable
- Vulnerable
- Imperfect
- Dependent
- Immature

Now, take each word and describe the ways in which your childhood needs were not met in those categories that apply to you. Then, take a moment and write a sentence or two about the ways in which not having those feelings honored has affected your life and relationships.

THE "SNEAKY" WAYS GIRLS ARE EXPOSED TO ABUSE IN THEIR HOMES

You have already seen that the definition of abuse isn't as narrow as physical abuse alone. It also includes verbal, emotional, and sexual abuse. Given that description, would you say that you grew up in a non-abusive, somewhat abusive, or highly abusive home?

Evidence has shown that girls raised in abusive homes, even those that are not physically abusive, experience the following:

- Increased rate of death by homicide and suicide

- More depression and emotional injuries, such as low self-esteem

- Higher risk for drug and alcohol use

- Earlier marriages and earlier pregnancies

- Continuation of abuse into adult relationships

- Inability to have a "normal" childhood and adolescence

- Early learning of denial as a coping mechanism

- Taking on roles inappropriate to their age and maturity level

If you were raised in a home that was abusive at any of the four levels (verbal, emotional, sexual, physical), you have been taught that this is acceptable behavior. Even though you may have hated how your parents acted toward each other and toward you, understand that you may be predisposed to recreate that behavior, if only to prove that you don't have to act as your parents did in the same type of situation. Sometimes women unconsciously seek out abusive relationships in order to solve, or put to rest the unfairness of their past; "I couldn't fix Daddy, but I can fix this guy."

In my book, *But I Love Him*, I outlined behaviors that may not always be perceived as abusive, but that clearly teach young girls to devalue themselves and set up the potential for them to enter an abusive relationship in the future:

- Men call women names, such as "bitch," "whore," "stupid," "ridiculous," etc.

- Men are considered superior to women. The behavior may not be blatant, but the attitude is displayed in various ways that make a woman feel incapable of doing "a man's work," such as hovering over her or laughing while she is fixing a car or working outside the home.

- Women are the butt of jokes ("stupid women" or "dumb blonde" jokes).

- Woman's body parts are referred to by vulgar words, such as "tits," "ass," "booty," and so on.

- The man of the family explodes in anger and leaves the house.

- Mom frequently cries over a difficulty with a man.

- Men usually have the last word whenever there is a difference of opinion and women remain passive in such a case.

- Mom tells her daughter that it is a woman's obligation to sexually satisfy her man, defer to his judgment, laugh at his jokes, take care of his every need, make herself available to his desires, not complain, "take what you are given," suffer through life, "forgive and forget," treat men as children, fix whatever is wrong in a relationship, be a helpmate.

- Mom gives her daughter the impression—either implied or directly—that she's nothing without a man.

Do any of those statements sound like your childhood home? Listen, this isn't "Bash Your Parents Week." It is just very important to understand where you came from and the possible impact your upbringing has had on your life. We all wish we had the *Leave It to Beaver, Father Knows Best, Ozzie and Harriet,* or *The Cosby* family. But let's face it: the reason why those shows were so popular is that their idealized families don't exist in real life. For an hour a week, we could immerse ourselves in the characters' lives and pretend our lives were perfect as well, if only for that limited time.

My mom and dad never slugged it out, although sometimes I thought it would be easier if they did. Then at least the anger might be gone for a little while. I came from an upper middle-class family and there were lots of rules about behavior. Well, lots of rules for the kids, not so many rules for the parents. Their only job was to present us as this perfect family and never let the cat out of the bag that they hated each other and probably didn't like us kids too much, either. The tension in my house was unbelievable. You couldn't crack it with a sledgehammer. Then, we'd go out—or they would—and you'd swear we were the ideal family.

My friends used to tell me, "You're so lucky to have such great parents. My parents fight all the time and I can't wait to get out of there. I love to come to your house, it's so calm and nice." What a crock! It made me feel a little crazy about what was real and what wasn't. Now, here I am doing the same thing as an adult: showing one face and feeling another. I've got kids who don't respect me, friends who only like me when I can do something for them, a husband who doesn't pay any attention to me, and when I go home for the holidays, it's still the same garbage with my parents.

— DEE, 46

THE EFFECTS OF DEPRESSED PARENTS

If you grew up in a home in which one or both of your parents were frequently depressed, you may not realize the effect it's had on your choice of relationships. Do you know what I mean by depressed? It's different than the occasional sadness we all feel that comes and goes with a shift in hormones, situation, or the seasons. Depression lasts most of the day, every day, for at least two weeks and it has at least five of the following symptoms:

- Changes in appetite: eating more or less than usual

- Sleep problems: not being able to fall or stay asleep or wanting to sleep much more than usual

- Low energy and feelings of fatigue

- Difficulty concentrating, making decisions, or thinking clearly

- Restlessness and irritability

- Feelings of worthlessness, hopelessness, or inappropriate guilt

- Excessive crying

- Chronic aches and pains that seem to have no cause

- Thoughts of death or suicide, or suicide attempts

- Loss of pleasure or interest in activities that used to give you happiness

Not only might these apply to one or both of your parents, you may find that you can also personally relate to many of the symptoms of depression. Scientific studies have shown that depression tends to run in families and there are genetic links. In addition, women statistically have far higher rates of depression than men. This could be an actual fact, or it may simply indicate that women are more open with their feelings and therefore report depression more often than men.

Is depression nature or nurture? A bit of both, actually. If you had depressed parents, you may be chemically predisposed to depression. Scientists have found that there is evidence that women who grew up in depressed homes have an increased risk for depression. In any case, growing up in a depressed home may have taught you many things that led to your abusive relationships.

In their book, *Growing Up Sad: Childhood Depression and Its Treatment*, Drs. Leon Cytryn and Donald McKnew state that a child's depression is clearly evident in the way she speaks and acts. She feels hopeless, helpless, worthless, unattractive, unloved, and guilty. In addition, suicidal thoughts may run through her mind frequently. Her facial expressions are sad, as is her posture, she often cries, there is a slowness of movement and emotional reactions, she has disturbances of appetite and sleep, increased irritability, and physical complaints for which there appear to be no causes. Does this sound like you when you were a young girl or teenager?

When parents are depressed, they can hardly take care of themselves, let alone their children. Therefore you may not have been properly cared for or nurtured. It's not that your parents didn't want to, they just didn't have the energy or concentration for the job.

So, how does this set you up to be the perfect candidate for abusive relationships? When her parents neglect a girl to some degree, she receives inconsistent parenting and learns to fend for herself. She may feel guilty about their sadness, and usually becomes a rescuer or helper in order to aid the depressed parent. She also becomes very attuned to their moods without their ever saying a word. She quickly learns—possibly just by their posture or the ways their eyes are cast—to read their moods and adjust accordingly. Due to neglect, she may fear abandonment.

Let's think about these descriptions for a moment. When a woman grows to learn that it is her responsibility to fix her parent's sadness, she does so with all the people in her life. If your child is having a bad day, you'd better see what's wrong and do something about it immediately. If your friend is sad about some difficulty that doesn't involve you, you're on the case. What if your supervisor is upset because her boss didn't give her the performance review she would have liked; you can't do enough to cheer her up. Sound familiar?

If a girl grows up anticipating her parent's moods, she now watches for signs of strain with everyone with whom she is in close contact and adjusts her own moods accordingly. That is the very definition of codependence: *I'm okay if you're okay.*

A fear of abandonment may be acted out in abusive situations in which a woman won't break off an unhealthy relationship for fear of being alone. She may even realize that she's being mistreated, but says to herself, "A family who loves you 50 percent of the time is better than no family at all."

When I was a child, my mother was very frequently depressed. Her marriage with my father was always in turmoil, yet she wouldn't end it. In the 1960s, a divorced woman was something of a pariah, and appearances, as well as social standing, were of paramount importance to her. This left her in a no win situation. She was desperately unhappy and unwilling to do anything about it. So, like many women of her generation, she took pills...lots of them: "uppers" to make her feel better and "downers" to calm her down and help her sleep. Unfortunately, my mother was also quite a dramatic, hysterical woman and whenever she had one of her "episodes," she started randomly grabbing at the many pill bottles on her dresser table.

As you can imagine, this scared the pants off of me. Although I was young, I knew what could happen when a parent took too many pills—she could go to sleep forever. Because of my need to protect my mother from herself, I often flushed all her pills down the toilet thinking this would end the problem. Of course, she just yelled at me and went back to the pharmacy. I recognize that my need to rescue my mother, judge her moods, and take care of myself, have all played a part in my own abusive relationships time and time again. Understanding that I was the child in the family, not the parent, and could not "save"

my mother from herself, helped to begin freeing me of my
unhealthy relationships.

THE EFFECTS OF SEXUAL ABUSE

According to the Safer Society Program, a project of the
New York State Council of Churches and a national
research, advocacy, and referral center on the prevention of
child abuse, it is a horrifying fact that one in three girls and
one in seven boys will be sexually abused by the time they
turn 18. If this has been part of your history, I personally
understand your pain. You are not alone. Sexual abuse can
happen to children of every race, religion, economic class,
and geographical region. Fathers, mothers, aunts, uncles,
siblings, teachers, caregivers, family friends, or strangers
can violate children. The vast majority of abusers are
heterosexual men who are at least acquainted with the
children and have gained their trust.

Although we may tend to define sexual abuse as
coerced intercourse, Ellen Bass and Laura Davis, authors of
the groundbreaking book, *The Courage to Heal*, clearly
delineate other terms of sexual abuse. You were sexually
abused if you were:

- Touched in sexual areas

- Shown sexual movies or forced to listen to
  sexual talk

- Made to pose for seductive or sexual
  photographs

- Subjected to unnecessary medical treatments

- Forced to perform oral sex on an adult or sibling

- Raped or otherwise penetrated [Dr. Murray's note: including with fingers or objects]

- Fondled, kissed, or held in a way that made you uncomfortable

- Forced to take part in ritualized abuse in which you were physically or sexually tortured

- Bathed in a way that felt intrusive to you

- Objectified and ridiculed about your body

- Encouraged or goaded into sex you didn't really want

- Told all you were good for was sex

- Involved in child pornography or child prostitution

Children who have been sexually abused truly are victims, as they have not had the power to object. They are the victims of ruthless and sick power and control games at the hands of adults who should have cared about them. These children did not have a voice, and didn't have a choice. They were not to blame, and if they continue to carry this shame and blame with them as an adult, there are certain emotional characteristics that may have been taken forward from childhood.

Bass and Davis do a tremendous job of outlining the effects that sexual abuse may have on the adult lives of children and I highly recommend you buy a copy of their book if it applies to your past. In brief, some of the ways that sexual abuse can affect your relationships later in life are:

1. *Low self-esteem and lack of personal power:* You may feel that you are an inherently bad person who doesn't deserve happiness. You may feel powerless and that you are still a victim. Perhaps if people close to you knew who you really were, they'd leave. You may have a lack of motivation, a failure to succeed, or a need to be perfect at everything you do. Perhaps you have self-destructive behaviors or hate yourself. You may have trouble trusting your intuition or feel unable to protect yourself in dangerous situations.

2. *Difficulty with feelings:* You may have difficulty recognizing your feelings or expressing them. Perhaps you are uncomfortable with negative feelings such as anger or sadness, or cannot experience a wide range of emotions. You may be prone to depression, anxiety, or panic attacks. Maybe your feelings appear to be out of your control and you cry "for no good reason" or become irrationally angry or violent.

3. *Uncomfortable feelings about your body:* You may not feel present in your own body some of the time or feel that there are times when you've left your body. Perhaps you are frequently unaware of the messages your body sends you, such as hunger, pain, tiredness, or fear. You may have a difficult time loving and accepting or intentionally damage your body.

4. *Intimacy issues:* Perhaps you have difficulty trusting anyone and have few, if any, close friends, a fact that may leave you feeling alienated and lonely. It may be difficult for you

to give and receive affection and nurturing. You may tend to get involved with inappropriate people or become romantically interested in those who are unavailable to you, such as married men. You may have been involved with someone who reminds you of your childhood sexual abuser. You may find that you often feel taken advantage of, have trouble making a commitment, or panic when people get too close. Maybe you can get close to friends, but can't make it work with a romantic partner. Perhaps you are clingy and dependent, expect people to leave you, or repeatedly "test" those close to you.

5. *Your sexuality:* You may be unable to remain present and focused during lovemaking or go through sex numb or in a panic. Perhaps you use sex to meet non-sexual needs or to keep men tied to you. You may find that you feel you cannot say "no" when a sexual request is made, so that you have sex when or in ways that you don't really want. You may not experience sexual desire or pleasure, and you may believe that those feelings are bad. Perhaps you feel that your worth is primarily sexual, have been a prostitute, or have used sex to control men.

6. *Children and parenting issues:* You may be uncomfortable or frightened around children. Perhaps you have been abusive to your own children or fear that you may be. You may have a difficult time setting boundaries with your children or balancing their needs with your own. You may also have a difficult time

feeling as close to your children as you would like or have a hard time being affectionate. You may also be overprotective of your children and see danger lurking in every corner.

ACTIVITY
The Issues of Sexual Abuse that You Carry with You

Although you were violated and demeaned during your childhood, you have survived to become a woman who now clearly understands that she wants to go beyond the abuse that has impacted her life. You are determined to move forward to healthier relationships with yourself and others. Bravo for you!

- Take a moment and look at the definitions of sexual abuse.

- In your journal, write down those to which you have been exposed and how old you were at the time the abuse occurred.

- Now look at the six ways the abuse may have affected your adult life.

- Which ones do you relate?

- Write those down as well. Give names of people, exact incidents, and how you felt.

Although this type of work can be excruciating, it is also very powerful and empowering. Sexual abuse is generally such a taboo that we may not discuss it or even dare think about it. We may be afraid to relive it. We feel guilty about it, although our abusers may not. Sexual abuse lives in a dark, scary place in our minds. Understand that so long as it remains hidden, abuse continues to have power over you and makes your decisions for you. Only by exposing it to the light can you begin to have power over it.

My sexual abuse was something I never spoke about, not even to my husband. He had no idea, but then he also couldn't understand my mood swings, my fear of having children, the reasons why I would push him away personally and sexually, and the multiple fears in my life. We were on the verge of divorce when a therapist asked me if I had ever been sexually abused. At first I denied it and was very indignant with her. She said, "That's okay. I understand where you are coming from because I had the same reaction when my own therapist suggested I deal with my childhood sexual abuse. If I've read you incorrectly, I apologize. But I don't think I have. We can begin dealing with it whenever you feel ready."

Wow! What a bolt between my eyes! I immediately began crying. All the walls came down. It was really hard work to talk about all that stuff and to actually deal with it. But it not only saved my marriage, it also saved all the rest of my relationships, and probably my life.

— TARA, 39

THE EFFECTS OF A NEGLECTFUL FATHER

This is a subject I have done quite a bit of research on, as the title of my doctoral dissertation was "The Effect of Father Neglect on Female Self-Esteem." I found overwhelming evidence of devastation caused by a father who lives in the home, but disregards his daughter or is emotionally unavailable to her. While a father's death is certainly very tragic, a neglectful father—one who doesn't care, treats his daughter in a careless way, or shows preference for his sons—is catastrophic in terms of her relationships later in life.

When a girl's father dies, she has irrevocably lost the first man she has ever loved. Try as she might to keep him alive in her fantasies, the relationship is over. She, her mother, relatives, and the community may actually "sanctify" him, making him a larger-than-life hero. In comparison, a girl who has lost her father due to neglect confronts no such finality. She ruminates rather than mourns. Her father is alive and most likely living in her home. She may see him every day, so she feels that perhaps—if she tries very hard—he will "come back" to her.

There are many reasons why a father's neglectful behavior of his daughter is so damaging. Since Daddy is the first man a girl loves, his particular relationship with his daughter is very important to her sex-role development. He is able to help create good feelings about herself as a female. As the first man to be attracted by her charms, a father's presence is crucial in his daughter's later development as a woman.

It is also Daddy who teaches her about the value of becoming a separate person. Dads come to their daughters from outside the profoundly intimate mother-infant connection. Their connection is essentially voluntary. If he is a loving, nurturing parent, a father's very presence illustrates the positive aspects of being an individual. Through his attention and interest, the baby girl learns that she can be a secure and important person.

Because of a dad's place of power in the family and community itself, it is he who shows his daughter a bridge to the outside world. It is through his example that the possibility of success as a separate person is initiated. Fathers give their daughters an ability to dare and a confidence in their femininity and their ability to achieve. While mothers tend to be their daughters' role model for nurturing or expressing themselves, fathers serve most often as their role model for achievement, self-esteem, and assertiveness.

So, what becomes of the neglected daughter as she becomes a woman? The evidence is very clear that she will have a pattern of frustrated relationships, primarily with men, both romantic and professionally, as well as in platonic relationships. Essentially, she will be going after what she can't have and constantly looking for the approval she didn't receive from her father. A woman may develop a Prince Charming complex, hoping that a man will love her enough to notice her and stay forever.

Neglected daughters are more likely than those with attentive fathers to describe themselves as "cautious," "serious," "guarded," "sad." They are also less secure about their body image and see themselves as less attractive and less feminine. They are less demanding of others and often state that they don't enjoy sex as much as they would like. Quite naturally, neglected daughters have a penchant for disappointing romances because specific experiences of their father were of disappointment, abandonment, and pain.

The rejecting type of man is, of course, easily recognizable to the neglected daughter. He is familiar in the feelings of self-doubt he brings out in her, and his ability to seduce and disappoint. She is more anxious and insecure with him. There is a definite correlation between low self-confidence and a penchant for relationships that reinforce that negative attitude. The woman becomes bored with men who appreciate her and shows a greater interest in men who are "unavailable," "older," and "bad" for her.

Fear of intimacy and rejection are all too familiar to the neglected daughter. Both protect against emotional involvement and anticipated pain. However, because of these fears, she may cling to an abusive relationship—be it with a male boss, friend, mate, etc. —and push away generous and loving men in favor of those who act similarly to her neglectful father. She may believe that she'll feel good about herself once someone adores her. Yet, it actually works in the reverse. When a woman loves herself, it enables her to attract men and women around her who will cherish her.

When daddy has neglected his little girl, she very often gives up her power to men. She is dependent and at the mercy of all men. He makes the decisions while she complies, either willingly or unwillingly. She may also have a fear of rage, which plays into her submissive behavior as well. She may feel unspoken rage toward her father but pushes it down because those feelings are dangerous to her. However, unexpressed anger usually turns inward and becomes depression, anxiety, and/or physical illness such as headaches, backaches, ulcers, colitis, or stomach ailments.

Well, that was a lot to think about, wasn't it? Have you recognized yourself and your relationship with your father or stepfather in anything written above? If so, perhaps some of your feelings, behavior, and relationships are beginning to make sense to you.

ACTIVITY
Ways that My Father's Neglect Has Harmed Me

If you have recognized yourself and your father in this section, you now have the opportunity to think more about the ways that this relationship has affected you. In your journal, write down the ways that you felt neglected by your father, either in your childhood, adolescence, or as an adult woman. Perhaps you'd like to write about all different stages of your life. How did it make you feel at those times? How do you feel now when you write about them? Sad? Angry? Resentful? Over it? Do you make excuses for your dad's behavior? How do you think your dad's neglect has affected you in your present-day relationships?

It's okay to think and write about your father's neglect. It is not hurting your father or being disrespectful of him.

It is a releasing, cathartic exercise that will enable you to begin letting go of the pain he caused you so you can live more successfully. He would want that for you.

> *I never felt like my father loved or even liked me. I felt like he tolerated me and resented that I wasn't a boy. Like I was his personal DNA failure. Whenever I tried to get close to him, he'd literally push me away. I remember trying to climb onto his lap and he pushed me off. He always had some excuse, and actually so did my mother. She'd say things like, "Oh come on now, Jana; you know Daddy's had a hard day." Or, my favorite, "Jana, you're too big to sit on Daddy's lap." I was a skinny five-year-old at the time. I just remember begging for his attention and feeling like there was something so fundamentally wrong with me that even my own father couldn't stand to be around me. I never suspected it was actually something wrong with him.*
>
> — JANA, 32

PARENTS WITHOUT BOUNDARIES

Boundaries are important. It is a line that marks or fixes a limit that enables family members, for example, to respect each other as individuals. In healthy families, there is a clear boundary between parents and children. While the parents can easily love their children and treat them with respect, there is no disagreement about what the parents' role in the family is and the fact that the children have full rights, but they are not the same rights as their parents. Parents are parents and kids are kids.

The type of boundaries you grew up with is important in determining the way you see yourself in your adult relationships. There are two basic types of boundaries in families: enmeshed and disengaged. Most families fall somewhere along the continuum.

Enmeshed families have very blurry boundaries. Parents hover over their children and may invade their privacy both in terms of space and invasion of thoughts. Frequently, children hear, "What are you thinking right now?" or "You can share all your private thoughts with me." Parents prefer to be pals rather than parents. These type of enmeshed parents put all their stock as people into whether or not their child gets a part in the school play, if their child is popular or gets good grades, and the like.

Enmeshed parents may tell their children personal information or use them as confidantes. Mothers may talk with their daughters as if they were girlfriends, discussing details of their sex life with the girls' fathers, disappointments they have with them, or looking to their youngsters for advice and solace. Enmeshed parents don't respect developmental stages. Whereas, it may have been wonderful for a daughter to see her mother or father volunteering at school when she was in elementary grades, it may be humiliating in high school. Even if she dares to express her feelings on the subject, her parents may act hurt and displeased, leaving the daughter to feel guilty and ungrateful for her natural and normal feelings of independence and separation.

Because enmeshed daughters are so involved with their parents, they fail to develop independent thinking and behaving, and don't learn the necessary skills for developing healthy relationships outside the home. In light of the fact that their parents hovered over every decision, they may become incapable of making good decisions for themselves and be given the message that they need someone to take care of them.

My parents were there every waking moment. I felt like I didn't have any time or thoughts of my own. At the time, I resented it but also felt a little guilty because I had so many friends who didn't have involved parents. Wasn't there a compromise? Did they really have to chaperone every school dance or talk with all my girlfriends into the night at every slumber party? I felt like I couldn't breathe.

— HEDDY, 28

A disengaged family has just the opposite dynamics. In this case, the boundaries are very rigid which causes each member to function on their own. They are distant, there is little talking or interaction, and children don't feel that they can request support when needed. The children's thoughts are controlled ("You shouldn't think like that") as is freedom of expression ("Don't talk like that. You don't know enough to have that opinion"). This leaves a young girl believing that she can't trust her own thoughts or opinions and feeling that having someone else control her is perfectly normal or desirable.

In *But I Love Him*, I quote a 15-year-old girl who speaks quite eloquently about how she felt in a disengaged family and her choice of boyfriend.

"My parents couldn't care less where I am or what I do. Everyone's in their own little world, and we hardly even talk to each other. There's a lot of stress in my house. I don't know if they would even bat an eyelash if they knew that I had sex for the first time at 14 and am doing it now with my boyfriend. He's not very nice to me, but it beats being in that house."

ACTIVITY

How Have Your Childhood Boundaries Affected Your Adult Life?

If you grew up in an enmeshed or disengaged home, you may see yourself in some of the descriptions I have related. Because lack of personal boundaries is a common experience in abusive relationships, it is important for you to understand the way in which your childhood boundaries have invaded your adult life. Take a moment to think and then journal about the following questions:

- How do you think boundaries—or lack of boundaries—have affected you in your relationships with your own family that you have created?

- Are you the same type of parent as your parents were to you?

- Can you see how your type of family has affected your relationships with your male and female friends? Your brothers or sisters?

- Do your parents still maintain the same type of boundaries with you now?

GROWING UP WITH CRITICAL PARENTS

The other day, a 39-year-old female patient was describing to me how critical her mother was and still is. She said, "Just the other day, we were at the bank together and I was endorsing a paycheck. She was watching me and then she took the pen out of my hand and said, 'Claire, you're doing that all wrong. You should sign your name and then write for deposit only. That way, if someone steals your check, they can't cash it. And look at your penmanship. Who can even read your name? It's like a child's scrawl.' Never mind that my check couldn't be stolen, since I was at the teller's window depositing it, or that this was my signature, something that was personal and unique to me. She's always been so critical of everything I've ever done and can't let it go. Nothing I've ever done has ever been good enough for her."

Hearing that made me feel so sad for her. This woman is intelligent beyond words, extremely attractive, and has a wonderful job. Everyone routinely adores her—except her mother—and herself.

Many times, the women who come to me with problems in relationships have grown up with highly critical parents. They often suffer from depression, anxiety, and physical problems, don't trust their own judgments, and have an extreme fear of making mistakes. Their inaction causes problems for them as does their need to please and be approved of and acceptable. They are often loyal to those who don't deserve it and create attachments to anyone who shows some type of kindness. They don't allow themselves to feel happy at their successes because they "know" that it will be torn down any moment. They may be jumpy and stressed out.

In a work environment, these women tend to work for overly demanding bosses without complaint, hoping for a crumb of approval, which rarely—if ever—comes. If their coworkers upset them, they keep quiet. Who are they to complain? They may be the "doormat" for their friends and accept needless criticism from them as well. They are the "dumping ground" for everyone's anger and disappointment because they'll take it. They allow their children to treat them in a disrespectful manner because they don't like to assume authority and are used to criticism.

ACTIVITY
Do You Have Critical Parents?

Like Claire, you may have been raised in a critical household. Perhaps you still can't do enough to please your parents—or anyone else, for that matter. Try as you might, there's always a little jab that comes at the end of so many comments they make, isn't there? Just because you haven't felt that you could speak up to them doesn't mean you can't speak up in your journal.

I'd like you to write about each and every incident you can recall when your parents were critical of you. Don't have that much time, you say? Then, just pick the ones that were especially damaging. Now, here's your chance for the comeback you thought of later but couldn't tell them. What would you like to have said to them immediately after their critical comment? "That's not fair." "I don't think that's true." "You've misunderstood what I said." "When you talk to me like that, it really hurts my feelings." "I know you are, but what am I?" Get the idea? No one is reading this but you. You can tell them whatever you want, no matter how angry, rude, or profane.

After you have completed this exercise, reread the comments. How do you feel now? Sad and angry? Did you laugh at their ridiculousness or your gumption for saying what you would have liked to say? Do you think you could really say anything such as this to them now if they were critical of you again? Why not? We'll talk about that later in the book and maybe you'll change your mind.

Hopefully, in this chapter you have seen the ways in which your parents helped shape you into the woman you are today, one who may have been treated unfairly at times or disrespected and dishonored for the unique and precious child she was. But now that woman is often courageous and willing to do what she needs to do in order to create greater success and break her pattern of abusive relationships.

In the next chapter, we'll talk about the relationships you've developed with your boss and coworkers.

CHAPTER
FIVE

Abusive Work Environments

THE REALITY TODAY is that the majority of American women work outside their homes. They work in large corporations, "mom and pop" outfits, and many places in between. The U.S. Census Bureau has estimated that at the turn of this century, women dominated the workforce and that 85 percent of all new workers were women and minorities.

Since most women have worked at more than one job and more than one company, they have been exposed to a multitude of bosses and coworkers. Because sexist and uninformed opinions of women are struggling to catch up with the present-day reality of women on the job, the Equal Employment Opportunity Commission (EEOC) has stated that gender discrimination and harassment is the fastest-growing area of claims against employers. Sexual harassment charges filed with the EEOC more than doubled from 1991 to 1997: from 6,883 in 1991 to 15,889 in 1997. I will discuss these legal issues later in this chapter, as well as the recourse that may be available to you in such a case.

In a recent study by researchers at the University of Michigan, 75 percent of working men and women described their work environment as abusive, with coworkers being the number one offenders.

Abusive work situations take many forms and it is important to note that both men and women can be perpetrators.

THE EMOTIONALLY UNSTABLE BOSS

I worked for a woman who never let up. Every day was a nightmare. She made up rules as she went along. She had a very volatile personality and would go off at the least little thing. I know she was having problems with her husband. Sometimes, I would hear her crying on the phone with him. I almost felt sorry for her. She was also extremely disorganized and it always seemed to be my job to fix whatever she messed up. I can't tell you how often I would wake up with a feeling of dread on work days and my heart would be racing all day just waiting for her to go nuts on me.

— SARAH, 34

Can you relate to Sarah's story? Many of you may have had a boss who treated you unfairly as a result of his or her own personal difficulties. Clearly, this is an unprofessional attitude and you should not be the recipient of a tirade for any reason. You deserve to be treated with respect and in accordance with your company's code of conduct every day of the week.

Why does it seem fair or necessary that you be the "whipping boy" for your boss' problems? Sarah states that she felt sorry for her boss, and you may have felt likewise. That's lovely. But you are not her gal pal or her therapist. There is plenty of psychological help available to anyone who is having relationship difficulties in their lives.

In looking back on your previous employers, if you find that you have had several bosses who have treated you in this fashion, it is probably not just bad luck. Of course, it is never permissible for a supervisor to act out against you, however it would seem reasonable to ask yourself, Why me and no one else? You're not a helpless victim in your own life. You have choices even if they don't seem great at the time. Allowing persons of authority to treat you in a rude and disrespectful manner may be another pattern of abuse in your life.

THE WORK-AT-ALL-HOURS BOSS

In my last job, I was constantly exhausted. I was a mortgage broker, which meant that I had to scare up strangers who wanted to refinance their house or take out a new loan. That's how I made my money. When I interviewed for the job, I told my supervisor that I was a single mom and would need to be out the door by 6:30 P.M. to pick my son up at day care. She said that wouldn't be a problem, but she expected a full day of work while I was there. I have always been very conscientious and a hard worker, so that wasn't an issue for me.

My first week there, I wasn't out until at least 7:00. My daycare provider said she understood that I was at a new job, but it couldn't continue to happen. My boss told me that if I were going to stay employed in my job, I would need to work at least ten hours a day. I saw that I was always the last one in every morning at 7:30 and the first one to leave at 7:00 at night. My workplace was becoming very hostile, as the other employees resented the fact that I wasn't working the hours they were. But then I also wasn't making the money they were. I received a minimum hourly salary, but the real money was in commissions for closing a deal. I only got paid for a maximum of eight hours no matter how long I worked.

My daycare provider gave me an ultimatum the third week on my job: to pick up my son on time or find other arrangements. What was I supposed to do? I had enormous pressure to perform at work, but my son was my first priority. I could have found other daycare situations, but was I supposed to leave him for 12 hours a day just to satisfy this boss?

— ABBY, 29

Abby brings up a situation that many women find themselves a part of—the care of their children being pitted against unfair expectations of working hours. Because single mothers make up the vast majority of women entering the workforce, the problem is doubly difficult. A woman may be the sole consistent provider for the family and she may also have little, if any, backup support in terms of childcare options. Many women feel they have to work the long hours their boss demands or else risk being fired.

You should know that the Fair Labor Standards Act of 1938 (FLSA), also known as the Wage-Hour Act, established protection for all workers with a minimum hourly wage and distinguishes between nonexempt employees (those who must be paid overtime for hours in excess of 40 hours per week) and exempt employees (those to whom the employer does not have to pay overtime). This law states that an employer cannot work nonexempt employees more than 40 hours a week unless they are paid at least time-and-a-half their regular rate of pay for the overtime.

Equally important, I feel, is for women to consider the types of jobs they take, especially when they have children. Jobs that are enormously stressful and require unbearably long hours are not conducive to a good quality of life for you and certainly not for your children. You may be reading this and thinking, *Dr. Murray must think that there are a million jobs out there and I have my choice of any of them. She*

102

doesn't understand that I am only qualified for this particular job and am lucky to have it. I can't just up and quit.

This is all very true. You may recall that in Chapter Two we discussed the issue of choice. Understanding that you always have choice in any situation is critically important, and even more so when you are in an abusive situation. Learning to prioritize your needs and wants is also crucial. If you find that you are working ten hours a day for a tyrant of a boss, your children are in daycare for twelve hours a day five days a week, and you not only don't have time with them, but the time you do have is spent in utter exhaustion and stress, then it is vital for you to take a close look at your life and the way in which you are living it.

What is your top priority? Your children? If you remember that love is a behavior, how is that being displayed when you are constantly too irritable and tired to engage lovingly with your top priority? You cannot expect young children to understand that you have to work long hours for a terrible boss because you love them and want them to have the best of everything. They understand that if you love them you will spend quantity as well as quality time together, neither of which are possible when you work in an abusive environment that taxes your time and emotional resources. I have never met a child who would trade a PlayStation for contented time with his mom. The "best of everything" for a child is wonderful time spent with you.

I will never forget the eight-year-old little girl I was seeing at my office a couple of years ago. Her nanny brought her to her appointments, as her highly successful father worked very long hours. Her mother had recently died of cancer and the child had withdrawn in sadness. This beautiful child had every toy and gadget known to mankind. She even had a battery-operated Mercedes-Benz play car that she was able to ride around her family estate. She had magnificent clothes and a top quality education at a prestigious private school. Her trust fund was huge. Yet, along with the children at the domestic violence shelter at which I had worked, she was the saddest child I had ever met because she had lost her mommy and felt completely alone.

I asked her about her favorite memory of her mother. She recalled that her mother's pain was especially horrible in the middle of the night. So as not to wake the rest of the household, she often went down to the kitchen and had a few bites of toast or read. One night, the little girl woke up and noticed that the light was on in the kitchen, so she went downstairs to see her mother breaking off little pieces of toast and trying to eat them. Wordlessly, the child pulled a chair very close to her mom and also broke off pieces of toast and ate them with her. They didn't talk, but the feeling of sharing and closeness was the most precious and important memory she had of her mother. Every time I recall that story, I cry, and it reminds me as a mother— and a working mother—that a mom's presence cannot be replaced by stuff they buy in their child's life. Tiny, special moments cannot be planned or predicted. They just happen, and if you are not there to share them, you've lost something that cannot be replaced.

If your top priority is advancing in your career, there are also other questions to ask yourself when working for the "all-hours boss." Is there balance to your life? By that I mean: Do you have some semblance of a personal life? Do you see friends? Do you exercise or engage in activities you enjoy? Do you have physical ailments that you know are work related? If you are too frenzied to take a bath, it is a good gauge that your life is out of control.

Some people are all-or-nothing thinkers. Everything is either black or white, right or wrong, all work or no work. They are not able to see the middle ground in most situations. If you believe that your only opportunity for advancement in your field—or merely keeping your job—

is to work horrendous hours that don't allow you any life outside your job, you may be an all-or-nothing thinker. You may be too stressed to sit down with a quiet mind for 30 minutes and come up with alternatives.

COWORKERS FROM HELL

I was new on my job as a graphic artist. I was working for a pretty big advertising firm and there were multiple accounts that needed design work done for print ads. There were seven of us in the department and it was very competitive. Everyone wanted to be a star and come up with the greatest artwork for the ads. We had a boss that encouraged backstabbing and gossip. In meetings, she would say things like, "Tom is way out in front of the rest of you in design production." Then, we would hear that Tom got a great perk like dinner for two at a fancy restaurant or a fat raise. If we were working as a team on a big project, she would let it be known that whoever made the most important contributions would get a trip for two to a vacation resort.

Can I just tell you what that did for the idea of working together? It was every person for himself. Coworkers were going into her office and making things up about others in the group. Some of my design files were stolen and passed off as the thief's. We had one woman who would say things to me like, "Carol, don't you think all this competition is ridiculous? We should just rebel and refuse to participate in that nonsense. We should just work together and do the best we can and let the rest of them squirm. Don't you think two heads are better than one? Especially two heads who have made a decision to work peacefully together?" I thought she was completely correct and was so glad to find a coworker who didn't want to participate in all that stress. We'd go out to lunch together and discuss the projects. We'd walk around the mall sometimes in the evening or get our nails done together. I was so much happier at my job knowing that at last I'd found a friend.

I guess you can imagine my shock when she decided to turn in the project three days early and she passed off all of my ideas as her own! I had nothing to turn in because she had already done it. I tried to talk to my boss and tell her what really happened. Of course, she didn't believe me and said it was sour grapes because I couldn't come up with one good idea. My "friend" was promoted and I was fired for non-production.

— CAROL, 39

Unfortunately, this type of behavior is not uncommon in almost all types of jobs. Abusers are everywhere: women who masquerade as your friends, men who just want to help you out. With the job market becoming increasingly more competitive, abusers are becoming even more frightened and will stop at nothing to get what they want.

It is important to remember that all abuse is intentional. The coworker you thought was your pal has made a conscious decision to hurt you because of her own greed, selfishness, jealousy, need for control, or personal unhappiness. This is not a person to whom you give a second, third, or sixteenth chance, even if she apologizes later. You may recall that in Chapter Three I discussed the cycle of violence, in which a period of abuse is usually followed by contrition and promises that things will be better. A coworker undermining your confidence or abilities is no different.

Sometimes, an abusive coworker is not as crafty as Carol's "pal." He or she might tell you, "You look terrible today. Are you having problems at home?" "Do you really want to wear that dress to the presentation? Maybe you have time to run home and change" (ten minutes before you give an important presentation), "I hope the boss doesn't notice that you're late" (said in a loud enough voice for the boss to hear), "You're so busy. Let me turn in your report for you" (with one page missing) and so on. These people gain your trust by appearing so helpful all the while planning your demise.

SEXUAL HARASSMENT AND DISCRIMINATION

I went to work for a friend of mine shortly after my divorce. I knew him from church and felt like he was a great guy for giving me a chance and a fresh start. I hadn't worked after I married my former husband, who was extremely physically and emotionally abusive for our entire marriage. This friend had a one-man operation that was moderately successful but could definitely use my help. I had a young daughter and since his business was in a two-room space, he allowed me to bring her and set up a little playroom for her. I couldn't believe how nice he was.

Soon, however, he started making me feel a little uncomfortable. One day when I came in, my desk, which was already close to his in the same room, was butted up against his desk. When I asked why, he said that since I was his assistant, he wanted me right next to him. I noticed that he glanced at my legs and breasts a lot. He began making comments about getting married and that my ex-husband was a fool for letting such a good woman go. He said that if I were his wife, he'd never once treat me badly. I never said anything and tried to do my work.

I began seeing a very nice man socially and my boss found out. Each day, he would drill me about my dates with him and pressure me for information about him. Even though he didn't know the gentleman, he tried to persuade me that he was all-wrong for me. My boss would leave little gifts, cards, or flowers on my desk almost daily when I came in. He'd talk non-stop about things of a

*personal nature. I told him that this type of behavior
made me feel uncomfortable and that it had to stop if
I was to stay. He apologized profusely and then proceeded
to do the same types of things, but would say that he felt
so guilty and sorry that he was doing it. He told me that he
thought of me constantly. I again told him that I cared
about him as a friend and was very grateful for the opportunity he was giving me to work and learn a new skill, but
that I would never think of him romantically and we didn't
have a future like that. He started quoting Bible passages
that referred to a woman's place in a marriage and said
that he could see me as his wife. Every time I moved my
desk further away from his, he'd move it back closer. He
wouldn't stop no matter how many times I tried to tell him
how bad it felt.*

*I was always nervous and edgy, dreading going to
work. It had an impact on my relationships not only with
men, but also more importantly with my daughter. When
I began rejecting him, he told me that having my daughter
at work was too annoying and that I'd have to make other
arrangements. Actually, she was really good and spent the
day watching videos, eating lunch with me, coloring, and
napping. Really, no trouble at all. The pressure got worse
and worse to the point where I became very depressed
and anxious. I finally quit without having another job
which was pretty terrifying but I thought that if I didn't get
out of there soon, I'd really crumble.*

— JANE, 38

The Equal Employment Opportunity Commission
(EEOC) has determined that this problem makes up the
fastest-growing area of claims against employers and it is
still extremely pervasive. Recently, as I was walking through
a major corporation visiting a friend, I heard two executives
joking around. "Sexual harassment isn't a problem; it's a
privilege," one fellow said to the other followed by gales of
laughter. "Well, don't you think it depends on what the

woman looks like and what she's willing to do before you decide who the privilege belongs to?" the second one responded with even more laughter.

Yup, Neanderthals still exist in the workplace. Before we go any further with this topic, let me first define some key terms that are important for you to know. This information is taken from a very valuable book, *Fair, Square, and Legal,* by Donald Weiss:

- *Protected class:* A group of people distinguished by their special characteristic(s) that has inhibited its progress: race, color, ethnic identification, national origin, religion, gender, age, disability, and veteran status. This term is important to you as a woman in the workplace because in accordance with Title VII of the Civil Rights Act of 1964, an employer cannot, under law, discriminate on the basis of a characteristic specific to any protected class, unless the characteristic is a bona fide occupational qualification (BFOQ).

- *Discrimination:* The decisions and actions that deny individuals in protected groups access to employment, advancement, benefits, training, and compensation permitted to other people in the organization.

- *Sexism:* A value system that holds that one person is inferior to another because of gender. For example, "Women are too emotional, especially during their periods." Sexism takes several different forms:
  - ➤ *Condescension:* Refusing to take someone seriously, (e.g., "Leave the difficult decisions to men").

> *Verbal abuse:* Making negative or derogatory comments (e.g., "I like watching your hips sway when you walk").

- *Exclusion:* Overlooking or denying someone access to places, people, or information, especially when opportunities for advancement are involved (e.g., excluding women from community organizations).

- *Tokenism:* Including a selected one or few members of a group for very visible positions; also called "window dressing."

- *Sex discrimination:* Employment decisions based on gender rather than on gender-neutral considerations, or different treatment of one employee merely on the basis of his or her gender.

- *Sexual harassment:* Unwelcome behavior of a sexual nature or with sexual overtones; sexual harassment takes two legal shapes:

  > *Quid pro quo:* a) Where submitting to sexual demands becomes an implicit term or condition of employment (e.g., "You can have a promotion but only if you have sex with me"); b) Making decisions affecting someone's employment or compensation on the basis of whether the person submits to or rejects sexual demands.

  > *Hostile environment:* Sexual conduct that has the purpose or effect of unreasonably interfering with a person's job performance or that creates an intimidating or offensive work environment. Whereas quid pro quo has a uniquely sexual

context, hostile environment does not;
it can exist for minorities, older people,
disabled people, and veterans as well.

- *Unwelcome behavior:* Conduct that "the employee
did not solicit or incite" and that "a reasonable
woman would regard as undesirable or
offensive."

- *Agency and employer liability:* Any employee
acting or speaking on behalf of the employer
and relying on his or her apparent authority
at the time he or she sexually harasses an
employee. An employer need not know about
a manager's sexual harassment of an employee
to be held liable for that harassment.

Gender-based discrimination takes many forms and
includes such issues as compensation, maternity (I will
discuss this issue in a separate section of this chapter),
discipline, promotion, and insurance policies, among
other more obvious harassment and discrimination such
as lewd comments and actions.

Lonnie Zilberman, a labor relations attorney in San Diego,
California, spoke to me about the issues of harassment and
sex discrimination, giving me a partial listing of common
forms of bias:

- Hiring or promoting a man who is less qualified
than a woman who was interviewed.

- Paying a woman at a lower rate than a man.

- Firing a woman when a man might only be
disciplined, or firing a qualified woman before
of or in lieu of a man.

- Making employment or promotion contingent upon meeting sexual demands. It is still harassment even if the other person appears to consent.

- Calling a woman names such as "babe," "honey," "girl," etc.

- Giving preferential treatment to a consenting sex partner in a way that discriminates against other female employees.

- Conduct of a sexual nature, such as lewd e-mail, jokes, or photos, touching a woman, making suggestive comments, ogling, staring at a woman's body, whistling, blocking a woman's way.

- Commenting on a woman's body or the sexiness of her clothing.

- Asking questions about her sex life or fantasies.

- Responding differently to a woman's requests than the boss would to a man's similar requests.

- Retaliating against female employees who rejects the boss' sexual advances or who file a claim of discrimination.

Mr. Zilberman also stresses that the conduct in question must be severe and pervasive.

I was on track to become an associate in a law firm. I worked harder than most of the men there and billed more hours than they did. I stayed later than almost anyone in the firm, certainly later than the male partners. There weren't any female partners but because I graduated near the top of my law school class, won numerous honors in school, and was such a hard worker, I was sure that in time I would be the exception. Maybe they'd never employed another woman as smart and as dedicated as I was.

When we had meetings, I wasn't asked for my input. A couple of times when a secretary wasn't available, I was asked to bring in coffee for everyone. When I had a strong opinion about a case, some of the other men would laugh or snicker, or say things like, "You go get 'em, pussycat," or "Are you on your period today?" One time, I caught one of the associates staring at my breasts and when he saw me looking at him, he stuttered, "Nice, uhh . . . suit." It was humiliating and disrespectful. I was given the puffball cases that hardly required a brain. And, surprisingly, all of my clients were women who were a little on edge. "You understand female hormones," my immediate boss would tell me when I asked why all these cases were going to me. Needless to say, after two years I left the firm. I could have tried filing a sexual discrimination suit, but knew I'd be wrapped up in court forever and just wanted to get on with my life and career.

— CATHERINE, 31

MATERNITY DISCRIMINATION

I worked as an assistant to the vice president of a fairly small company of about 100 people. I had worked with him for almost five years when I became pregnant. My husband and I had been trying to conceive for three years and had done fertility treatments for the last year of that time. I didn't tell anyone at work because I felt it was our private life. When I became pregnant, even though I was so excited, I still didn't let anyone at work know because my doctor had told me that with fertility methods such as ours, the risk of miscarriage was reasonably high.

After the first trimester was over, I let my friends at work and my boss know the good news. He was not happy, to say the least. I know he was concerned for himself and thought that I would leave for good, which I really wanted to do but financially it wouldn't be possible. I did everything for him; he was pretty inept by himself. I know he depended on me a lot and was worried about how he'd manage without me for the three months I was entitled to. I had also saved up an additional month of paid vacation so I would actually be gone for four months.

My boss began treating me differently. He was nasty and sometimes outright hostile. Once, he told me, "You know, if your replacement does a good job, I may not need you anymore. You might want to think about a different job when you decide you've had enough of a crying baby." Can you believe that? I checked my employee handbook and told him that I was definitely planning on coming back to work for him when my maternity leave ended and that according to the rules the company set out, he would need to take me back. He made my life so miserable until I left and then again after I got back that I decided to find another job with another company. I couldn't imagine working there anymore.

— DAISY, 27

The Family and Medical Leave Act (FMLA) of 1993 protects against discrimination in several ways. It entitles employees to take a reasonable unpaid leave of up to 12 weeks in a 12-month period for medical reasons, for the birth or adoption of a son or daughter, and for the care of a son or daughter, spouse, or parent who has a serious health problem.

In order to qualify for FMLA, you must work for an employer with 50 or more workers within 75 miles of your work site. You also must have been working for your employer for at least 12 months before the leave is requested (although the 12 months need not be consecutive), and have worked at least 1,250 hours during that 12-month period.

At the time of this writing, California, Connecticut, Massachusetts, and Montana, as well as Puerto Rico have laws requiring preferential treatment for pregnant women such as maternity benefits and other management decisions.

WHAT CAN YOU DO IF YOU BELIEVE YOU'VE EXPERIENCED DISCRIMINATION?

The good news is that you've now read all the ways in which the law protects your rights as women. The bad news is that while record numbers of lawsuits have been filed, legally proving sexual discrimination or harassment are very difficult, time consuming, and oftentimes expensive to pursue.

Let's say that you have tried talking to your supervisor without success or feel intimidated to do so. Your first line of defense in making a claim against your boss is with your company's Human Resources (HR) Manager. He or she is well versed in the laws of your state and the rules of your company. The HR manager has an obligation to interview you, write up your claim, and investigate your allegations thoroughly without bias. He or she should be able to give you an approximate date as to when he expects to complete the investigation and share his findings with you as well as any disciplinary actions that will be taken against the offender, if deemed appropriate. You should also consult your company's policies and procedures booklet that you received at the time of your employment. If you don't have one, ask your HR manager for one so that you can be clear as to your level of protection and options you have.

If you work for a small company that does not employ an HR manager, you may contact the EEOC, which is listed in the front of your telephone book and also in the resources chapter at the end of this book. You can also call or write to the Department of Fair Employment and Housing, which will also be listed. Both entities also have a Website at which you can gain further information or e-mail a specific division.

While the offending harasser may be fired from his job for misconduct, the standard adopted by most state laws is that "in order for an employer to terminate an individual for alleged misconduct, the employer must make a good faith determination that sufficient cause existed based on reasonable grounds." The legality of good faith and reasonable grounds can best be explained by a California Supreme Court case of *Cotran vs. Rollins Hudig Hall International, Inc.,* which was in the judicial system from 1993–1998.

Ralph Cotran was a senior vice president of an insurance brokerage firm and in charge of its West Coast operations. In 1993, two female employees made reports alleging that Cotran was sexually harassing them. In separate interviews by the company's HR manager, both women told of several similar incidents. They both claimed that Cotran had made obscene phone calls to them at home and work; he'd exposed himself to them while in the office, and mastur- bated when he was alone with them in his car. Cotran denied the allegations, however he was suspended pending further investigation, which lasted two weeks. During that time, more than 20 employees were interviewed, resulting in two other female employees stating that they had received strange phone calls from Cotran. At that time, the company fired Cotran.

Cotran sued his company for wrongful termination. He claimed that the company had implied that his discharge was only for just cause and they didn't have cause since he did not harass anyone. This may seem unreasonable to you, since we can both agree that what he did was certainly sexual harassment, right? Well, Cotran then stated that he didn't harass the women because in fact he had had consensual sexual relationships with them. He said that he had not disclosed this during the company's investigation because he felt "ambushed." The court rejected the company's defense that its decision to fire Cotran was lawful because it had been reached honestly and in good faith. The jury in the case found that Cotran had not engaged in any of the behavior on which his termination was based—sexual harassment—and awarded him $1.78 million in damages.

Now, before you get your nightie in a knot, you should know that the company appealed the jury verdict, stating that "an employer need only reasonably and in good faith believe that the employee engaged in conduct that was inappropriate in the workplace." The California Supreme Court agreed and overturned the original jury verdict.

Okay, so all's well that ends well, but remember that it took five years for this decision to reach a conclusion. Although Cotran was not at the job site for those five years, the two original female employees who made the claims had this upheaval in their lives for all that time. I am not at all telling you that you should not pursue a claim of sexual harassment no matter how long it takes. I am merely trying to make you aware of the emotional factors and time factors that may be involved in a case of sexual harassment.

How can you be certain that your case constitutes a claim of sexual harassment or discrimination? It may appear that the answer is quite simple based on the list that attorney Zilberman put forth earlier in this chapter. However, this is not always true.

In the case of *Saidu-Kamara vs. Parkway Corp.* in 2001, U.S. District Judge Joyner found that since the female employee could only point to four incidents of sexual misconduct by her assistant manager over an 18-month period, while it was "loathsome and inappropriate," it was sporadic and isolated incidents of harassment. Therefore, it did not qualify as a hostile work environment. The judge stated that in order to prove that Ms. Saidu-Kamara's workplace was hostile "the discrimination complained of must be pervasive and severe enough to alter the conditions of the victim's employment and create an abusive working environment."

Ms. Saidu-Kamara was a parking lot attendant in Philadelphia for two years. She claimed that she was discriminated against when she was fired for sleeping on the job while two other male employees were merely given warnings for the same behavior. She claimed that her supervisor began sexually harassing her within a few months of her employment by grabbing her, making sexual comments, inviting her repeatedly to spend the evening with him. She also claimed that he told her he could provide money for her to take care of her children if she would go out with him. She further alleged that he touched her breasts on two occasions and patted her buttocks once as well. Although she repeatedly complained of her supervisor's behavior to the manager, he did nothing to stop the harassment.

The supervisor's lawyers argued that the allegations did not add up to a hostile environment because the incidents "occurred too sporadically" and were not severe enough, and that Ms. Saidu-Kamara had only formally complained of one incident of unwanted touching.

In the end, Judge Joyner agreed with the defense that the alleged harassment was not pervasive and regular. "Title VII does not extend to all workplace difficulties, even where the conduct at issue may be crass and unwanted. Allegations of isolated or single incidents of harassment do not constitute a cognizable hostile work environment claim," he stated.

These cases let you know a few things about sexual harassment and discrimination in the workplace. 1) While you feel that your superior or a coworker is abusing you, it will be difficult to prove. 2) These charges require enormous time, energy, and possibly money (some lawyers take these type of cases on a contingency basis, which means that their fee is predicated on your winning a cash settlement of which you give them a percentage). 3) You may not win your case.

To make sure that you are well informed about your company's responsibilities, here is a listing, also from Donald Weiss's book, *Fair, Square, and Legal,* of what you should expect from your HR manager if you file a claim of sexual harassment or discrimination. I offer this list because otherwise you may not have any idea of the level of expectations from your company, and also you develop a power position when you know what your rights are and insist on them:

- In your initial meeting, you should feel comfortable with the HR manager and have a sense that he will handle your case in a fair, thorough, and unbiased manner. You should feel that while he must remain neutral, he has a sense of empathy for the information you are revealing.

- He should get all the facts: who, what, when, where, why, and how.

- You should find out if he interviewed other employees for their input on the case, and if so, why? If there are other people he should interview, give him their names. Perhaps there were witnesses to the abuse or you have discovered that the abuser has done similar things to other women in the company.

- You should determine whether your issue is with the actual harasser, your company (what are your company's policies and procedures in this case), or both. If you recall the case of *Saidu-Kamara vs. Parkway Corp.,* she alleged that she made complaints to the company manager, but he didn't take action against the harasser. In that case, she had an issue not only with the abuser, but her company for their failure to investigate her claims and take action deemed necessary.

- He should assure you that there would be confidentiality in his investigation of your claim.

- He should reiterate that your company has a legal obligation to maintain a harassment-free workplace.

- You should be encouraged to come back to the HR manager with any additional information or documentation. You may forget all the details of the incident(s) at the time of your initial interview due to stress, but he should have an open-door policy to you as you remember important facts.

- He should assure you that your claim is serious to him and the company and that he will keep you apprised of relevant information, and certainly his findings at the conclusion of his investigation.

ARE ABUSIVE WORK ENVIRONMENTS A PATTERN IN YOUR LIFE?

You may recall that earlier in this chapter I encouraged you to think about this question. It is very important for you to be honest with yourself about this issue. Many of us who have worked for any length of time have met male coworkers or bosses who were a bit rude and obnoxious, but not to the point where we would consider them sexually harassing. Remember, a man complimenting you on the way you look in a dress may not be harassment. For example, it is not inappropriate for a man to say, "That color looks nice on you," while it is inappropriate for him to say, "The way you look in that dress really excites me sexually. I'm going to have fantasies about you all day now."

See the difference? Sometimes, I think that we have become so politically correct that we have forgotten that men and women can peacefully co-exist and appreciate each other.

If a man tells you that the color of your dress looks nice on you, and it makes you feel extremely uncomfortable, that may be a personal issue within yourself that you need to examine. If the man in question has not made lewd comments and gestures to you previous to his compliment, perhaps you have some unresolved feelings in other areas. Are you healing from an abusive marriage and any attention from a man causes you to wonder if he is being charming in a way that your ex-husband was in the beginning of the relationship? Have you been the victim of childhood sexual abuse?

Attorney Lonnie Zilberman told me that the vast majority of women filing sexual harassment and discrimination lawsuits have a history of abusive relationships. In other words, they have a pattern of abusers in their lives, not just this one issue with their boss or coworker. This is a critically important concept for you to consider in your growth as a woman and as a person who makes conscious decisions about her relationships and her part in acquiring and maintaining those relationships.

ACTIVITY
My Pattern of Abusive Work Relationships

In doing this exercise, I'd like you to think long and hard about all the places you've worked and all the people you came into contact with in those jobs who made you feel uncomfortable for one reason or another. Set up your paper this way:

Person's name	Position in the company	What she/he did	How I felt	What action I took

Once again, I'd like you to look for patterns. Were most of the perpetrators men or women? Were they coworkers or people in positions of authority? Was the offending behavior of a sexual nature? Unkind and demeaning comments about your job performance? Betrayals of confidence?

How did you feel in the aftermath? Angry? Betrayed? A loss of confidence in yourself? Depressed? Hopeless? Awkward? A feeling of dread at the thought of going to work each day?

Lastly, how did you try to resolve the situation? Did you speak up for yourself immediately? Did you report the behavior to the offender's immediate supervisor? Did you make a claim with the HR manager of your company? Did you keep quiet? Did you tell a friend or spouse but didn't take any other action? Did you quit without giving the true reasons why you left?

This list will very quickly help you to see if there is a pattern in your working relationships. Most likely, there is. Please know that not every woman, or even most women experience this type of behavior on the job. It would not be genuine for you to think that these types of things happen to everyone with estrogen. It's simply not true, and it only serves to minimize what has been done to you and allows you to deny your pattern. This does not allow for responsibility, growth, and change. It only keeps you stuck and destined to repeat the same mistakes for quite a while to come.

You may have noticed some interesting patterns in your list. Maybe all the abusers were women who demeaned your skills and appearance and didn't give you a chance to advance. Funny, wasn't that the way your mother treated you? You never looked quite right enough, she always seemed to have an issue with your weight, and couldn't seem to compliment you on a good grade in school.

Maybe your workplace abusers were a combination of men and women, and were not your bosses, but your coworkers who stabbed you in the back and gossiped about you. Do you remember the girlfriends you had in high school who did the same thing? You kept them in your life much too long because you were afraid that if you gave them up, you wouldn't have any friends at all.

In your "how I felt" list, some familiar feelings may have come back that you felt in an abusive marriage or childhood home: fear, hopelessness, depression, anxiety, and the like. Your actions may have been the same as well: not speaking for yourself, thinking it must have been your fault anyway, and desperately trying to find a way to fix it and get in the abuser's good graces again.

Do you see where I'm going with this? Your less-than-satisfactory work relationships may be part of a larger picture, especially if you have had several abusive work experiences. While there is absolutely no excuse whatsoever for your boss or coworkers to treat you in such a way, it is also up to you to set your expectations for the ways in which you will allow yourself to be treated. It is also up to you to make those expectations known either in words or in your behavior. Remember, abusers can spot a woman who is willing to be abused as soon as she sets her toe in the doorway. The reason why you are chosen, rather than another woman in your company is because that other woman makes her high expectations known.

CHAPTER
SIX

Abusive Friendships

HOW IN THE WORLD CAN YOUR FRIENDS BE ABUSIVE, you may
think? Just the phrase *abusive friend* seems to be an
oxymoron. If a person is abusive, she must not be a friend.
Likewise, if a person calls herself a friend, she wouldn't
dream of abusive behaviors toward you. Right? I wish that
were so.

Let's think for a moment about possible abusive behaviors
that might be perpetrated by a friend. Remember, you have
already expanded your notion that all abuse is physical.
Try to recall times when your friends were verbally or
emotionally cruel to you.

> *I used to tell my best friend everything. I was having a
> really bad time in my marriage a couple of years ago and
> she was my safe person to vent with. She seemed to
> understand everything I was talking about and was so
> sweet. I would always say to her, "Please don't tell anyone
> what I talked to you about, okay?" She would always tell*

me, "Sweetie, of course not. I wouldn't do that to you." My husband and I got some good counseling and were able to reconcile.

One night we were out for dinner with my friend and her husband and we were talking about this great therapist that helped us so much. My friend's husband says, "Dee, how did she help you get over the betrayal you felt when Tom was cheating on you? I don't mean to embarrass you, but if you don't mind talking about it, I could pass it on to a gal at work who is having the same problems you two were." My husband looked at me with shock and disgust knowing that I was telling my friend about all of this. I looked at my friend with shock and disgust knowing that she betrayed me as much as my husband did.

— DEE, 43

You may have "friends" like Dee. I know I sure did. I felt like I could tell my best gal pals anything only to find that they have then spilled the beans to their husbands. If I had the nerve to call them on this betrayal, they would just pooh-pooh my feeling with a snappy line like, "Oh Jill, don't be silly. You know Jack and I don't keep secrets from each other. But I'm sure he won't tell anyone else. Who's he gonna tell anyway?"

Friends like that don't get it. You have shared something very personal with them and asked them to respect your confidence. It is not up to them to decide whom else you can or cannot trust with the information. You trusted them alone. And don't believe the line that your friend's husband isn't going to tell anyone else. Many men are horrible gossips! They aren't usually interested in mundane details, but really go for juicy stuff.

Another type of abusive "friend" behavior is the pal who feels she must be excruciatingly honest with you, because "who else cares about you enough to tell you the truth?" Well, there's honest and then there's too honest.

An honest friend whispers in your ear when you are at lunch with others, "Honey, why don't you excuse yourself to the ladies room? You have spinach in between your teeth and I don't want you to be embarrassed." After you've gone to the ladies room, a too honest/cruel friend tells your lunch companions, "She went to the bathroom to get the spinach out of her teeth. Poor thing. Since she and Randy have been fighting so much lately, she hardly knows which end is up. We should all be supportive of her. It looks like they may split up." If you wanted the other women at the table to know that information, wouldn't you have told them yourself?

How about the friend who tells you her version of the truth even when you don't ask for it? Let's say you've just gotten a new dress in which you think you look smashing. You've recently lost ten pounds and worked hard at the gym. Today, you are daring to wear a dress that's shows off your new buff body a little more than usual. You greet your pal with a big smile and before you can say a word, she looks you up and down and says, "Oh honey, what were you thinking when you bought that dress? Your hips look enormous!" Up until that moment, you thought you were looking good. Your kids had complimented you on the dress—even your teenage daughter—and your usually critical mother just had to confess that she thought you'd never looked better. When exactly had you asked your friend for her opinion?

This is a different scenario than if you take your friend shopping with you and say to her, "I trust you to tell me the complete truth. How do you think I look in this dress?" If your hips do look a little wide, a kind friend might say, "You know: gray just doesn't do anything for your eyes. They are so beautiful and you know they are your best feature. Let's find another dress that plays up your eyes." Or she might even say, "That dress is the perfect color. Good choice, but why don't we look for a more flattering cut? You look great in a V-neck style." Has she told you that your hips look enormous? No, she accentuates the positive without letting you walk out the door with an unflattering dress.

A gossipy friend is not a friend. Not just one who will tell her husband anything, but the friend who tells everyone anything. She likes being the one with the information. If the ladies want to know what's going on in the neighborhood or in the carpool line, she's the one they ask. Be absolutely certain that if your friend shares a piece of gossip with you, she's gossiping about you behind your back.

What about the friend who uses and abuses you? She drops her kids off at your house while she runs a couple of errands—"I'll do the same for you next week"—and then picks them up three hours later than she said she would; in other words, after dinner. Funny how she does this time and time again. Funnier still that when you try to take her up on her offer to watch your kids, she's always busy.

Some women will turn their backs on a friend when the going gets rough. They are real fair-weather friends. They like you when you are charming and funny and don't remind them that there are problems in the world. But, if your life takes a 180-degree turn, they can't be bothered.

When I separated from my former husband, the "friends" I'd had for nearly ten years completely abandoned me. All of them, except for one sweetheart who wasn't part of the "group." This is absolutely true. I lost almost every single friend. These were women with whom we'd shared kids' birthdays, the trials and tribulations of going from half-day kindergarten to full-day first grade, bad haircuts, weight gain and loss, in-law problems, anniversaries, everything. Well, everything except the unspeakable: being a single woman. It was devastating. I was never given an explanation as to why I was so unceremoniously dumped and given outcast status.

I'm sure I was a psychotic maniac. I know I was no fun for a long time. Divorce is not a good time. But isn't that the time when you really need your friends? That experience taught me a lot about the type of friends I would look for afterward. (By the way, as a short note that might make you chuckle: I didn't hear from any of those women again until four years later when my book, *But I Love Him*, was published and I became something of a media darling. All of a sudden, they took such an interest in my career and my life. They wanted to be my friends again! Needless to say, that didn't happen!)

Do you remember in Chapter Two when we spoke of abuse as an intentional behavior? It's still true in this chapter. No one does anything without a payoff. No one. Think about it for a moment. If you smile at a stranger and she smiles back, that's a lovely payoff, isn't it? It makes you feel good to make another person feel good for no reason at all. Payoffs don't have to be monetary or a promotion at work. They don't have to be, "If you do this for me, I'll do that for you." Not all payoffs are what they appear.

So, let's follow that logic a bit further. If abuse is intentional and no one does anything without a payoff, what payoff is your friend getting by being cruel to you? Usually the payoff is that they have the opportunity of feeling superior to you. They have the upper hand. You get to look pathetic. They look smart. They get to feel altruistic. They see you devastated, which—if they have a horrible life— makes theirs look a whole lot better. It's one of the reasons why we watch soap operas. Your life may be the pits, but at least your niece's transvestite husband is not sleeping with your grandmother! See how it works?

Now, here's the harder question: What is your payoff for remaining friends with an abusive "pal?" That will be your activity for this chapter.

ACTIVITY
Why Do You Stay with Your Abusive Friends?

In this chapter, we've talked about different abusive behaviors that you may have experienced with your friends, reinforced the truth that all abuse is intentional, and the fact that no one does anything without a payoff. Now is the moment to think about the cruel behaviors you've put up with in the name of friendship.

Friend's name	Their abusive behavior	Their payoff was	My payoff was

Because this is a book about changing your patterns of abusive behavior, I'd like you to look at the types of behaviors you've experienced and what your payoffs have been. Do you see some similarities? I know this is difficult for you to experience and confess to.

Later in this book, we are going to work on ways for you to develop new and healthier relationships and ways in which you can keep abusive friendships from entering your life again. At this moment, it is most important for you to realize your friends' abusive behaviors and why you stayed in relationships with them when you were being hurt. It is the first step in true change.

CHAPTER
SEVEN

Abusive Family Members

I T IS A SAD FACT FOR MANY WOMEN that members of their own family are their primary abusers. If you are in this situation, the very people that you believe are going to love and accept you when no one else will are the people who hurt you the most: mother, father, sister, brother, son, daughter, or husband. I am also including boyfriends in this chapter. For although you are not married, when you are in a committed relationship with a man he usually feels like family to you.

In Chapter Five, you read about the ways in which your family of origin may have "taught" you to accept an abusive relationship in your life. In this chapter, we will expand that knowledge into the ways in which your childhood home may have been recreated in the home you've made as an adult. We will also look at the ways that your parents and/or siblings may continue to abuse you today.

As you read the balance of this chapter, it is important that you remember that love is a behavior. As you experience the stories that other women have related, ask yourself, "Would I consider that loving behavior?" Constantly reminding yourself of that truth will be crucial in breaking your own patterns of abusive relationships.

ABUSE IN YOUR OWN HOME

My four-year-old son has started saying, "Shut up, Mommy." Can you imagine? If I had said something like that to my mother, I would have been knocked from here to Kingdom Come. I don't know where he gets the idea that he can talk to me that way.

— MADELINE, 32

Where do you think Madeline's little boy got the idea that he could talk to her in a disrespectful manner? If you are thinking that he heard his father talk to her that way, you're correct. If you're thinking that he has heard characters on television speak that way—and get big laughs—you're right again. Did you think that he tells her to shut up because he can? She doesn't stop him, or she says something ineffective like, "Oh darling, nice boys don't talk to their mommies that way. Now, let's go get an ice cream cone."

Madeline has been so verbally and emotionally abused all of her life that, although she doesn't like to hear demeaning names thrown at her, even her own small son knows she's easy prey for abuse. Furthermore, she doesn't think enough of herself to be an authority figure to him and lay down the law. His father is certainly teaching him to be a junior abuser—as is television—but so is Madeline. Kids will always get away with as much as you let them; and she's letting him.

You may have the same situation in your home. Perhaps your daughter tells you that you're stupid. Maybe your son flips his middle finger at you. You may have children that hit you. You may also have children who treat you like a slave. They don't help you with the household chores or have any consideration for your level of fatigue or stress. They expect you to cook their favorite meals—even if they're different from the rest of the family's—wash their clothes, drive them around at any time they wish, and buy them whatever they like. They feel entitled to have everything they want and to do anything they please.

If your husband or boyfriend is your abuser, you also have a very difficult life. Many wonderful books have been written on domestic violence and they are listed in the resources at the end of this book. In Chapter Two, I also discussed the various levels of abuse—verbal, emotional, sexual, and physical—and gave some simple examples of each. Go back and review them as many times as you need.

Many women I know are in abusive relationships and don't even realize it. They just know that they feel a vague, nagging unhappiness much of the time, but blame it on hormones (or lack of them), fatigue, boredom, a "midlife crisis," or their own selfishness or neediness. Listen to what a few of them have to say:

> *My husband likes to choose my clothes for me. It makes him happy. What's the big deal if I let him do it? Isn't marriage about making the other person happy?*
>
> — ALANA, 41

> *My boyfriend doesn't like me to go out with my girl-friends without him. He's such a worrier. I know I should feel grateful that he cares so much.*
>
> — HAILEY, 27

It used to make me a little crazy when my boyfriend called me six or seven times each day while I was at work. I thought it was a bother. He'd call for little reasons, mostly asking what time I'd be home or who I had talked to that day. He's such a good person other than that, so I've just learned to accept it.

— NANCY, 30

My husband calls me names when he drinks and accuses me of sleeping around with almost everyone. It makes me cry, but he's just an angel when he doesn't drink and he's always so sorry. I know he doesn't mean what he says; it's just the alcohol.

— DEB, 38

I don't know what it is about my husband; he needs me to be home every night. My mother is Italian and has invited me to go for a chef's tour of Tuscany with her and I can't go because he would miss me too much. My friends went for a girls' spa weekend a few times and asked me to go, but he raised such a fuss and pouted so much that I felt sorry for him and didn't go.

— BEVERLY, 36

My boyfriend is a real girl watcher. When we are out together, he looks at other women and makes comments like, "Look at the rack on that girl," or "What a babe!" If I get upset, he tells me I'm being too sensitive because, after all, he comes home to me every night. He told me that all guys are just wired that way and looking at girls is normal. That might be so, and I guess I can't stop him from doing that when he's with his guy friends, but does he have to do it in front of me?

— KELLY, 29

He touches me all the time when we are out together, especially with his friends. He'll kind of massage my butt or plays with my breasts a little. His friends give him a smile, but it humiliates me. I feel like a slut.

— LAURA, 32

He lies to me all the time. Even about little stuff, like going to the market. He'll say he's going there to buy ice cream and come home an hour later. I know he didn't just go to the market, so I'll ask him where else he went. He still insists he only went there, but there's no ice cream, so he'll tell me he already ate the whole container. If he'd lie to me about going to the market, what else is he lying about to me? I can't trust him about anything.

— CHLOE, 34

My husband is a very physical man. He's very demonstrative and uses his hands a lot in conversation. When he's been upset or excitable, he's pushed me a few times. It hasn't hurt me, or anything. He's also grabbed me by the hair before. He's not doing it to be mean, it's just the way he is.

— MONICA, 38

The women above have demonstrated instances of verbal abuse (name calling), emotional abuse (jealousy, possessiveness, controlling them, checking up on them, making them feel crazy, humiliation, commenting on other women), sexual abuse (inappropriately touching them), and physical abuse (such as pushing and grabbing hair). These are not uncommon occurrences in a day-to-day abusive relationship. Do any of those situations look like loving behavior?

As women, we are taught to believe that one of our main jobs in a relationship is to please our man. Think of the articles in your favorite women's magazine, whether it is *Ladies Home Journal, Redbook, Good Housekeeping,*

135

Woman's Day, Cosmopolitan, or the many others that are published. There is always at least one in which the tone of the article is how to fix your relationship.

Basically, there are three types of articles: how to snare a man, how to keep a man in your clutches, and how you must fix what's wrong. Titles such as, "How to Give Him a Kiss He'll Never Forget," "Ways to Stop Fighting," "Ten Steps to a Happier Marriage," "Is Your Marriage Headed for Trouble? Take Our Quiz and Find Out Now!" and the like make sure you never forget that it is you who must repair your ailing relationship.

Whenever I lecture to groups of men and women, I usually ask the men in the group if any of their men's magazines have articles like the ones above. They usually laugh nervously and admit that they've never seen any.

When the man in your life begins to make casual remarks about your attractiveness, such as comments on your weight, hairstyle, or choice of clothes, that is the time to begin evaluating whether you want to believe his comments. Do not automatically assume that he's correct. It is just his opinion, not the law. He may then feel it's helpful to you to point out examples of women he thinks you should look like to make his point. Do you feel hurt? If so, you have the right to tell him!

Does your man ask you where you've been, where you're going, what time you'll be home, who you will be with, who you spoke to, etc? Our partner has a right to a certain amount of knowledge regarding our whereabouts. It is considerate to let him know where you will be and the approximate time you'll be home. You can tell him, "I'm going to the movies with Jean. I'll probably be home around 10." If he expects more information than that, it is excessive and prying.

I see couples in my practice that phone each other several times each day. They don't think it's unusual and feel they are just staying in touch. Calling your mate or being called by him once or maybe twice in a day is a nice way of staying connected, but when there are consistently multiple phone calls back and forth—or perhaps one of you calls the other several times—that is needy, dependent, possessive, and jealous behavior.

Touching a woman's private body parts in public is never acceptable. Men do it to display dominance and control. It demonstrates that you are his. This is especially true if he does this behavior in front of other men. Touching you in private, in ways that make you feel uncomfortable, is not acceptable either and it is your responsibility to tell him. If he does not stop, then it is obvious that he doesn't respect you. Your body belongs to you, not him.

Pushing and shoving, grabbing or restraining, or any other physical actions like this are not acceptable even once. I am frequently asked, "If a guy pushes you once, does that make him an abuser?" My answer to that is usually, "It may not make him an abuser, but that is abusive behavior. It is up to you to decide how many abusive behaviors are acceptable."

I have mentioned some of these behaviors because they begin slowly and may even seem flattering. You may shrug them off once or twice or deny that they even occurred. At a certain point, however, it becomes part of your daily existence and you forget that it's wrong. It's just "who he is."

It is your responsibility alone to put your foot down and speak up whenever your children, mate, or anyone else says or does something to you to which you object. If they get angry or pout—you've hurt their feelings—you can remember that one of the things you do not have control of is their reactions. If a loved one becomes upset because you request not being spoken to in a demeaning fashion, what does that say about them? What does it say about you if you decide you'd rather be spoken to in that way than to risk hurting their feelings? What about your feelings?

I do want to emphasize, however, the critical importance of removing yourself from a highly abusive situation. Remember that abuse always escalates. It never diminishes unless something dramatic is done, and even then, the "cure" rate for abusers is extremely low. By dramatic, I mean that the abuser is arrested and sent to jail or ordered into a 52-week batterer's treatment and anger management program by a judge. Your leaving the home—even with your children—may not inspire your mate to wise up; it may just make him angrier and blame you for taking his children away from him.

Conjoint therapy (also known as couples counseling) is not the answer. Whatever reason he gives for his cruelty has nothing to do with you. It's all about him. I will not counsel couples together if there is abuse involved in their relationship. I will see them separately or refer one of them out to another therapist. They each have important personal issues to resolve. If there is some resolution, I may then bring them together, although I will admit that that situation is rare. Usually, the abuser does not want to stop blaming the woman or she has made a decision to stick with him no matter what. That is her mind-set for the time being.

I do highly encourage her—and you—to heed the following advice if you are in an abusive relationship with your partner.

- Know that the police are there to help you if you need it. You are not "bad" or a "bitch" if you call them. Your mate is "bad" for terrifying and abusing you. He is merely seeing the consequences of his chosen behavior. You and your children are entitled to live without fear and violence.

- Keep the phone numbers of domestic violence shelters in a place where you can easily find it. You can get their phone numbers by calling 800-799-SAFE, which is the National Domestic Violence hotline.

- Have a plan for leaving. If it becomes necessary that you have to flee your home, pack a suitcase in advance with extra money, a credit card, a change of clothes for you and each child, a toothbrush and toothpaste, each of your children's favorite toy or security blanket or teddy bear, each of your birth certificates, documentation of health records for your children, and any photos you can't bear to part with. Once you leave, it may be a long time before you can return home. In the meantime, your children will need to attend school wherever you are, which will require their birth certificates and health history. If you share a car with your partner, have an extra car key made and hide it in a drawer so that if you need to leave in the middle of the night, you will not need to jingle keys or in the worst case scenario, if he hides your keys to prevent you from leaving, you will still have your extra key.

- Do not tell your family where you are going. Your abuser will contact them immediately and try to find out where you are. You can contact them and let them know you are fine and will call them when you are settled.

ABUSIVE PARENTS AND SIBLINGS

I have already discussed with you some of the abusive actions you may have experienced in your childhood home. This helps to explain the person you have become and the way that you view the world and your relationships. In this section, I'd like to talk with you about the ways in which that abusive home life continues to affect you today.

The same parents who criticized the way you made your bed are now the parents who make comments like, "Joe is doing well now. Why don't you get a housekeeper?" "I wouldn't let my dog live in a mess like this." "Do you remember when we used to find dishes under her bed? If we go into her room, I'll bet we'd find the same thing now." "You shouldn't let the children live with such dirt. It's unhealthy." "You'd think you could vacuum once in a while." "I know you have a new baby, but that's no excuse. When I was a young mother, I just put you in your crib while I cleaned the house. If you cried, you cried. No baby ever died from a temper tantrum."

Sometimes, the criticism is so underhanded, you don't realize you've been insulted until after they've left and you have that familiar sinking feeling. Then it's too late to say anything—even if you would have—and all you are left with is anger and hurt.

My mother used to make little comments like, "You'd be so pretty if you'd just wear a little makeup," or "If you wore a push-up bra, you'd look like you had a chest." What do you think that did to my feeling of attractiveness? I didn't feel I could confront her until I heard her making remarks to my daughter about her appearance when she was very young. Then it had to stop, and of course, since I had all that anger simmering for 30 years, I didn't gracefully say, "Mom, Jennifer is beautiful exactly the way she is. I'd appreciate it if you wouldn't speak to her that way again."

140

Oh no. It came out in a vicious attack; not only on this subject but also on everything else under the sun and on ways I'd felt violated by her criticism all those years. She gave me a look that said, "You need some serious help."

Did it keep her from being critical to my daughter and me in the future? No. So I decided to limit my contact with her until I felt that I could be strong with her each time she made an inappropriate comment. The outcome was that her criticism did lessen in time because she wasn't getting the payoff she wanted, which apparently would have been our undying gratitude for letting us know we were inadequate in her eyes.

Sibling rivalry can be horrifying when you are young and just as bad as adults. Competing for your parents' attention when you are 35 may be subtle yet just as real as two kids fighting over who gets to sit on Daddy's lap. Who has the better job? Who has the nicest house? Whose child learned to read when he was three? Yes, but the other sibling's child was potty-trained at 18 months! One sibling insists on picking up the entire check for Mother's Day brunch—because Mom is there—while the other siblings seethe. One sibling always takes Dad to his doctor appointments or goes fishing with him. Get the idea?

Don't get me wrong. Sibling rivalry is not necessarily abusive behavior, but it can be. Take my brothers, for example. Two of them live near me and whenever they came to my home, they would take great delight in making fun of my most cherished items. They would pick up certain items and make jokes about them or hide them so I couldn't find them. Yes, these were grown men, not five-year-olds, but it still hurt my feelings. In a couple of instances, they broke an item and didn't volunteer to replace or repair it, or even apologize.

One of my brothers used to love to make fun of my appearance. He had apparently learned from my mother that this is an effective way to hurt me. One day, he said to me, "My, aren't you looking like Queen Elizabeth today."

I replied, "With those ears, aren't you looking like Prince Charles today."

He was so taken aback that I actually stood up for myself instead of just giving him a glaring look that he had to laugh and say, "Good one."

"We are much too old for you to be making fun of me as sport," I told him, and he stopped.

ACTIVITY
How Is Your Family Abusing You Today?

You have thought about past parental abuse already. Now is a good time for you to look at your present situation with your own family and your family of origin. Do you feel resentful or used by them? Do you dread holidays or visits from your family? Do you feel ineffective as a parent? Let's take a look at these feelings. You may want to use your journal for additional space or privacy.

I feel uncomfortable about my relationship with (check all that apply):

- ❏ My husband/boyfriend
- ❏ Daughter(s)
- ❏ Son(s)
- ❏ Mother/stepmother
- ❏ Father/stepfather
- ❏ Sister(s)
- ❏ Brother(s)

Situations in which I've felt uncomfortable or abused as an adult:

_____

_____

_____

_____

_____

My responses to these situations were:

_____

_____

_____

_____

_____

Once again, look closely at your responses. This is a book about patterns of behavior and the ways to change them. You may find that if your father or brother was your abuser as a child, you may never have resolved those feelings. So, not only does he continue to be your abuser, you now have difficulty with your mate or son. Likewise, abuse from a female family member could cause you difficulty with your daughter.

The situations in which you've been hurt may have a similar quality to them as well. Perhaps your appearance or intellect was criticized, you didn't feel listened to, you were spoken to in a disrespectful manner, your feelings weren't considered, etc.

Your responses are most likely similar, too. Perhaps you feel hurt but don't say anything, lash out in an extreme way, silently punish the offenders by being passive-aggressive, or cry, etc.

Looking at these patterns again later in the book will be very helpful as you begin changing them and practice interacting in healthier ways.

WHAT HAPPENED
TO YOUR LIFE?

Introduction

What Happened to Your Life?

THIS WASN'T THE LIFE you were born to live, was it? You weren't meant to have so many folks in your life treating you badly. Now that you've seen the effect of your childhood experiences as well as what abusive relationships look like in the real world, let's begin to figure them out.

What are the difficulties your destructive relationships have had on your psyche? How do they run your life and make your decisions for you?

The first issue I'd like to discuss with you is your self-esteem. It is not possible for you to have gone through all that you did and come out of it with a high self-concept. Likewise, it is impossible to have positive self-esteem and allow others to treat you that poorly. What true self-esteem is and the ways in which it helps you make all your decisions may surprise you. We know one thing for sure: It's time to raise yours up.

When fear, shame, and guilt are the triplets that invade your life, nothing good can come of it. These are all negative, destructive emotions that have a decidedly destructive effect on you. When you live each day in these feelings, you are not living an authentic life. You aren't making plans or decisions based on strength, but on weakness. Also, a pattern of keeping dark secrets, not only from others, but yourself as well, has not served your life in an empowering way. We can fix all that; just give yourself a chance.

When you are in a downward spin, good coping skills usually go out the window. Suddenly, you may find that you are sleeping more, drinking more, shopping more, or using other nonproductive ways to deal with your situation. As you have already found out, when you fail to handle your problems in a real way, you may be able to cover them up in the moment, but it does nothing to eliminate them. You can run, but you can't hide from challenges in your life. Isn't it time for you to look at your destructive relationships differently and cope with them in a healthy, productive way? You deserve a lot more than you've been giving yourself!

Are you able to help everyone but yourself? Are you the gal that "fixes" other people's problems? Do you accommodate weaknesses in others while not looking at your own? Are you a great little helper, the one who can rescue those in your life from their own failings? You may think you can, but actually you can only "fix" yourself. I know you've tried to help your family or friends out of good intentions, but it doesn't work, does it? Do they even appreciate your help? Does it keep them from making the same mistakes time and time again? No, not really.

So let's start concentrating on you and the ways in which your attempts at being a rescuer/helper has hurt your own life. Maybe, the way to communicate with others is part of the problem. I'd like to show you a more effective way of speaking with others and the ways in which that can have a powerful effect on your relationships.

Let's go!

148

CHAPTER
EIGHT

The First Consequence
of Your Abusive Relationships

Low Self-Esteem

SELF-ESTEEM. We hear that word tossed around willy-nilly, but how many of us really understand what it is? It seems as though it would be important to possess self-esteem in order to be happy and successful, doesn't it? With high self-esteem, you can chart your own course and wake up each day and feel good about life. Yes, with high self-esteem you can practically rule the world . . . or your little piece of it, right? Well, yes and no. Let's talk about what self-esteem is, the ways in which your unhealthy relationships have harmed it, and, most importantly, how you can get it back and use it to create success in your own life. Or, if you never had high self-esteem, the way you can achieve it for the first time.

WHAT IS SELF-ESTEEM?

When I was a kid, I could never do anything right. My mother was always pulling at a cowlick I had in my hair, and I had to wear glasses to try and correct a slight cross-eyed problem I had. A few times, I heard my mother saying things to friends like, "God made a mistake with Gina. She has such a gorgeous brother. It wouldn't have been so bad if the boy had the bad hair and bad eyes instead of the girl. It would be more acceptable. It's such a shame." God made a mistake with me and now I'm unacceptable! How horrible is that? These were things I couldn't fix. I was doomed from the beginning.

— GINA, 44

Perhaps you had the same type of parents that Gina did. You may have been ridiculed for your appearance, the way you thought, your grades, or just the fact of your being. If that was your case, I'm sorry. You didn't deserve that type of treatment. Positive self-esteem is perhaps the greatest gift a parent can give a child. It is their obligation to show and tell their child that she is the most amazing creature on earth and that she is loved and accepted just as she is.

When a child—especially a girl child—doesn't receive these loving messages early in life, it negatively affects every part of her life: the way she functions in school and later at her job, her relationships with her peers, the way she feels she belongs—or doesn't—in her family and in society, how high in life she is likely to rise, and her choice of relationships with men, as well as the length of time she stays with an unkind partner.

Nathaniel Branden, known as the "father of self-esteem," states that, apart from problems that are biological in origin, he can't think of a single psychological difficulty that is not traceable to poor self-esteem: depression, anxiety, fear of intimacy or success, alcohol or drug use, underachievement at school or work, spousal abuse, emotional immaturity, suicide, and crimes of violence. Isn't that amazing?

Self-esteem has two parts: a feeling of personal competence and a feeling of personal worth. In other words, self-confidence plus self-respect equals positive self-esteem. It reflects all that you do and your judgment about your right to be happy. When you have low self-esteem, you not only feel wrong about certain issues and challenges in your life, you also feel wrong as a person, that you are somehow defective. You may be plagued by feelings of inadequacy, insecurity, self-doubt, guilt, and a sense that you are not enough as you are.

The following is a list of feelings and behaviors that are common to women with low self-esteem. How many of these do you identify with?

1. I try to please others instead of myself.

2. I don't really know what I need, or if I do, I tell myself that it is not important.

3. I find it easier to feel and express anger about injustices done to others rather than those done to myself.

4. I anticipate other people's needs.

5. I feel best when I'm giving to others and uncomfortable or guilty when others give to me.

6. I find myself attracted to needy people.

7. I over commit myself.

8. I blame myself for everything.

9. I pick on myself for the way I think, feel, look, and behave.

10. I reject compliments or praise.

11. I feel different from most other people.

12. I think I'm not good enough.

13. I fear rejection.

14. I take things personally.

15. I feel like a victim.

16. I tell myself I can't do anything right.

17. I am afraid of making mistakes.

18. I feel a lot of guilt.

19. I have a lot of "shoulds" in my life.

20. I believe other people can't possibly like or love me.

21. I lose sleep over petty problems or other people's behavior.

22. I am afraid to let other people see who I am.

23. I feel controlled by people or events.

24. I try to say what I think will please other people.

25. I don't have the word "no" in my vocabulary.

26. I avoid talking about myself.

27. I think that most of what I say is unimportant or uninteresting.

28. I make a lot of apologies.

29. I let other people hurt me.

30. I don't trust myself, my feelings, my decisions, or other people.

31. I am overly trusting of others before I actually get to know them.

32. I am afraid of my own anger.

33. I am afraid to make others angry.

34. I lie to myself.

35. I don't remember the last time I felt happy, content, or peaceful with myself.

36. I look for happiness outside myself.

37. I desperately seek love and approval.

38. I am afraid or uncomfortable being alone.

39. I find myself seeking love from people who are incapable of loving.

40. I try to prove that I'm good enough to be loved.

41. I fall into serious relationships quickly.

42. I stay in relationships that don't work.

43. I don't say what I mean.

44. I feel safer feeling hurt than angry.

45. I have sex when I don't want to.

46. I find it difficult to have fun and be spontaneous.

47. I remain loyal to people who have hurt me.

48. I make lots of excuses for other people's behavior.

49. I often feel hopeless about the future.

How many of those items applied to you and your life? It would be difficult to calculate a specific number of points that are needed to "qualify" for low self-esteem. More than a couple does not bode well for a happy life. In looking at the 49 sentences, you may have recalled situations in your life when the statement was true. It may have been very painful to realize how low your self-esteem really is.

Let's think about your feeling about yourself in terms of the relationships you've chosen. The higher your self-esteem, the more likely you are to form healthy rather than destructive relationships, since health is attracted to health. If you came into a relationship with a poor self-concept, it became lower and lower the longer you remained with that person. Every time another person treated you unkindly, it merely validated the bad feelings you already had about yourself.

What would you need in order to feel worthwhile and good about yourself? According to Dr. David Burns in his book, *Ten Days To Self-Esteem*, many people base their own self-worth on the following characteristics:

- *Looks:* People who are exceptionally attractive, charming, and popular are sometimes considered to be "special" and desirable.

- *Intelligence:* We often think that very brilliant and talented individuals are more worthwhile.

- *Success:* Our culture emphasizes the importance of productivity, accomplishments, and wealth.

- *Personal effort:* We may feel like we are worthwhile as long as we are trying hard and doing the best we can, regardless of how our actual skill or performance compares with that of other people.

- *Fame and power:* Some people think that famous, charismatic, and influential people are superior.

- *Love:* We often feel worthwhile if we are loved and cared about.

- *Happiness:* Many people think that they are worthwhile as long as they feel happy and satisfied with their lives.

- *Altruism:* We may think that we are worthwhile if we are kind, generous, and loving.

- *Race or religion:* We may think that we are worthwhile because of our race, belief in God or other religious beliefs.

Basing your self-esteem on what you do rather than who you are is always a dangerous proposition. Let's think about that idea for a moment. External things like appearance, money, success, and the love another person has for us can come and go. Oftentimes, we don't have perfect control over these things. Those of us that are of a "certain age" can attest to the fact that body parts are going to sag no matter how many leg lifts and abdominal crunches we do. Goodness knows I've spent a fair amount of money on lotions and potions that promise fewer wrinkles! Almost anyone who has achieved wealth and success can give you a list of their failures along the way quicker than their list of accomplishments.

I remember watching Maria Shriver on *Oprah* as she related all the jobs from which she'd been fired and the many boyfriends who had dumped her. Here she was, a gorgeous woman from the wealthy Kennedy family, with great intelligence, a terrific career as a television journalist and best-selling book author, living in more than one very expensive home, having lovely children, and married to the *Terminator* (Arnold Schwartzenegger) for heaven's sake. She couldn't possibly be like the rest of us. Well, apparently she was. Even Oprah was surprised and said so, to which Maria replied, "Do you want to do the entire hour on my failures, because I can do that!"

When we rely on outside forces to determine our level of self-esteem, it is called other-esteem. As I mentioned, other-esteem is very tenuous and fragile. The word self in self-esteem requires you to feel good about yourself for other reasons.

Take a look at this list and decide how many of the items apply to you.

1. I am a considerate person.

2. I am a good mom most of the time.

3. I am a person who usually tries to do what is right.

4. I am a child of God.

5. I am a woman who does her best as often as possible.

6. I am a gal who tries to move ahead when obstacles get in my way.

7. I am a person who wants to gain knowledge about myself in order to do better in life.

Do you qualify for any of those statements? Yes, I thought so. When you look at that list and understand that those are intangibles—that is, you cannot directly measure them—and you also have perfect control over them, you can begin to feel better about yourself.

Look at the above list again and compare it to the other list that involves looks, intelligence, success, fame, power, love, race, and religion. Ask yourself this question: What is the benefit to me in attaching my self-esteem to external qualities? If I base my self-concept on my appearance, what will happen when they fade? What will happen when I am older and can't recall all that I used to know? What if I never become CEO of a company, an Academy Award-winning actress, President of the United States, fall in love with the same kind person for the rest of my life, or find out that my higher power didn't intend for me to feel superior to others by virtue of the color of my skin?

Wow! That's a pretty hefty list to accomplish. So, what would be the benefit to you? What are the negative consequences to basing your personal esteem on those factors?

Now, what is the benefit for you to base your self-esteem on the fact that you are a good person who does her best under difficult circumstances and wants to learn more about herself so that she can make good decisions? What are the negative consequences to basing your personal esteem on those factors?

Are you getting my point? In the first instance, they are all external factors over which you have little or no control of your destiny. In the second instance, it's all about you and factors over which you have perfect control based on your own decisions and behaviors. That feels good.

Most of us have the impression that only people with high self-esteem do wonderful things and accomplish amazing feats. Not so. Actually, it's the other way around. First, you do something that's a little difficult or uncomfortable to you; something that you thought you couldn't do. Shazzam! In doing this task—whether you are 100 percent successful or not—you begin acquiring more self-esteem. As you do other difficult things, your self-esteem grows and grows. You think to yourself, I'm a pretty awesome woman for even attempting this. Who would've thought I'd even try (to ask the boss for a raise, tell my parents I don't like the way they treat me, let my kids know they can't speak to me that way anymore, tell the room mom I can't chaperone the next—and fiftieth—field trip, or kick my ungrateful boyfriend to the curb)? Pretty soon, you get a reputation as a gutsy woman and people have tons of respect for you. Gee, who would have thought you could do that? Me . . . and, most importantly, you.

ACTIVITY
Under What Circumstances Is My Self-Esteem the Lowest?

In your journal, write down and answer the following questions:

- When I think of self-esteem, what images pop into my mind? In other words, what does self-esteem mean and look like to you?

- What situations make me feel less worthwhile?

- What do I think about myself in these situations? What do I tell myself?

- How has low self-esteem sabotaged my happiness, creativity, relationships, and personal success?

- What one thing can I do for myself today that will help me begin to feel better about myself?

(Hints: Take ten minutes alone for quiet and solitude, look in the mirror and say one good thing about yourself, begin reading a biography of a woman you admire or to whom you somehow relate, eat lunch outdoors, rent a happy movie, make cookies with your kids, swing on a swing, exercise, spend girl-time with an emotionally healthy female friend, bring fresh flowers into your home, etc.)

Do something else from your list tomorrow.

CHAPTER
NINE

The Second Consequence
of Your Abusive Relationships

Emotional Fear

I was in a series of crazy relationships. My boyfriend of four years was really controlling and started considering my feelings less and less. He was talking about having kids and I was seriously considering it, even though each day he made me feel terrible about myself. Then, I also had friends who were creeps. I think they intentionally hurt my feelings sometimes because it made them feel better about themselves. I was really unhappy where I was working. My boss was so ungrateful for all the effort I was putting in. My parents lived far away—which was probably for the best, since they are always criticizing anything I do. But I didn't even have them for support. I felt like my whole life was in the toilet. I couldn't imagine how I would get myself out of this nightmare. I was scared to stay in it and scared to get out of it, because it was my whole life. I mean, everyone in my life was really bad for me.

What was I going to do? Blow them all off and be completely alone? When I was finally forced to look at that question, it was pretty easy to see that I thought it was better to keep abusive people in my life—and let them continue to abuse me—than to be on my own. How crazy is that?

— BETH, 36

IF YOU ARE ANYTHING LIKE BETH, you have asked yourself the same questions. I have found that the fear of being alone is only one of many fears most women have when they make a decision to discontinue their destructive relationships. In fact, emotional fears are really one of the many by-products of the time you spent in abusive relationships.

Here is a list of the most common fears and concerns that women experience when they have been in one or more abusive relationships in their family of origin, with a mate, children, friends, or in a work environment:

- I don't know how to live on my own anymore.

- I'm afraid of making more poor decisions.

- Have my kids been damaged by my abusive marriage?

- I'm really concerned about money.

- I think about going back to my abusive relationship (with my mate, friend, boss, coworker). Does that mean I'm crazy?

- It's been so long since I've worked, I don't think I have any good job skills anymore.

- I feel like a complete mess.

- I'm afraid of everything.

- Sometimes I think, "It wasn't that bad." What's wrong with me?

⊙ Most days I feel like I'm going crazy.

- I'm so depressed that I don't know how I'm going to function day-to-day.

- I think of myself as a total loser.

- I feel like a nervous wreck most of the time.

- I feel defective and useless.

- How can I teach my kids to be strong and be in good relationships when I've been such a bad role model?

- I don't trust anyone . . . including myself.

- I second-guess everything I do.

- I can't imagine ever being happy again.

Boy, how many of those statements have you made? When you've been in even one unhealthy relationship, it robs you of your spirit. When you've been in several of these relationships, the outcome can be almost catastrophic in terms of your mental health and well-being. Sometimes, fear seems to rule your life. Let's take a look at some of the fears above and try to get a handle on them.

Fear is an interesting—and necessary—response to a stimulus. Oftentimes, fear is a learned behavior. In childhood, we are taught not to talk to strangers because they might be mean and take us away from our families. Therefore we learn to fear people we don't know. In some families, the mom might say, "Just wait until your father gets home," so we learn to fear our fathers. If your mom was an alcoholic who was prone to rages when she drank, you learned to behave in a quiet, submissive fashion so as not to anger your mother out of your fear of her. And so it goes . . . .

As adults, we carry those types of fears into our grown-up lives and learn to accommodate them. We accept a boss with a temper because we know how to bend our behaviors to his. We make excuses for cruelty in friends or spouses or even our own children because we fear their responses: verbal or physical violence, emotional withdrawal, projections of their own feelings of self-loathing, or leaving us.

Sometimes fear is rational, but most often in adult life, it is irrational. It is merely a conditioned response. You may be used to feeling afraid in a certain situation, and so you feel afraid in many situations.

A woman who has been in an abusive romantic relationship has very real fears when she leaves her abuser. During their time together, he has intimidated her with threats of violence against her and/or her children, pets, or her other family members. He may have threatened to leave her, take her children away from her, or a myriad of other disgusting threats at which abusers are good. He conditioned her to feel fearful all the time, either because he would occasionally follow through on his threats, or because she was just so afraid that she feared he would act them out. She may now fear that even in her current safe situation, he will act on the old threats. This may be true, but usually is not.

Women who have survived abusive mate relationships almost unanimously have an over-exaggerated feeling of their ex's power. Of course, it is helpful to be cautious and not act in an unwise or unsafe manner, but many women live in constant and debilitating fear of what their abusers will do to them next. It prevents them from moving forward.

Women who have suffered abuse at the hand of their boss or coworker have fears as well. Because a boss is in a position of authority and control, a boss can make decisions to terminate employment and therefore a woman's livelihood. A coworker may have damaging information about a woman—real or perceived—that can produce the same effect.

The subject of abusive parents has been dealt with in several chapters of this book. When adult women look at their fears surrounding their parents, they almost always laugh. As adults, they continue to fear their parents' disapproval, criticism, and withdrawal of love. Since they are no longer dependent on their parents for their basic needs, it now becomes a question of preference in having unkind and conditionally accepting parents in their lives. However, initially, the fear feels just as real as it did in childhood.

Abusive friends also leave their marks in terms of fear. Women rely very heavily on other female relationships for nurturing and acceptance. As women, we reveal a great deal of ourselves to our friends, which makes us very vulnerable when they go south. We fear that these other women to whom we have been very close see something defective in us, which is why they are acting unkindly. We imagine they know the "truth" about us, which is that we are weak, stupid, ineffective, uncaring, and unlovable. Who could possibly know you better than your best girl-friend (unless the answer to that question is my abusive mate or my abusive parents)?

Abusive kids are a whole matter unto themselves. When children are abusive, it brings out the fear that we haven't been good enough moms. If we had done a better job, they wouldn't treat us that way. If we aren't even good enough to be loved by our kids, what hope is there?

When we are coming from a fearful place, we are doing several self-destructive things at once. Let's take a look at a few of them so that after you identify them, you can go about changing them.

IRRATIONAL BELIEFS

It is true that our perceptions create our reality. That is, the way that we view the world and our own situations are the only realities that we tend to accept as correct. Here is an important perspective, however: *Just because you believe a thought is true doesn't necessarily make it true.* If I were to say to you, "Look at the sky. Isn't it a beautiful shade of green?" Obviously, you would look at the sky and see that it is not green, but that it is blue. I might insist and am persuasive to the point that you question your sanity. My reality is that the sky is green, but it is not *the* reality.

When you have emotional fears, you may be engaging in a great many irrational beliefs, such as:

- *All-or-nothing thinking:* This is also known as black-and-white thinking or dichotomous thinking. It means that you look at events or thoughts in absolute black-or-white categories. Someone may be all good or all bad, completely trustworthy or not at all trustworthy under any circumstances, etc. When you are engaged in all-or-nothing thinking, there is no room for shades of gray, which is actually where most of reality lies.

- *Generalization:* This type of irrational belief sees you viewing a negative event as a cata-strophic pattern of defeat. The word "always" fits into this type of thinking as in, "I always mess up job interviews," "I always disappoint my friends and family."

- *Discounting the positives:* You insist that your positive qualities don't count and that any of your accomplishments are unimportant.

When you are complimented for a job well done or your lovely appearance, you might say, "Oh, it wasn't a big deal. A monkey could have done that job," or, "This old dress? I think it makes me look like I'm sitting in a tent."

- *Jumping to conclusions:* This irrational belief is comprised of two parts: mind reading and fortune telling. When you engage in mind reading, you make assumptions about the ways in which others think about you without any evidence whatsoever. How many times have you gone to work to find that your boss snaps at you as soon as you walk in the door? Your initial reaction might be that your boss is angry with you for some unknown reason, or a reason that you devise. The truth is that your boss's mood probably has nothing to do with you and began long before you arrived at work.

  When you are a fortuneteller, you predict that events will turn out badly without any evidence whatsoever. But, because you are Magda the Fortuneteller, you just know that it's true. Before you go to a job interview, you know you won't get the job. You also absolutely know that you will never know happiness in your life again. You know that all your future decisions will be bad ones.

- *Magnification or minimization:* When you magnify events, you blow them way out of proportion. If one of your coworkers dislikes you, then no one at work likes you. When you minimize events, you shrink their importance significantly. Women in abusive situations use minimization a good deal of the time: "My friend didn't mean to insult me. She's just having a bad day." "My husband just pushed me down once. Is once in three years really that bad?" "My son is disrespectful to me, but it's not personal. He's just having a difficult school year." "You might say that my mother was abusive to me when I was a child, but she was a single mother and doing the best she could."

- *Should statements:* You criticize yourself, and perhaps others, with words such as "should," "shouldn't," "must," "ought," and the like. You make absolute and highly critical statements. "I should be a better mother," "I shouldn't ever have gotten involved with my husband," "I must do a perfect job on this report," "I ought to have a better career by now," etc. When you criticize yourself in these ways, you don't give yourself any wiggle room for improvement or salvaging a situation.

- *Labeling:* You give yourself labels such as "loser," "stupid," "jerk," "idiot," and the like. In other words, you are verbally abusive to yourself.

- *Blame and personalization:* You may blame others for situations you now find yourself in and deny the ways in which your own behaviors and attitudes contribute to the problem. As a point of reference, I discussed the idea of victimization earlier in this book. When you take the role of victim in your abusive relationships, you deny any complicity in the problem. When you personalize a situation, you blame yourself solely for a situation you may not have been entirely responsible for. Very often, women in abusive situations don't look at the part others played in their situations and take the entire problem onto them. Abuse is always a two-way street.

- *Emotional reasoning:* You make decisions based on your feelings without looking at concrete evidence. For example, you may think, I feel like a loser so I really must be a loser, I feel like no one likes me, so I'm sure no one likes me, or I've been sad so long, I don't even need to try anymore.

ACTIVITY
My Irrational Beliefs

Let's think back to some of the common emotional fears I listed at the beginning of this chapter. These may be some of the fears you experience yourself. Look at each one and try to identify which irrational belief you are seeing:

- I feel like a complete failure (so I must be one). *Emotional reasoning, Labeling.*

- I'm afraid of everything. *All-or-nothing thinking.*

- Sometimes I think that the abuse wasn't that bad. *Minimization.*

- I feel like I'm going crazy (so I must be crazy). *Emotional reasoning, Labeling.*

- I'm so depressed that I don't know how I'm going to function day-to-day. *Fortune telling.*

- I think of myself as a total loser. *Labeling.*

- I don't trust anyone. *Generalization, All-or-nothing thinking.*

- I can't imagine ever being happy. *Fortune-telling.*

- I'm afraid of making poor decisions. *Personalization, Fortune-telling.*

Now, in your journal, make a list of your own irrational beliefs and identify the distortions you are using to keep them alive.

EXTREME TALK

I find that when people are operating in crisis or fear mode, they talk in very extreme ways. The statements above of, "I'll never be happy again," "I don't trust anyone," "I think of myself as a total loser," and "I'm afraid of everything" are good examples of this type of negative and extreme self-talk.

You may have used similar extreme language or others such as, "My life is horrible," "I'm the worst mother in the world," or "What my friend did was so disgusting that it's totally unforgivable."

The language we use is very powerful and informs our feelings about the situation and decision-making associated with it. Be very careful about the words you use with yourself and others in describing your relationships and your feelings about them. You may be catastrophizing the situation, which puts you in a helpless position. From that lowered place in your own life, it's very difficult to pick yourself up and fight for what you deserve.

ACTIVITY
Ways That I've Used Extreme Talk
in My Abusive Relationships

Here is an opportunity to take back a good deal of your power, think about your relationships differently, and reduce your fears. On a page in your journal, list the extreme words you have used to describe different unhealthy situations in your life. You can use some of the examples I stated above to help you.

After you do so, are you able to see the ways in which these words were so powerful that they left you paralyzed with fear? Now, think of some powerful and healing words that can help you describe the same situations. Do you notice the way in which your mind-set immediately changes from "victim" to Superwoman?

I have found that I use the word "never" a lot, as in, "I'll never be able to understand this," or, "I never do anything right," or, "I never sound as smart as my sister." It became a habit. I didn't think it was any big deal until I started looking at the ways it affected my life and kept me in a constant state of helplessness and depression. I began forcing myself to say things like, "I don't understand this right now, but I'm sure that if I work at it, I'll be able to master it," or, "I didn't do it right this time, but next time will be better," or, "I don't need to compare myself to my sister or anyone else. I'm unique and great as I am." You can't believe how just minding what I said changed my life.

— SUE, 41.

NEW WAYS TO EXAMINE YOUR FEARS

I'd like to teach you some other ways to look at the emotional fears in your life so that you will be the mistress of your own life, rather than letting irrational beliefs control your decisions.

- *Examine the Evidence:* Look at your list of fears and the irrational beliefs you attributed to them. Now, one by one, ask yourself, "What is the evidence for this fear?" Just because you feel like you can't imagine ever being happy doesn't mean that it's true that you will never be happy. You are not Magda the Fortuneteller and you don't know what the future holds.

  So, along those lines of reasoning, give me the evidence for a particular fear. Pretend that I'm a Supreme Court judge and you are a trial lawyer, so you'd better come up with some pretty persuasive evidence. Remember, feelings don't count in a court of law. Hard, cold evidence is the only standard by which a case is decided.

- *Conduct an Experiment:* Look at another of your fears. When women have survived abusive relationships, they are not only depressed while engaging in the relationship, but also equally depressed in the aftermath. The fear that, "I'm so depressed that I don't know how I'll function day-to-day" is common. It builds on itself so that you imagine not being able to work, take care of your children, and take care of your own basic needs. This fear then spirals downward, in which the "logical" conclusions become: If I can't keep a job, I'll lose my home. If I don't have a home and I can't take care of my children, they will be taken away from me. I will be a homeless woman without any hope of getting my kids back. Do you see how these fears, the irrational thoughts behind them, and the extreme talk can leave you unable to move?

Do you remember the science experiments you conducted in school, such as putting one of your baby teeth in a glass of cola and seeing how long it took to disintegrate? (I swore off all soda products that very day.) Why not conduct your own experiment to test out your theories.

Take the fear, "I'm afraid of everything." When you are accustomed to living in fear, it is very common to feel this way. Why not take an hour and sit quietly in your home. Are you afraid of your couch? Are you afraid of your refrigerator? Are you afraid of your bath towels? Okay, so you're not afraid of everything in your home. Go to your local mall. Sit on a bench and look around. Are you afraid of every person that passes you? Are you afraid of the clerk at the store in front of you? Are you afraid that you will have a heart attack and keel over right there and then? No? Well then, given these two simple examples, I think it might be fair to say that you're not afraid of everything.

- *Look at Your Double Standards:* Think of another fear, let's say, "I feel like a total loser." If you heard your best good friend say that, what would be your reply? Why, you'd be shocked and indignant. "You are not a total loser," you'd cry. "You're a terrific friend with so many good qualities, I hardly know where to start!" Why should you be able to get away with saying that about yourself?

If you aren't your own friend, who will be? Sure, you have some not-so-great characteristics. Who doesn't, including your best friend? But you are willing to overlook the times she's been 20 minutes late to meet you for lunch when you were ravenous, or the times she's had something hanging from her nose or between her teeth. She may have lost jobs or had a creep as a boyfriend or husband. Would you say that makes her a "total loser?" No, of course not. Give yourself the gift of applying the same standards to you as you would to a friend or loved one. Give yourself the same encouraging messages you'd give her.

- *Use Substitute Phrases:* Do you remember when you were in school and walked into your classroom to find a substitute teacher? Wasn't that a great feeling? It usually meant that you had a "pass" for the day. She might have said, "Boys and girls, I know you were supposed to have a test today, but Miss Palmer didn't leave the questions for me, so instead we are going to watch a *Flipper* rerun and talk about our ocean friends." Substitutes were wonderful.

    You now have a chance to use the same idea in dealing with your fears. You can use substitute phrases, which will give you a break and an opportunity to stop testing yourself. For example, instead of telling yourself, "I feel like I'm going crazy," which leaves you frightened and powerless, substitute a phrase such as, "Life has been difficult lately. It's taken all my strength to keep my head above water." Instead of telling yourself, "I'm afraid I'll continue to make bad decisions," substitute a phrase like, "I'm going to begin thinking about letting only kind, healthy people into my life from now on. I deserve that much." Can you see the impact this type of substitution can have on eliminating your fears?

In the next chapter, we will discuss the ways in which keeping your abusive relationships a secret—perhaps even from yourself—and holding shame and guilt has kept you from achieving the happiness and success you deserve in your life.

CHAPTER
TEN

The Third Consequence
of Your Abusive Relationships

Shame, Guilt, and Keeping Secrets

WHEN A WOMAN IS ACTIVELY ENGAGED in an abusive relationship of any kind, she becomes supremely adept at keeping the unhealthy aspects of it a secret. She usually doesn't tell anyone about the way she is being spoken to or treated. Instead, she exaggerates what she perceives to be the parts of the perpetrator's behaviors and personality that she finds endearing—or at least bearable. These are the parts that entice her to stay. Why? Because she feels ashamed that this is happening to her and guilty that she has "caused" her abuser to treat her in such a heinous fashion. And, if she is in an abusive partnership, she feels guilty that her children have been witness to these acts. So, secrets, shame, and guilt work together in a type of terrible triad, swirling in and around each other every day.

The secretive, shameful, and guilt-ridden aspects of a destructive relationship are very powerful reasons why women not only remain stuck at the time, but also remain stuck after they've left. These feelings are so intense that it is difficult to move past them. You may have felt that way as well. Well, not anymore. Starting right now, I promise you that you will begin to have control over these destructive feelings. This will allow you to live a more honest and powerful life.

WHY HAVE YOUR DESTRUCTIVE RELATIONSHIPS BEEN SUCH A SECRET?

When I was a little girl, it seems like my whole life was a secret. My family didn't have a lot of prestige in the community, but I think my mother liked to believe we did. She was very competitive with other women and unhappy with the fact that our last name wasn't Vanderbilt. We were just an ordinary middle-class family. But you'd never know it by the way my mother acted, which was pretty snooty and high-society. I don't know what she was thinking. Anyway, when I was two, my father left my mother. I never got the real story as to why it happened, only her side of it.

When I was three, my mother remarried and by the time I was five, my stepfather was sexually abusing me. I didn't tell my mother at the time because he told me not to and threatened me that if I did, he'd start hurting my older brother, too. I know that my mother knew about the abuse, though. I started wetting my bed, having horrible nightmares, and being incredibly frightened of her husband. She never asked about it and I think she didn't want the reality of what was going on to be told to her, because then she might have to kick him out and be alone again. It would be a big embarrassment to her to be divorced, especially so soon after she remarried. People might talk! So, we had this implied understanding that we would keep all this a big secret for her benefit.

My parents fought a lot, but when we were out in public, we had to act like this happy, perfect family. My stepfather would hold my hand, which would tear me up inside, and my mother let him because it gave the illusion that he was a happy family man with a great, well-adjusted daughter.

When my brother was 14, he started rebelling big time. He was running away, taking drugs, not going to school. Instead of getting to the causes of his problem behavior, my mother kept everything hush-hush and I had to also. There was a reason why he was away: He was visiting his father (whom we never saw again after he left). He wasn't going to school because he was sick again. And he wasn't using drugs; that weird behavior you saw was just typical adolescent stuff.

Everything was a big lie. I couldn't stand the pressure of having to keep all the stories straight or just living in my house. I guess it wouldn't be hard to predict that, when I was 15, I became involved with a boyfriend who was pretty terrible and also got pregnant by him when I was 16. That—and my abortion—was a secret, too. I kept going from one bad relationship to another and of course, I was keeping them a secret from my family. Each one was worse than the next and I kept the entire bad parts secret from not only my family, but also my friends.

I was really on a terrible roller coaster until I ended up homeless and addicted to cocaine. It took a lot to confess all the secrets of my life and begin living truthfully.

— JENNA, 26

Let's talk about secrets and the reasons you learned to keep them. You may recall that earlier in this book I discussed the ways in which your childhood experiences may have inadvertently "taught" you to accept subsequent destructive relationships. Let me reiterate a few of those ideas and you can gauge whether you think that they fit for you and whether or not you have brought those behaviors into your adult life.

If you grew up in a household in which one or both of your parents were heavy drinkers or drug abusers, keeping it a secret took up a good deal of your time. You may not have felt comfortable inviting friends to your house because you didn't want them to know of your parents' substance abuse problem. If one of your parents had this difficulty, your other parent may have encouraged the secretive—and possibly, dishonest—behavior. Keeping secrets about what happened in your family was a given, a way of life.

If you were raised in a home in which an appearance of normalcy, or perhaps perfection was stressed, you learned that "we don't air our dirty linen in public." Perhaps your parents argued frequently, or yours was a domestic violence household. Maybe one of your brothers or sisters acted inappropriately—according to your parents' standards—and was the "black sheep of the family." Nobody needed to know that one of your siblings had a problem with drugs, was pregnant before marriage, got poor grades, was arrested for shoplifting, or wasn't accepted to the college of her choice. Because your parents felt defective in their roles and competitive with their friends, it was your responsibility to keep all the family secrets and act as if everything was hunky-dory.

You may be able to think of other examples in your young life in which keeping family secrets was a necessity if you were to remain in your parents' good graces. What would the consequences have been if you spilled the beans? So, there you were: a young child with so much responsibility and so much dishonesty. Sometimes, it was difficult to discern reality from fantasy, wasn't it?

When keeping secrets is a part of family life, it becomes very easy to bring that attitude into adulthood. You keep your destructive relationships a secret from anyone else in your life, perhaps even to yourself, which we call "denial." You don't let on that you are being spoken to in a cruel and demeaning fashion. You don't say a word about the fact that you are being sexually or physically violated. You don't tell anyone that you are frightened or depressed. It's all a great, big secret, which quickly becomes a great, big lie.

Please don't feel as though I'm picking on you here. Hey, I've been there, done that, bought the tee shirt. I've had many destructive relationships, kept every one of them a big, ol' secret and even lied to the faces of those who were concerned about me. I became so good at it that I should have won an Academy Award for Best Actress in an Unhealthy Relationship. I may have won several years in a row!

ACTIVITY
What Are the Secrets You Have Kept?

You have kept many secrets, both in childhood and in your adult life. When you were young, you may have kept them as a means of assuring your own survival. Whereas this may have been a good idea at the time, it no longer fits into your new life of greater health and authenticity. We all have many times in our lives when we'd like a "do over," a chance to say or do something differently if we only had the opportunity. Here is your do over, your moment to "confess" the secrets you have not shared before and the ways in which they have damaged your life—if only to yourself. Structure your journal page like this:

My secret	My age	I kept that secret because	What I have to say about it now

WHAT ARE SHAME AND GUILT . . . AND ARE THEY ALWAYS BAD?

Dr. David D. Burns, in his book *The Feeling Good Handbook*, defines shame and guilt in this way: "You believe that you've hurt someone or that you've failed to live up to your own moral standards. Guilt results from self-condemnation, whereas shame involves the fear that you'll lose face when others find out about what you did."

While shame and guilt are the fraternal twins of emotions, there are real differences in the way they are felt and expressed, and like human fraternal twins, they each have their own identities.

SHAME

John Bradshaw states, in his wonderful book *Healing the Shame that Binds You,* "In itself, shame is not bad. Shame is a normal emotion. In fact, it is necessary to have the feeling of shame if one is to be truly human. Shame is the emotion that gives us permission to be human. Shame tells us of our limits. Shame keeps us in our human boundaries, letting us know we can and will make mistakes, and that we need help. Our shame tells us we are not God. Healthy shame is the psychological foundation of humility. It is the source of spirituality."

Bradshaw further states, however, that healthy shame can be transformed into shame as a state of being. "As a state of being, shame takes over one's whole identity. To have shame as an identity is to believe that one's being is flawed, that one is defective as a human being. Once shame is transformed into an identity, it becomes toxic and dehumanizing."

So, while healthy shame has the power to motivate you to examine your life and decisions, toxic shame becomes the core of depression, character disorders, feelings of inadequacy and failure, violence, and a whole host of inwardly and outwardly destructive behaviors and thoughts.

Toxic shame is loneliness and isolation. Because a shamed person cannot expose her true self to others and believes she is flawed and defective as a person, she views herself as untrustworthy in relationships. Because a shamed person cannot expose her true self even to her own self, there is a sense of total self-abandonment and soul loneliness. She has lost her true identity and feels a powerful sense of alienation within herself and the outside world. When a woman feels toxic shame, she can be in a room full of adoring "fans," be the CEO of a successful company, or win the lottery and she still feels lonely, tormented, and "wrong." She must spend an enormous amount of energy keeping up her false front both to herself and others.

Can you see how the intense feelings of toxic shame have directed your decisions to find and maintain destructive relationships? It is crucially important for you to understand that you have not been the only participant in this feeling while in these relationships. Your abusers have felt even more powerful toxic shame and that is the very reason for their abusive behaviors. Let me explain this concept.

Often, when one feels overwhelming toxic shame, the way to protect against the repercussions of that is by acting "shameless" and transferring one's own toxic shame to another person, namely you. These kinds of transference behaviors are the very ones you have found to be abusive: power and control, arrogance, criticism, rage, blame, being judgmental, perfectionism, and patronizing attitudes. These types of behaviors take the focus off the person experiencing toxic shame and place it directly onto you. Your response to these behaviors may have been your own shame-based behaviors of people pleasing, care taking, and envy.

Since you now understand that all abuse involves the need for power and control, I will further explain this one aspect of the way in which toxic shame is presented to you. When one lives with the fear of exposure for what he believes to be a defective self, controlling behaviors are a surefire way to insure that no one can ever see through him and shame him again, removing the risk of vulnerability. This involves attempting to control another's thoughts, behaviors, and reactions. This destroys the equality necessary for healthy relationships. Those who feel inferior are always on the lookout for ways to control others, thereby (falsely) feeling more powerful, secure, superior, and unafraid. Those with a need for power and control therefore find another person with shame that is expressed in the forms of people pleasing behaviors so that they can reenact their own victimization from childhood when they were shamed by their parents.

When you have self-love and self-acceptance, you are always the person with true control—control over your own thoughts, behaviors, and reactions. You love and accept yourself unconditionally and strive for generosity and equality in your own relationships.

ACTIVITY
Healing Your Toxic Shame

Recovery from toxic shame is a many-pronged process and it doesn't happen quickly. Just as it took many years for you to develop this self-destructive emotion, so too will it take concentrated effort for you to now learn to face yourself and the outside world with new and more loving attitudes. It may involve pain, which is the exact feeling shame attempts to avoid.

The most important step in the recovery process is to develop healthy social contact. If you have spent a good portion of your life in destructive relationships, you may understandably feel that you are in no position to decide which people are healthy versus unhealthy. The easiest way to learn about this is through a 12-step program. Two groups that I find enormously useful are Al-Anon and CoDA.

You may associate Al-Anon with alcoholics, and with good reason, since it is essentially a group to aid people who are dealing with an alcoholic loved one. However, the tools of personal empowerment and choice-making you will receive are priceless. The messages of individuality are adaptable to anyone's life and difficulties.

Codependents Anonymous (CoDA) is a wonderful group for those who find themselves drawn to unhealthy, abusive people and react in a self-shaming, people pleasing manner. CoDA will help support your quest for authenticity in a loving manner.

Once you feel comfortable with the members of your group, you will need to begin honestly sharing your feelings with those who prove to be trustworthy and show that they believe your emotions are valuable. It is important to be able to see yourself mirrored in the eyes of a non-shaming, healthy person. Likewise, if you are able to establish yourself as healthy and trusting enough to eventually aid in another person's recovery that will be wonderful. However, it is crucial that you guard against your people pleasing tendencies. It is important to honor the reality of your own recovery from toxic shame. It is absolutely all right for you to accept another person's grace and support without giving anything back except the hope for a more honest life. When you are experiencing a healthy person, that is more than enough for them. You do not have to do or be anything additional.

Toxic shame is hidden and frightened to face the light. Writing and speaking about your feelings of shame will force it to come out of hiding and, like a vampire who faces the light of day, it will begin to self-destruct. Make time every day to journal your experiences of shame and the feelings of loneliness and falsity it has created. Or, if you don't enjoy journaling, you can speak it aloud to yourself or your trusted friend. When you begin to truly experience toxic shame for what it is, it has less and less power over your life.

If you know that your feelings of shame are based on your childhood experiences and who your parents convinced you that you were, find some photographs of yourself as a child and scatter them around your home. That little girl was not treated in a wholly loving way. She was taught to feel things that really didn't have anything at all to do with her. That child lost the best parts of herself at a time in her life when she should have felt joyful and confident. Speak to her. Tell her about her true self. Educate her on all the lovely things about herself that she wasn't told then. Help her to understand that she is perfect and precious just as she is. Accept and love that incredible little girl.

Externalize the shaming voices in your head. Understand what they are telling you and speak back to them. Your original shaming voices have been internalized and have become your voice. It is time to replace those voices with a new, positive, and self-loving voice. Looking in the mirror each day and telling it one wonderful quality is a good start. In addition, when the destructive, self-loathing voice starts to play in your head, replace it with an affirmation of goodness and clarity. You can actually tell the toxic voice, "Stop! You don't know who I am. I have allowed you to run my life for too long. It's time for you to go away. I no longer need you or want you. I am in control now."

It sounds a bit like an exorcism, doesn't it? In a way, it is. Exorcise the demons of self-doubt and self-hatred from your life. Experience the magnificence that is the real you!

Finally, learn to recognize the people and situations that trigger your shame spirals. This will be easier than you think if you look over all of the past activities you have already done in this book. Is it your critical mother? Your remote, unaccepting father? Perhaps it is your friend who tries to make you feel guilty as a mother or constantly competes with you in petty ways. It could be your mate who tells you in so many ways that you are "less than." Your boss may be unyielding in her blame or you may have coworkers who sabotage your trust. Maybe your own children are so argumentative that you feel as though you are in a constant, losing battle with them.

You can practice the assertiveness techniques you will learn later in this book. You can also understand those who have shamed you or attempt to shame you from the view you now have: they feel their own toxic shame and are unwilling to deal with it at present. That doesn't in any way mean that you have to put up with it or allow it for yourself. Create a boundary between your understanding of an unhealthy person's personal challenges and what you are deserving of yourself. Realize that just as you have had to put forth tremendous energy and honesty in dealing with your own shame, they will have to do the same for themselves when and if they find it valuable. You cannot do that for them, nor should you even attempt it. Realizing this is another important step in healing your life.

GUILT

As women, we really know how to dish out guilt and how to take it. I am reminded of the joke I was e-mailed recently by a friend, which perfectly describes the ways that we can make our children feel guilty. A 40-year-old man calls his mother and hears that her voice sounds weak and sick. "What's wrong, mom? You sound terrible," he says. "Oh, I feel terrible. I haven't eaten a thing in four days," she replies. "Oh, mom, that's horrible. Why haven't you eaten in so long?" he asks. "I was afraid that if I went to the refrigerator, I'd miss your call."

Well, yes, we know how to make our kids feel guilty for the stretch marks, varicose veins, and permanently wider hips that we have as a result of our pregnancies. But, if we are good at giving guilt, we are probably even better at receiving it.

Guilt isn't always a bad thing. Oftentimes, it motivates us to do the right thing or get things done. It can also help us make the correct decisions in our lives. When my children were younger, I told them that when they were unsure about whether a decision was good or bad, they should ask themselves these questions: If I do this, will it disappoint my parents? If I do this, will I feel disappointed in myself at a later time? If I do this, will God think it is immoral? If the answer to any of those questions were yes, it would be easy to see that it was not wise to embark on what they were considering. That's essentially good guilt in a nutshell. Good guilt therefore involves your actions rather than an attack on who you are as a person.

Psychologists have found that people who feel guilty tend to be understanding and forgiving in addition to having a keen ability to build strong relationships. There's good news and bad news in that finding, however. Sometimes it is not appropriate to be understanding or immediately forgiving of another person's abusive behaviors. It is not wise to build strong relationships with just anyone, especially with an unhealthy destructive person.

Bad guilt always involves a feeling of being defective or not good enough. We need to compensate for those feelings by overdoing in another area. For instance, feeling guilty about being a working mother is the number one trigger for women. We feel guilty when we are at work because we aren't with our children and may be seen as an indifferent, uncaring mother. We feel guilty when we take time off to be with our children because we are neglecting our job responsibilities and may be seen as slackers at work. We may feel guilty that we enjoy our work and wonder what's wrong with us that we can't feel wholly content staying home and caring for our children and home as our entire job. On the other hand, we may feel guilty if we stay home with our children because we are not contributing financially to the household or because other women tell us in so many words that our "brains will turn to mush." We may feel guilty that we got a higher education that we are not using in the workplace.

Of course, there are those for whom guilt is a foreign concept. They don't have a personal code of moral ethics or a sense of consequences. Rules don't apply to them and they feel no remorse. We call these people psychopaths or sociopaths. We also call them abusers.

I think that there are times when it is certainly appropriate to feel guilty. In writing this book, I have had to confront many uncomfortable feelings of my own. Like you, in this chapter, I have assessed my own shame and guilt feelings. I have thought a lot about a very disturbing incident in which—feeling frustrated and out-of-control— I brandished a belt in front of my son when he was only five-years-old. I threatened that if he didn't obey me, I would hit him with it. I will never forget the look of terror in his eyes. He was terrified of the woman that he loved most in the world and with whom he trusted and felt safe. He was terrified of the woman who told him so many times that she loved him and showed him that he could trust her and feel safe with her.

As I recall that incident now, I am reminded of the identical look my brothers had on their faces as my father chased them through our childhood home with his belt aimed at them. Even though I was not the target of his anger at those times, I remember the feelings of horror I had in watching this display. I remember hating him at those times. My father was frustrated and out-of-control, just as I was. For both of us, intimidating someone younger, smaller, and powerless made us feel superior and in control of the situation and ourselves. While my father has never apologized to my brothers for his abhorrent behavior, I have repeatedly apologized to my son. Although he has accepted my apologies, it does not assuage my guilt, and perhaps that is beneficial as it helps to keep my own power and control issues in check and prevents me from repeating the same types of mistakes.

So, you can readily see the difference in that example of good guilt and bad guilt. Good guilt would say to me, "Threatening your child with physical pain is wrong." Bad guilt would say, "You are a terrible mother." The former condemns my actions, while the latter condemns me as a person.

On and on it goes, in which guilt leads to more guilt and no matter what you do, you're guiltier than when you started! It doesn't seem as though there is an escape.

There are ways to confront your feelings of guilt and take control of your life.

ACTIVITY
Healing Your Guilt Feelings

As you've seen, there is good/productive and bad/ unproductive guilt. When you are in a destructive relationship, a vast majority of the guilt is unproductive. It is, in fact, one of the many ways your true self is trying to tell you that if you feel this bad, maybe you shouldn't be in this relationship. After all, it is nearly impossible to feel joyful, contented, and also have a sense of bad guilt all at the same time.

You may feel guilty because your abusers blame you for anything that goes wrong in their lives. They may make themselves appear weak and pathetic so that you will feel guilty for things you've never even done. You may feel guilty because you are subjecting your children to an abusive romantic relationship and know that they are being hurt by it. Or it could be that your guilt stems from the fact that you know you have a pattern of destructive relationships and understand that you aren't treating yourself kindly.

Here are some techniques that will help you attack the inappropriate, useless guilt that has been running your life:

- *Cost-Benefit Analysis:* In this very effective exercise you list the advantages and disadvantages of feeling guilty in a given situation. For example, if you feel guilty that you have damaged your children by exposing them to a domestic violence relationship, you might make a list as follows:
  - *Advantages:* 1) Feeling guilty keeps me from having to make a decision about leaving my abuser. In this way, I can just beat myself up without actually having to do anything about it.
  2) Feeling guilty reinforces my feelings

of being a bad mother. 3) Feeling guilty allows me to overcompensate with my children by bowing to their every want and wish.

➤ *Disadvantages:* 1) Feeling guilty keeps me stuck in my abusive situation. 2) Feeling guilty shows my children that I am not strong enough to handle them or the situation. 3) Feeling guilty makes me depressed and therefore unable to care for my children adequately. 4) Feeling guilty keeps me from making good decisions, therefore role-modeling behavior I don't want for my children. 5) Feeling guilty keeps me stuck.

If you were looking at that list, would the **advantages** or disadvantages win for you? Most probably, you looked at the second list as the better choice.

When you feel guilty, think of the ways it is benefiting your life and the ways in which it is harmful. In most instances, you may end up thinking to yourself, why did I spend so much time feeling guilty for something that doesn't have anything to do with my emotional growth?

• *Re-attribution*: When we are accustomed to feeling guilty, we automatically assume that we are "bad" and blame ourselves completely for the problem. This time, I'd like for you to think of a situation that makes you feel guilty and instead of jumping on the "Me, Me, Me Ship", think about the many factors that may have contributed to that problem.

For instance, your husband may have berated you for not taking his best white shirt to the cleaners and therefore he cannot wear it to the big presentation he has to give today. What a terrible wife! Now, he'll be a total failure at this meeting and it will be all your fault. How could you have made such an error? True, he has other white shirts, but this one is special. It is his lucky white shirt. Whenever he's worn it on important occasions, things have gone his way. You're so inconsiderate. You are just about useless!

Hold on there, horsey.

Okay, he doesn't have his special shirt. But before you go out on a limb, let's think about the factors that may have contributed to this problem:

1. He never told you he had this important presentation until this morning.

2. You didn't know his shirt needed to go to the cleaners because he didn't put it in the dry-cleaning pile.

3. You had a sick child this week or many projects of your own to take care of and couldn't get to the cleaner.

4. His shirt may be "lucky," but if he doesn't feel confident enough in his own abilities to wear another shirt, maybe he's not as prepared as he should be.

5. We're talking about a shirt here, not world peace.

6. Doesn't he have two good arms that could carry a little white shirt into the cleaners if he needed it so badly?

When you really think about it, making yourself feel guilty for every situation that comes up makes you think you are actually more powerful than you really are. That's kind of a power trip, isn't it? Why not focus on solving the problem at hand instead of using all your energy feeling guilty?

Is there another solution? When you are feeling guilty, you are not taking action. Think of your guilt-provoking situation in a new way. Let's take an example of forgetting your mother's birthday. You didn't call or send a card or gift. Now, she's giving you the guilt trip, sighing heavily over the phone, telling you, "It's all right. I can't expect to be as important to you as I used to." Before you go into a full-blown guilt attack, pretend your friend was telling you this tale over a cup of tea and a few mint Milanos. What would you tell her?

1. Why don't you just call your mom, apologize, and plan to take her somewhere special next weekend?

2. You could set a boundary with your mom and tell her that while she is important to you, you had a hectic week at work and with the kids, so like so many other things that week, it truly slipped your mind.

3. You can give your mother the responsibility for finding a solution to this egregious flaw in your character and say, "You're right, mom. I was being inconsiderate. What can we do as two adults to get us back on track?" When she sighs deeply and says, "Oh nothing. It's all right," choose to call her bluff and say, "Okay, then."

4. Hey, isn't this the mom who makes you feel guilty for breathing?

Forgive yourself. This is often easier said than done, as you saw in my personal example involving my son. But, when you are feeling unproductive guilt, it is important to ask yourself, "Is this a character flaw, or was it just a mistake?" In other words, is the reason for your guilt an enduring pattern of unrepentant errors or did you just mess up this time?

Say you don't turn in a project on time at work. Because of this, your boss berates you in front of the rest of the staff and shares his disappointment in a memo to her boss. Not only do you feel justifiably humiliated, you feel guilty because you were asked to perform a task that had a clear deadline and didn't come through. This might be good guilt since you undoubtedly had ample time to complete the project. However, if you find yourself repeating the mantra, I'm a bad and horrible person. I'm a complete failure as a human being, over and over in your head, you have a case of bad guilt that's not only false but is harming your life.

Look at this thought closely: Do you always or usually turn in work projects late? Do you have a pattern of com-promising your company's standing in its work community? If the answers are yes, then perhaps this is truly a flaw of pro-crastination and inconsideration that plays itself out harm-fully in other areas of your life as well, and one that you might want to get some help with. If the answers are that this was a one-time error that was due to circumstances beyond your control, then your guilt is overblown.

Remember, good guilt is about your action—not turn-ing in the project on time—while bad guilt attacks your character.

You might also want to take a look at the idea that you are dealing with a demeaning, abusive boss.

So, as you have seen in this chapter, guilt, shame, and keeping secrets come from many sources, have many outlets, and result in keeping you stuck and not allowing you to move forward on a path of emotional health and gratifying relationships. I hope that in the future you will be aware of people and situations that contribute to these feelings and behaviors and take them as a red flag that perhaps this is not a good place for you to spend your precious time, energy, and spirit.

CHAPTER ELEVEN

Poor Coping Mechanisms and Ways to Change Them

I closed my eyes to anything I didn't really want to think about. I just pushed it away if it got too close to me. Soon that wasn't working, so I began drinking during the day. I ate too much. I shopped too much. I slept too much. Nothing worked.

— ABBY, 34

ACTIVE INVOLVEMENT IN AN ABUSIVE RELATIONSHIP requires enormous effort. In order to stay in it—and justify the reasons for staying in it—a woman must use extraordinary methods that she wouldn't in any other circumstance. In this chapter, we will discuss the most common methods of coping with destructive relationships:

- Denial
- Minimizing
- Delusion

- Substance use

- Compulsive behaviors (commonly thought of as "addictions")

- Not accepting help

When you are able to become aware of and identify the coping mechanisms that you have used to maintain your sanity while engaged in your unhealthy relationships, then you can learn new and productive ways to live more fully.

DENIAL

Sigmund Freud called denial one of our most basic defense mechanisms. When the mind feels threatened, relevant information that would enable us to view the situation clearly, simply "disappears" so that we don't have to deal with it at the time.

When you are in an abusive relationship of any type, one of the reasons you may not leave as quickly as you should is that you are not looking clearly at the entirety of the abuse. If you were, it would be difficult to justify your reasons for staying involved. If you were engaged in a destructive relationship with a friend, for example, you'd be hard pressed to tell yourself, "My friend betrays the personal information I share with her, she undermines my confidence, she says one thing and does another, she has no respect for my time or feelings. . .and I'm choosing to keep her as my very best friend and continue to put up with her abusive behavior."

Do you see how ridiculous that would sound? That's the reason denial is so handy. Until you are prepared to make the decision to remove that friend from your life or at the very least confront her on her behavior, you continue to pretend that either it doesn't exist or it doesn't bother you.

Here is a good way to remember what denial really is:

Don't
Even
k**N**ow
It's
A
Lie

Denial also has another sneaky component, which is that you may be able to clearly define other people's relationships as abusive, but deny that yours is pretty much the same. Very often I hear patients in my office deny that their parents' abusive behaviors affected them in any way. Most likely, they will go so far as denying that their parents were abusive to begin with, even though there is overwhelming evidence to the contrary. It is almost as though by looking squarely at the reality of that behavior, they feel that they have to take responsibility for their parents' choices or that it would brand them personally as "defective."

Denial often begins as a survival tool in childhood. If a young person lives in an abusive home, there is very little opportunity for her to leave. She is dependent on her parents for everything she needs. Therefore, what good is it to look at the horrible situation in which she's stuck? What can she do about it? She begins to protect herself emotionally by pretending the abuse doesn't exist or doesn't affect her. That works so well that when she finds herself involved in an abusive relationship as an adult, she naturally tries the same coping mechanism, only to discover that she is increasingly unhappy without knowing why.

MINIMIZING

Minimization occurs when you reduce the significance of what you do, think, and feel, or when you make the seriousness of what another person has done to you seem less important than it really is. This is a very common coping mechanism in abusive relationships of all types.

When I worked as a therapist in a domestic violence shelter, I often heard a resident tell a group of other residents, "I'm not like all of you. My husband never broke my bones or anything like that. He just pushed me around and called me names or left me without a car or a phone for days at a time. But you guys were really physically battered. You guys were really abused. I feel so sorry for all of you. I probably shouldn't even be here and should give my bed to someone who really needs it." Can you see how this woman minimized the seriousness of her abuse?

This type of minimizing one's own abuse allows destructive behaviors to continue unchecked. It somehow has a deserving quality to it. Again, as with denial, if the speaker were to look at the seriousness of her abuse, she would have to make a decision about it that she might not be prepared to do at the time.

It is not possible to compare abuses against other abuses. All abusive behavior is heinous. Very often, in minimizing the effect of abuse, I hear women say that verbal and emotional abuse is not as bad as physical abuse. I hear others deciding that abuse by a boss is not as serious as abuse by a parent, or that abuse by a child to a parent is just "kid stuff" or "a teenager expressing his independence" or that "boys will be boys." I hear that having a friend betray another's trust is not as bad as a husband calling his wife names. On and on it goes, showing that these women feel a need to quantify the depravity of abuse. They use minimizing to allow themselves to feel better about the abuse they are suffering and somehow make it "okay."

Abuse is abuse. Bad is bad. It should never be allowed. It is never deserved. One is not worse than another. End of subject.

DELUSION

Delusion is more serious than denial or minimization. When a woman is deluded, she believes one thing in spite of the fact that there is clear and compelling evidence to the contrary. Again, it is a form of ego protection that has the effect of keeping her in an abusive situation.

Women who are in domestic violence situations often believe that because their children were not physically abused by their fathers, but "only" heard their heated battles or the sound of their screams as they were beaten, the children were not adversely affected and certainly not abused. This is a common delusion. Can you see how much more serious this can be than denial and minimizing? Even when presented with reams of evidence demonstrating that merely living in a violent household is highly damaging to children, a woman may delude herself into believing that the evidence is incorrect or that the evidence may be true with respect to other children but not hers. Because she doesn't want to confront the truth of the situation, this woman may displace her own anger onto the bearer of the facts.

Delusion grows out of shame and guilt. In the example above, I'm sure you can see that if a woman were to confront her delusion about abuse not damaging children, she would have to confront her own shame and guilt at subjecting her children to this type of life.

SUBSTANCE USE

When a woman is engaged in a series of destructive relationships, she quickly learns what "works" for her; that is, the way she can survive it and function in her daily life. One of those coping mechanisms is to use drugs and/or alcohol to numb her reality and her feelings.

Substance use as a form of numbing and stress relief is readily accepted in our society. Going to a bar after work to "unwind" is seen as so normal that it has become a social occasion and a way for people to connect with each other. Bars have "happy hours" to entice overstressed, emotionally beaten business people into their establishments to drink away their problems and relax. There's an implicit message: Don't think about the reasons why you feel so distraught that you need to numb yourself, just have a few drinks, and forget about it until tomorrow, when you will face the same situation again. Don't ever get to the root of your difficulties, just adjust your reality.

And so it begins. If your mate or children are mistreating you, you may have a little drink or a hit of marijuana in the afternoon to get you through the rest of the day. Nothing's wrong with that. Maybe your critical parents are coming for a visit and so you steel yourself for the onslaught of raised eyebrows and backhanded compliments by tossing back a couple of Valium. When having lunch with your competitive friend who always seems to have a way of letting you know that she's a better mother, wife, and all-around "together" gal, you can order a martini or two during the meal. Why not?

Those behaviors work so well and you feel so much better afterwards that you decide that you have the right to feel that mellow all the time. Why shouldn't you feel good? And if a drink, a pill or two, or a joint works, are you hurting anyone? Just a little bit every once in a while is okay. Then a little bit every couple of days is fine. Then, just once a day is really dandy—and it doesn't mean that you're an addict, just that you've learned how to control your stress and anxiety. Too bad everyone can't be as together as you. Worries? Problems? Stress? Bad thoughts and feelings? That's for other people. You've got your own little secret to peace.

Drug and/or alcohol use doesn't allow you to look at the reality of your life. It keeps you in a state of unreality where you can cope just fine, thank you very much. You may never have to wonder why you are living such an unhealthy life with destructive relationships that would necessitate your altering the reality of the situation and compromise your health and safety just to survive.

COMPULSIVE BEHAVIORS

There are many compulsive behaviors that numb feelings: shopping, eating (or not), gambling, and sex. All are designed to reduce anxiety and give you momentary excitement or the illusion of self-control when you actually feel that you have none.

Compulsive shopping is almost accepted as a way for a woman to relieve tension or anger. If you feel bad, go to the mall. Need a lift in your life? Buy a few pairs of shoes and maybe a purse to match. Did your boss yell at you, insult you, and make you feel small? A few hundred dollars at the Clinique counter ought to take care of that. Did your husband lie to you and cheat on you again? Charging up his credit cards is quite a nice revenge. We laugh at those types of behaviors and the comments you would typically hear might even be followed by a chant of, "You go, girl!" But when shopping repeatedly becomes a way out of dealing with your feelings, it's a problem.

Compulsive shoppers get a "high" out of scarfing up scarves. They shop aimlessly and almost unconsciously. They buy so much that they don't have a place to put it. If you look at the compulsive shoppers' purchases a year later, you will find unworn shoes, tags still on dresses, and bags and bags of unused accessories. They keep their shopping a secret from their husbands until it is too late and they have placed their families in financial peril. It is an emotional disease.

Eating disorders, of course, are out of control in North America. There are two types of compulsive eating disorders: overeating and anorexia/bulimia.

Many of us were taught in childhood that food is love. We may have fond memories of Mom's meatloaf and mashed potatoes, and turn to those foods—or any foods—when we are tense and need some self-care. We may have been told that there are "starving children in other parts of the world who would kill for that pork chop," so we joined the "clean plate club" out of guilt. As adult women, we still feel that we need to finish everything on our plates. . .and maybe on our kids plates and high chair trays as well.

Compulsive overeating is mindless and "stuffs" unpleasant feelings down. This is not to be confused with hormonal cravings for specific kinds of foods. Personally, mid-cycle, I'm quite aware that I have the capability of doing bodily damage to anyone who gets between a Reese's Peanut Butter Cup and me. When food is used as a coping mechanism, you feel soothed and anesthetized at the time that you are eating. You decide that you will deal with the guilt later.

An anorexic initially uses food as a weapon of control for various reasons: her parents' need to over control her, their desire for perfection, to show herself that she is in charge years after sexual molestation, and to quell her own self-doubts, as well as a myriad of other reasons. Even though she is desperately hungry, she feels proud that she can choose not to eat. She can prepare gourmet meals for her family without ever taking a bite. She can fool her parents by moving her food around her plate so it appears that she's eating, or eat a small amount and over-exercise off the 20 calories she took in. Tragically, her anorexia begins to control her and then takes over her life. Her health and her very life may be compromised.

A bulimic binge eats and then purges the food. Again, it begins as a tool of control. She can enjoy eating anything and everything she wants and then, clever girl that she is, she can just throw it up or use laxatives and be done with it. However, the enjoyment factor is a fallacy. Bulimics don't even taste their food, but use it as a means of coping and calming themselves and defending against unpleasant feelings. Many times those unpleasant feelings are associated with abusive relationships. While the woman is binging, she feels the illusion of calm and numbness, however immediately feels anxious, frightened, and guilty, needing to dispose of the evidence. This is a very physically dangerous practice as it severely harms the body's chemical balance.

NOT ACCEPTING HELP

Many women in abusive relationships are ashamed and secretive. They remain stuck, therefore, because they will not avail themselves of the help offered to them so that they can get out.

I will never forget a woman I was counseling in the domestic violence shelter. She was a well-known real estate agent in her community but kept up a wonderful front, all the while being humiliated and sexually demeaned by her husband. She never told a soul what was really going on in her life and maintained a magnificent illusion of control and happiness. By her description, she had a beautiful home. You can imagine that fleeing to a shelter was possibly the lowest point in her life. While she kept that fact a secret from everyone she knew, and didn't allow us to contact even her closest relatives or friends, she was also worried that when she was able to leave the shelter, she would find that her husband had closed all of their joint bank accounts, leaving her destitute after a lifetime of work.

Accompanied by shelter staff, she went to her bank and quietly asked to remove her money from a specific account. Even though the staff members kept a respectful distance, they could see that she was so quiet in her request that the account manager had to lean his head in, straining to hear her small voice. His answer was to give her a mountain of paperwork and excuses as to why her request was denied, since her husband was also on the account and was not authorizing such a large withdrawal.

In the self-esteem group I led the next day, she tearfully told the rest of the women her sad story. She said she again felt violated and victimized by the bank employee. "All men are jerks and just power hungry idiots," she declared to the confirmation of the other residents', "Mmm hmm, you said it, girl."

"I'm sorry," I said. "I must have missed part of her story. Was there a victim here? I didn't catch that." The women all looked at me as if I had a room temperature IQ and gently explained to me that the woman in question had requested her money and been denied. "That must have been a terrible experience for you, but I guess I don't understand why you just left the bank without asking anyone else to help you. It's your money, after all, not theirs."

"Oh, the bank president saw me leaving in tears and asked if he could help me, but I just wanted to get out of there," she said.

"Why didn't you take him up on his offer of help?" I asked her.

"Oh, he didn't really want to help me. He just felt like he had to ask since he saw me crying."

"Why, I had no idea you were actually Magda the Fortuneteller [remember her from a previous chapter?]. You just knew that even though he asked to help you, if you accepted his help, his answer would have been, 'Just kidding,'" I said, while the women laughed. "You're not a fortuneteller. You're embarrassed and therefore afraid to accept help."

I gave her the assignment of going back to the bank— with myself and the rest of the group as support—and demanding her money. To my amazement, a few days later, she walked into the bank, went over to the account manager who didn't help her previously, and said in a very loud, courageous voice, "I am a survivor of domestic violence. My husband tried to crush me but didn't succeed. He will come into this bank and try to close our accounts and steal my money so that I'll be flat broke and have to go back to him. I'm living in a shelter and have no intention of allowing that to happen. I am a customer here and demand that you give me all of the money that is in my accounts right now. And if you don't help me, I will ask the president of your bank to help me. Which would you prefer?"

Well, you can't imagine the stunned silence in that bank, quickly followed by cheers and applause not only by the tellers and other bank employees, but also by every customer waiting in line! Needless to say, the account manager hopped to it and the president attended to her personally, offering her a new, individual account with free checking. As she filled out the forms, customers came over to congratulate her on her strength and courage. One woman quietly told her that she was living in a domestic violence situation and hoped that one day she might be as brave.

CHANGING YOUR
POOR COPING MECHANISMS

You have now clearly seen the ways in which you may have kept yourself stuck in your destructive relationships by altering the reality of what you were living. There is no need to blame yourself. That would just be a way of re-abusing yourself like your perpetrator did. You can choose to use the philosophy offered by Dr. Maya Angelou, who said, "You did what you knew at the time. When you knew better, you did better."

Self-destructive coping mechanisms are difficult to change on your own. Because they are used as a way to prevent you from dealing with the truth, they are hidden even from you. Have you ever tried to confront an alcoholic on his drinking? Not only are denial and minimizing the hallmarks of alcoholism, there are also such deep reasons why he "needs" the substance to cope with his world that it is impossible for him to see the severity of his problem on his own. That is much the same with you.

Identifying your unhealthy coping mechanisms, the way they work, and your reasons for using them are a huge first step. When you can step back from yourself and see your situation clearly, you can help yourself.

In ridding yourself of these unhealthy traits, it will be helpful to enlist others for support. If one of your prime coping mechanisms is not to accept help, this will be especially difficult. If you are dealing with shame, guilt, and secrets, it will seem very frightening. Still, your mission is to clean your life of all toxic relationships and it is best done with assistance and support.

There are many support groups that can guide you through the steps to health and recovery. Their national phone numbers are listed in the resource section of this book. Let me give you a few ideas of places to begin:

- Codependents Anonymous (CoDA)

- Alcoholics Anonymous (AA)

- Al-Anon

- Narc-Anon

- Sex and Love Addicts Anonymous (SLAA)

- Gamblers Anonymous (GA)

- Overeaters Anonymous (OA)

- Specific support groups sponsored by your house of worship

- Pastoral counseling

- Private therapy

In any group or therapeutic setting, it will be important for you to uncover the roots of your coping mechanisms. Some questions to unravel might be:

- Where did you learn them?

- Were they helpful at one time and then ceased to be useful and ultimately destructive?

- Why did you choose to use them rather than seeing the reality of your relationship(s)?

- Do you use different coping mechanisms with different abusive people?

- Do you follow a predictable pattern of coping? For example, do you begin with denial, then proceed to alcohol use, then abuse, overeating, compulsive spending, and finally, not accepting help?

Try not to be fearful when embarking on this quest. I understand that it is a new way of living that may feel uncomfortable. Poor coping mechanisms are like shields to deflect against an attack of horrible, difficult feelings and a reality that is not what you deserve. Wouldn't it feel so much better to throw away the need for the shield instead? You can do it. I believe in you.

ACTIVITY
What You Can Do Instead …

You have seen the ways in which destructive coping mechanisms may have hurt you and allowed you to prolong your abusive relationships or keep you going from one to another. Now, I'd like you to take out your journal and begin deciphering ways to break that pattern.

Abusive person or situation	Coping mechanism used and how	What I can do instead

What are some of the more positive coping mechanisms you can choose? Sometimes, when a woman has used unhealthy coping mechanisms most of her life, it's difficult to imagine that she can choose differently. Here are some examples of healthy coping mechanisms I suggest to women:

- Call a supportive friend or family member (someone who will tell you how brilliant and magnificent you are!)

- Journal your feelings

- Hit the road . . . on a bike or with your walking or running shoes

- Take a bath

- Go to the gym

- Read a relaxing book and get totally involved in their lives

- Play with your kids

- Plan your next career or life move

- Plant flowers or a tree so you can see that growth also comes in difficult times

C H A P T E R
T W E L V E

The Rescuer/Helper Personality

*If only I loved him more. If only I listened to him better.
If only I fixed his favorite meals as well as his mother did. If
only I was a better lover.*

— CHRIS, 32

A s women, we can recognize and share Chris' anguish.
Many of the messages that we received in our girl-
hood homes—and from society at large—set us up for
future destructive relationships. As a child, you may have
been told by your mother, or seen from her example that
your success as a partner depended upon you taking the
role of the non-complaining happy helpmate who squelch-
es her own needs in order to take care of her husband or
children's wishes.

Looking at the most popular women's magazines, we
can see that each issue has at least one article discussing
how a woman can snare a man, keep a man happy, and if
he's not happy, it's your fault and you need to fix it fast

otherwise he'll leave you. Quick! Take the quiz and find out how extreme your deficits are and then read the author's tips on ways you can change. "Are You the Best Lover You Can Be?" "How to Keep Him Happy in the Bedroom," "New Ways to Understand His Moods," "Ways to Help Him Through a Difficult Time," and "Dinners He's Sure to Love."

The same type of articles are now being filtered down to teenage girl magazines so that they're sure to understand—at the time that they begin their relationships with young men—that they're totally responsible for not only the happiness of their relationships, but their boyfriends' personal happiness as well. "Ten Ways to Kiss Him so He'll Never Look at Another Girl," "How to Have the Clear Skin He'll Love to Look at," and "Prom Dresses He'll Love."

Other articles we find include the ways in which we are falling short as mothers. Studies are cited to provide evidence for our lack of adequate mothering abilities. Whether you work in or out of the home, there's a good reason why you should feel guilty. Are you really feeding your children healthy foods or are you—gasp—one of those moms who drive through fast food restaurants once a week or try to pretend a frozen pizza is a nutritious meal? Do you let your kids watch too much television or play too many video games? Uh-oh, you must be lazy and therefore are damaging the little ones for the rest of their lives. Is your child actually acting out his "terrible twos?" You poor dear; too bad you don't know the secrets of better mothers. Here, read the ways in which they handle it better than you do.

I challenge you to find a single article in any men's magazine that stresses the importance of being a good partner to a woman, a good father to your children, and taking responsibility for the happiness of the relationship.

So, you see, as women we've been sold a bill of goods. We've been taught early on that we should take the role of a rescuer and helper in all of our relationships. It doesn't matter whether you are the CEO of a Fortune 500 company; you're not doing enough for your employees. You're not doing enough to help a friend in need. And your parents; well, if you were a better daughter they wouldn't have to treat you the way they do, now would they? Boys are not raised with such emotional responsibilities. They are taught to help and rescue themselves, not others.

RELATIONSHIPS WITHOUT BOUNDARIES

When you are operating in caretaker mode, you frantically do all that you can to ensure that your loved one feels valued and supported, often to your own detriment. You violate your own boundaries in order to be seen in a more favorable light. The following is a list that more fully explains this idea. When you give up your boundaries in a relationship, you:

- Are unclear about your preferences.

- Do not notice your own unhappiness since pleasing is your main concern.

- Alter your behavior, plans, or opinions to fit the current moods or circumstances of another (i.e., you live reactively).

- Do more and more for less and less.

- Take as truth the most recent opinion you have heard.

- Are satisfied if you are coping and surviving.

- Make exceptions for a person for things you would not tolerate in others. For example, your friend is habitually 20 minutes late or is gossipy, which would really bother you in any other person.

- Are manipulated by flattery so that you lose objectivity.

- Try to create intimacy with a narcissist.

- See the other person as causing your happiness or excitement.

- Feel hurt and victimized but not angry with the other person.

- Act out of compliance and compromise.

- Do favors that you inwardly resist—you cannot say "no."

- Often feel afraid and confused.

- Frequently become involved in dramas that are beyond your control or don't involve you personally.

- Commit yourself for as long as the other person needs you to be committed.

- You don't have a bottom line.

How many of those items apply to you and your life? I recently saw a patient who was such an extreme caretaker that she'd volunteer to do all kinds of exhausting, time-consuming favors for others without complaint. Although they never repaid her kindness in any way—it was just expected of her—she continued her loyalty to them even after incidents in which some of these folks were deliberately cruel to her. I questioned her motives for her furtive desire to help and she replied, "That's just what good friends do for each other." I tried to explain that the "each other" piece was missing from her equation, to which she told me, "That doesn't mean that I shouldn't be a good friend to them." There was no limit to which this lovely woman would go to please these ungrateful, callous "friends."

ANOTHER EXPLANATION OF CARETAKING AND HELPING

There is another way to look at your rescuer/helper tendencies: You're a narcissist. Yes, you read that correctly. You're wondering how I can label you a narcissist when you are constantly doing and looking out for the good of others, right? Well, let's think about this for a bit.

In the shame and guilt chapter, you saw the ways in which a person who feels flawed and defective also feels helpless and powerless. When taking care of others, she can alter those feelings and feel helpful and powerful. Therefore, the true goal of the rescuer/helper is to care take so that she can feel better about herself, not for the good of the person she's caring for. Yes, the fact that the other person may feel better in the end is a nice side benefit, but not the true source of the desire to care take. Rescuing distracts the helper from her feelings of inadequacy and therefore is a way to alter her own mood.

Think for a moment about the feeling of power it gives you inside when you do for others. Aren't you a great person? Sometimes, the underlying feeling is that the other person is actually weak and helpless and you, mighty person that you are, are the only person who can help the situation. Without you, where would they be? It's up to you to save them either from themselves or from the outside world. Wouldn't you call that a narcissist?

Enabling and rescuing are actually very damaging; not only to you but also to those you feel you must help. When you constantly rescue your children by bringing them the homework or lunch they forgot, or standing up to the coach you think has not treated your child fairly, you are robbing him or her of learning how to fix things themselves. You are not teaching personal responsibility or consequences for actions. You are not allowing them to do things on their own which leaves them feeling inadequate, defective, and dependent. You are stealing from them; you are stealing their opportunity for a sense of achievement and personal power. You are inhibiting them from learning how to go out into the world successfully, which is your main job as a mother.

IS BEING NICE ALWAYS NICE?

Let me just tell it like it is up front: The goal of a nice person is her own self-image and not the other person. In their book, *Creative Aggression*, Dr. George R. Bach and Dr. Herb Goldberg state that being nice is actually a way of manipulating others. They feel that when a nice person is in action, it is her attempt to avoid real emotional contact. In that way, she can bank on the fact that no one will see her as she truly is, which is shamed, defective, and flawed.

John Bradshaw, author of *Healing the Shame that Binds You*, further states that the people pleaser: 1) Tends to create an atmosphere wherein no one can give any honest feedback. 2) Stifles the growth of others, since she never gives any honest feedback. This deprives others of a real person to assert against. Others feel guilt and shame for feeling angry with the nice person. Nice behavior is unreal; it puts severe limitations on any relationship.

ACTIVITY
What Will Happen If You Stop Rescuing?

Acting as a rescuer/helper/people pleaser in most of your relationships denies you your true feelings and creates an imbalance with others. That is not a healthy relationship. I'd like for you to think for a while about people or situations in your life in which you feel compelled to help, often at a detriment to your time, energy, and feelings. Take them one at a time and ask yourself the following questions (I will use an example):

- *In which instances am I most likely to overextend myself?*
  When my child asks me for something.

- *What sort of things does he ask you for?*
  For me to take him somewhere or buy him something.

- *What feelings does it bring up for me at that time?*
  That I should comply.

- *What will happen if you don't comply with his requests?*
  He'll be angry and throw a tantrum or try to wear me down.

- *How do you feel when he does that?*
  Exhausted, fed up and that it would just be easier to go along with what he wants.

- *If you were not to comply, what would he say to you?*
  He would tell me that I'm not a good mother and don't care about him.

- *Would you believe that?*
  I might, although I would also know that he's just saying it to push my buttons.

- *Why would you believe it?*
  Because sometimes I'm not a good mother. What's the big deal about taking him somewhere or buying him a little toy?

- *Is it possible to be a perfect mother all the time?*
  No.

- *Will he really love you any less if you don't do what he wants?*
  Probably not.

- *Will the world stop spinning if you don't do what he wants?*
  No.

- *Will he be damaged for life?*
  No.

- *Will you be a better mother if you teach him limits and respect for his mother?*
  Yes.

Making a practice of asking yourself logical, rather than emotional questions is a very helpful way to begin ending your need to rescue and please. Think for a moment about the type of people who might reject you if you declined to help at the church bake sale, drive their kids to and from school each day, consistently stay late at work when you have a family at home waiting for you, or do, do, do for them when they could easily do the tasks themselves but just don't feel like it.

Are those people respectful of you? Do they care that they are inconveniencing you? Do they care that you are tired and that they know they're taking advantage of your weaknesses? Why would you want to help people who think so little of you? So that they will like you? Why on earth would you care if cruel, unfeeling people liked you or not? Are you really so desperate and unworthy that it doesn't matter who people are as long as they like you?

I often think that a better way to judge myself is not by the people who like me, but by those who don't. I would feel that I had done something very wrong in my life if terrible people thought I was great!

COMMUNICATION SKILLS

The way in which you communicate your needs and wants is very important. It allows others to understand what you expect of them and of yourself. When you are a people pleasing helper, you usually neglect or deny that you have needs or wants, and gain a feeling of esteem by giving to others.

There are four types of communication. As I describe them, try and imagine which kind of communicator you are and which category the abusive relationships in your life fit into.

- *Passive:* A passive communicator doesn't ask for anything she wants. She feels that if those around her really cared about and understood her, they would just know what she wanted or how she was feeling. An example of passive communication might be a woman who has worked hard in and out of her home all week and would like to go out to dinner on Friday night. She doesn't tell her husband of her desire, but decides that since they've been married for five years, he should know how tired she is on Friday nights and offer to take her to dinner. Because he is not Marvin the Mind Reader, he comes home and asks, "What's for dinner?" as he does every night. She breaks down into racking sobs and accuses him of not loving her, doesn't speak to him for the rest of the night, does a lot of pouting, and denies him sex for two weeks. Totally confused, he repeatedly asks her what's wrong, to which her reply is, "Nothing," or "If you don't know, I'm not going to tell you."

- *Passive-aggressive:* The passive-aggressive communicator begins in much the same way as her passive counterpart: not clearly stating her needs, expecting others to know what she wants, and then silently brooding when she doesn't get it. However, this woman's motto is "Don't get mad, get even." When she doesn't get what she wants, she plots revenge. She might deliberately show up late to the birthday luncheon of a friend she perceives to have slighted her, hold up a team work project until the last moment because she doesn't feel that the others in the group have treated her fairly, or come home three hours late just to worry the husband who didn't remember to take her out to dinner last Friday night.

- *Aggressive:* The aggressive communicator makes demands rather than requests. Often they are in a loud voice accompanied by gestures or fist pounding. He expects compliance. He doesn't care about excuses and feels entitled to make the demands he does. He doesn't want to hear that you can't work late because you have a sick child at home, or that you can't travel two hours each way to visit your mother every third day, that you didn't get the laundry done because you weren't feeling well, or that you don't have the time or interest in bringing the snack for the entire Little League team again because it's not your turn and you've taken other parents' turn for the last five weeks. Too bad, too sad. His wants are more important than yours. End of subject.

Now, just because I've used the pronoun "he" in these examples, make no mistake about it: Women can be highly aggressive in their communication manner. Maybe that woman is your mother, daughter, gal pal, coworker, or boss. Take a close listen when you feel verbally attacked by a man or woman. Chances are they are extremely aggressive in their communication.

- *Assertive:* The assertive communicator is respectful and mindful of another's time, energy, and abilities. She directly asks for what she needs and wants in a clear, direct, and non-abusive manner. She doesn't begin her request with, "If you really don't mind and I'm not bothering you too much, I mean you can say 'no' if you want, but can you. . . ." She doesn't anticipate a negative response because she is asking for something completely reasonable and has treated the person fairly in the past. She is also capable and comfortable declining a request without overstating her apology.

ACTIVITY
Asking for What You Want and Saying "No"

All right, now we're down to the tough stuff. You could easily recognize what type of communication you usually engage in and how others relate to you as well. Now, you are going to practice stating your needs with the expectation that others will respect what you have to say (well, maybe they will be shocked and displeased in the beginning, but they will get over it).

State what you would like in a clear, respectful manner. For example, "I have worked hard this week and would like to go out to dinner on Friday night." That wasn't so hard was it? Now, follow it up with specifics, such as, "I think Rosie's House of Ribs would be fun. Why don't we try to get a 7:00 reservation or would 7:30 work better for your schedule?" That's very clear, and nine out of ten times you will find that you get what you want. You've directly stated what you want (dinner out), where you'd like to go (Rosie's), and asked your partner to choose among two times that you pre-selected in which he can make the final decision. It's a win-win situation!

Here's another example. You have a "pal" who betrays your confidences. This could be tricky because you want to keep her as a friend and are afraid of hurting her feelings with direct confrontation (even though she didn't mind hurting your feelings, to be sure). You could say, "Susan, do you remember when we had the conversation about my frustration with Steven?" She replies that she does. "I asked you not to let it go any further than the two of us and have found out that you told Julie and Barbara. I know that they are your friends also, and perhaps you didn't think you were doing any harm, but I need to tell you that it really hurt my feelings and made me feel humiliated. I can't understand why you went back on your word to me. Can you explain it?"

Why would it be incorrect for you to ask your friend to explain why she chose to hurt and betray you? You might have a decision to make about whether you want to keep her as a friend, a casual acquaintance, or wipe her off your list entirely. Doesn't she owe you an explanation? You are the hurt party, not her. If you are afraid that asking a friend to be accountable for her actions is going to ruin your "friendship," might I suggest that you reconsider the meaning of the word "friend?"

All right, you have a boss who wants you to work late, even though you promised your daughter you'd take her out for pizza tonight. You tell your boss and he laughs it off. "She can eat pizza tomorrow night, for crying out loud. This report has to get in tonight!" Your response might be to agree, sulk, call your daughter, and apologize while she cries and says, "You promised!" How can you be assertive in this situation?

Well, first you need to decide to whom you are going to be assertive—your boss or your daughter. Or, you can compromise by being assertive with both. You might say to your daughter, "Mr. Wheeler has asked me to stay late to finish up an important report tonight. It doesn't look like something I can back out of without hurting my job. It was unfair of him to ask me so late, but I need to help him out, so I will be one hour late and then we will go out for pizza. If you feel hungry before then, why don't you have some cheese and crackers?" Then, you can tell your boss, "Mr. Wheeler, I can stay an extra hour to help you with the report. I take my obligations both to you and my daughter very seriously and don't want to slight either one of you. I promised her I would take her for pizza tonight and I try my best not to break my promises to my children. So, I'll work as hard as I can until 6:30 and then I'll have to leave."

Now, I'd like you to practice saying "no." It's really just as easy and direct as saying "yes," and you can even be a nice girl and say "no." Here's how it's done: "Thank you for asking, but I won't be able to do that this time." How about that? Just a few, little words. No apologies, no explanations, no feeling bad. You will usually find that the asker is so dumfounded that she won't even go further. If you like, you can quickly change the subject in a charming way, or merely get off the phone or otherwise end the conversation.

Apologies are not necessary because you don't have anything to feel sorry about.

You are asked to bake three-dozen cupcakes for the class party. "Thank you for asking, but I won't be able to do that this time." Easy-peasy. You don't need to feel badly afterward. They will find someone else to make the cupcakes or they will make them themselves. Or, if all else fails, your child will not be permanently scarred if she doesn't have a cupcake. The whole world doesn't depend on whether you can do this one thing for someone else!

How about the person who calls you urgently for a favor, or not even so urgently? If your immediate knee-jerk reaction is to say "yes" and then wonder later why you did that again, here's a snappy reply, "Let me think about that and get back to you." Good, huh? Why wouldn't you be allowed the respect of thinking about it for a bit? Why does he need his answer this minute? His lack of planning does not constitute your emergency.

"I need a mom to chaperone the field trip on Thursday," the teacher tells you. "I always know I can count on you." "Well, let me think about it and get back to you." If she becomes defensive and states that she needs a reply right this instant, I guess you have to say, "Thank you for asking but I won't be able to do it this time." She'll get over it . . . and she'll find another mom to chaperone. You're little darling will still go to the Natural Science Museum, even if you don't.

How would you feel saying those lines? Frightened? Powerful? As you become accustomed to speaking assertively, you will find that everyone in your life has greater respect for you and stops treating you like a doormat. They simply find a new doormat. There are plenty to go around.

I taught these techniques to the women in the domestic violence shelter at which I counseled. Here were a group of women who had not said "no" in a long time. Many times, there would have been severe consequences if they had. One woman in particular, Jo, was being walked all over by the other women in the shelter. In our group session one day, I gave her the assignment of saying either, "Thank you for asking, but I won't be able to do that this time," or "Let me think about it and get back to you" every time one of the women or children made a request. Then, I assigned the other residents to ask her for things nonstop for a week. I told them to be very demanding.

The results were hilarious. They began by asking her to cook dinner each night or trade chores with them, then it escalated to babysitting all the kids at the shelter while the other mothers went out to lunch and finally, "Jo, I want you to paint the entire house," or, "Jo, I'd like you to build a new deck for me." By the end of the week, she was very skilled at saying "no" or that she needed a bit of time to mull over her answer!

PART
FOUR

THE FUTURE
LOOKS GREAT!

Introduction

The Future Looks Great!

LOOK AT HOW FAR YOU'VE COME! You began this book a short while ago with an inability to understand the ways in which your patterns of destructive relationships have hampered your life success. Already you have done a tremendous amount of work and earned the privilege of looking toward a bright future.

In these last few chapters, we still have many ideas to discuss so you can put yourself on a positive path toward happiness. The first is your personal power. Yes, you have power and it's time to harness it. What are your goals? What would you like to achieve? Don't know where to begin? Not anymore!

You understand how your abusive relationships have hurt you. Can your abusers ever change? Can you help them in that process? In your day-to-day life, how do you handle an abusive boss, mate, parents, kids, and friends? Yes, there are real life strategies for dealing with those people who have helped to keep you down.

Speaking of kids, what kind of adults do you hope yours will become? What do you wish for them? The same life you've experienced? Probably not. Therefore we will discuss healthy ways of raising your children and helping them to make good decisions. You can end the cycle of abuse inside your home and family.

Lastly, it's time to begin new and healthier relationships. Perhaps you are ready to date, but you don't want to make the same mistakes with partners that you have in the past. How can you be sure that you won't fall into the same traps? How can you choose new friends who will treat you with the respect you deserve? What about your parents and siblings? You've already learned new techniques for dealing with your family members, and now you are going to consider a different concept of "family."

I'm so proud of the work you've done to this point. You're in the home stretch. It's time for you to create your future!

CHAPTER
THIRTEEN

Taking Your Life Back Right Now

Personal Empowerment
and Goal Setting Strategies

YOU HAVE BEEN WILLING TO LOOK at many parts of your previous relationships, communication style, your family of origin, and you have examined your fears. You have already made the largest and most difficult change in your life: the decision to allow healthy relationships into your life. Those destructive relationships are now part of your painful past. So, are you willing to take another step toward changing the future? Because if you are, then let's start taking action now!

PERSONAL POWER . . .
WHAT'S THAT?

Personal power is not a mystery or only available to a select few. There are rules to achieving power. Anyone can learn these rules and create success by using them.

In order to gain personal power, you need to be accountable for your own life. No one but you has this responsibility. It is an awesome task, but a rewarding one as well. The good news is that every positive accomplishment you have from now on will be yours alone. You will have done it on your own and through your own efforts. Isn't that exciting? The bad news is that if you fail, you won't be able to blame it on anyone else. It is time to stop playing the blame game with your abusers. From now on, you are going to have to work hard on your own success.

> *Whenever I got a new job, my husband would do something to mess it up. If I needed a ride to work, he'd take me so that I got there late. He'd call me on company time and I'd get in trouble with my boss. He always had his reasons for doing this ridiculous stuff. But the end result was that I couldn't keep a job for more than a few weeks. Pretty soon, I just gave up and stayed home, which was part of his plan of course. Then, I was financially dependent on him and couldn't leave ... he thought.*
> — BECKY, 32

Do you remember at the beginning of this book when I discussed the idea that you have the free will to do almost whatever you'd like in your life? The only limitations you have are those you place on yourself. Free will gives you choices and these create outcomes. There are always consequences for every choice you make. You have seen those consequences in the choices you have made to remain in abusive relationships. Other choices can have better consequences, such as success and happiness. Can you see that your free will makes you responsible for the outcome of your life?

Albert Einstein said, "We are what we think about ourselves every day." In your life, you will create exactly what you feel you deserve. Therefore, if you want a different life than you have now, it is important that you give yourself positive messages of encouragement to support it.

You have free will in your thoughts as well as your behavior. You can choose to think of yourself in any number of ways. So, ask yourself the following question.

How do I choose to think about myself? Am I:

- Weak?
- Frightened?
- Frail?
- Strong?
- Confident?
- Powerful?
- A failure?
- Not good enough?
- Magnificent?
- Successful?

- Unlovable?
- Stupid?
- Angry?
- Thoughtful?
- Loving?
- Generous?
- A quitter?
- Resilient?

Do you relate more closely to the negative comments than the positive ones? Remember, negative voices are the voices of your abusers and anyone else who has ever spoken unkindly to you, including yourself. It is these voices that are helping to disable you. You have a choice about whether or not you listen to these voices and how you choose to respond. Who says that you have to agree with them? Now, you have the opportunity to discard unkind voices and listen to your own clear and powerful voice.

CHOICES

Choices are for other people. I made my choice when I married him.

— SYLVIA, 41

To make new and better choices, you first need to understand those you have made in the past. Let's take a look at whether you've been living your life actively or reactively.

By that, I mean:

- Have you pursued your own interests?

- Have you spoken up when things didn't feel right?

- Have you thought about your own goals and gone after them?

- Have you made a personal plan as to how you can succeed at your goals?

(These are active choices.)

Or did you:

- Adjust your moods and plans to your abuser's moods and plans?

- Defer what you wanted in life until "the time was right"?

- Keep quiet when you should have stood up for yourself?

(These are reactive choices.)

I have found that in most destructive relationships, the latter situation is usually true. There would have been consequences for trying to live a better life, wouldn't there? I'm going to encourage you to become more like the woman in the first list.

> *When I was a young girl, the whole house revolved around my dad. Whatever he wanted to do, we did. Whatever he wanted to eat, my mom or I fixed. If he was in a mood when he got home, we knew the distance we were supposed to keep and how much we were allowed to say to him. When he accused me of something that wasn't true, I went along with him and apologized instead of making waves. It was just easier that way. I'm 35 now and my relationship with my dad still hasn't changed and I've had other relationships that seem to follow the same path.*
>
> — FAVA, 35

ACTIVITY
Getting to Know What I Want

If you have been living a reactive life until now, it is time to ask yourself the following important questions. Write down the questions and answers in your journal, knowing that you may not have the answers right away. You have the right to change your mind about them whenever you want. No one is going to judge you.

1. What do I want from my life?

2. Who do I want to become?

3. When I have the answer to #2, how will I act? How will I feel? What will it look like?

4. What will I have to overcome in order to have what I want?

These are very deep questions. You may not have asked them before. Furthermore, you may not ever have known that you had the right to ask them of yourself. As women, we are often "trained" not to think for ourselves. We are taught that we must put others first, and to do otherwise is selfish and narcissistic. But think of it this way: Have you ever been on an airplane? Do you recall the emergency instructions you were given by the flight attendant? "If there is a loss of cabin pressure, an oxygen mask will descend." You were told to put on your mask first and then help your children. Why? Unless you think of yourself first and you are safe, you cannot be of any help to your children.

The same is true of everything you do. You will be more able to help others if you take care of your own needs first. Remember the airplane story as you read through the rest of this chapter and do this important and empowering work on yourself.

> *When I started speaking up for myself and telling the truth of my life, all hell broke loose. My friends turned on me. The women I worked with thought I was nuts. My family accused me of lying or being ungrateful because my former husband provided for my kids and me financially. Was a trip to Hawaii supposed to be a trade-off for the torture I was living in my real life? I guess they thought so. It was then that I realized he wasn't the only abuser in my life.*
>
> — ABBY, 45

ACTIVITY
What Does Personal Power Mean to You?

Let's begin examining what personal power is to you. This will help you define your goals more clearly. Make a check mark next to each description that fits for you. Feel free to think about these words and mark more than one response.

Is personal power about:

- Money?
- A nice house?
- Spirituality?
- Contentment?
- Freedom from fear?
- Education?
- Knowing that your kids are okay?
- A good job?
- Self-confidence?
- Self-knowledge?
- Self-reliance/not having to depend on others?

Which responses did you select? If you chose items such as job, house, money, or education, that's completely fine. Remember, no one is judging your responses. Now you know that what you value in the most immediate future is a plan that includes steps to accumulate the basic necessities in life and reach a concrete, visible goal. If you checked more items involving internal needs, those are also a good place to start taking charge of your life.

You may not be your only critic on the road to personal expression and evolvement. Others in your life may not enjoy the "new you." They are used to the passive woman they have come to know and use for their own benefit. At this point, you have another decision to make: Is your success more valuable than the opinions of those who would keep you down? If you are passionate about your success, then your family and friends will eventually come to accept and appreciate it as well. If not, it will be time for you to have a talk with them and ask them to examine their own motives for keeping you "stuck."

Only you can decide what you need in order to feel more powerful and successful in your life. Others may have ideas for you and will try to tell you what you need, but yours is the only voice that matters. You are the only person in the world who is going to be living your life. Those people can decide what they need to make their own lives a success. So far, how has listening to others tell you what you need worked out for you?

> My mother used to tell me that I didn't need to go to college like my brothers. I would be a good wife to an important man some day, and what good was art history and geometry going to do to help me with that? While I was waiting for Prince Charming to show up, however, I had to work and make some money. Because I didn't have any real education, I had to take minimum wage jobs in which my bosses were real jerks to me. They knew the power they had over me. What was I going to do? Quit? Without any education, I'd just be going to another job like this with other jerky bosses.
>
> So finally the "Prince" shows up and I get married. My husband told me all I needed was an allowance, a roof over my head, food to eat, and sex from him once a week-the way he liked it, of course. I can't believe I fell for this garbage for so long. Now, at 39, I'm divorced from the guy, back in college and almost ready to graduate. I have worked at some great places in the meantime and have so much more confidence in myself. It was very hard and I had a lot of obstacles to overcome, both within myself and financially. I really feel proud of myself for doing all this. For the first time in my life, I feel like I have a future.
>
> — MAGGIE, 39

I invite you to remember an important concept as you waltz through your life: *If something is working, do more of it. If it's not working, do something else.*

Think about the number of times a plan, behavior, or thought has not worked out well, however you kept repeating it expecting a different result. That, my girlfriend, is the definition of insanity. Therefore, if your friends, coworkers, or family insist that you would be a fool to try a different and perhaps riskier plan, or that you stick with what you know, remember the ideas above. If it hasn't worked to your satisfaction before, why continue to do it and expect something different to come of it?

ACTIVITY
What Would I Do If . . .

Let me ask you two more questions in an effort to crystallize what you would like to accomplish:

- If you knew that you had three months of health left, how would you want to spend those three months?

- On your deathbed, what would you be sad that you had never accomplished? What passion had you denied yourself?

Get as clear as you possibly can with these questions. They will help you on your path of success and—more immediately—as you go along in the rest of this chapter and book. You may want to do this in your journal.

Now that you have gotten this far, and have a clearer vision of what you need to make your life more fulfilling and more complete, it is time to start taking action. If you have been living a passive existence, this will be difficult for you to comprehend. Be patient with yourself. You are learning new skills, establishing new brain pathways, and thinking about yourself and your abilities differently.

TAKING ACTION

You gain strength, courage and confidence by every experience in which you really stop to look fear in the face. ... You must do the thing you think you cannot do.

— ELEANOR ROOSEVELT

Benjamin Franklin said, "Well done is better than well said." What did he mean by that? Well, you can go around talking about all you are going to do with your life, but how far does that really get you? About as far as your mouth.

I am guilty of doing this on a regular basis in one strange area. I dream of winning my state's lottery and about what I would do with the money. But do I ever purchase a ticket? No, because I feel it's a foolish dream, a waste of money, etc. However, I do not count on that money and understand that the only money I will have is the money I earn, so I develop strategies to make my life more successful in the category of money whenever that is a concern to me.

You see, in the real world—as opposed to the world of dreams and fantasies—people don't care about how you "feel." They care about the way you behave. Imagine that your child is at soccer practice. It is time to pick him up, but you are tired and depressed and you are in bed. You look at your clock and see that you should be at the soccer field but make no effort to move. Does your child really care about how you "feel" at this time? Does he care that you feel tired and blue? Does he care that you feel like you should be picking him up, but are not? No, he's alone at the field after all the other kids go home and that's the only thing that matters to him—and rightfully so. Try telling your boss that you "feel" badly that you didn't finish that important report. Try telling a judge that you "feel" that you have a good case, but have no hard evidence to support it.

Life does not reward your feelings. It rewards your actions. So, don't "feel" like you should be successful. Do something about it!

I remember very clearly that when my book, *But I Love Him,* was published, many people would say to me, "You're so lucky!" In the beginning when I heard that comment, I was resentful. Did those people think that a book just fell out of the sky and a publisher picked it up and decided to put it into print? In truth, I actually found the publication of my book quite unremarkable and easy, but not at all a matter of luck. Does that sound contrary to you?

Let me explain. When I thought of writing my first book, I had a very clear idea of what I wanted to say in it. No, it didn't come to me in a dream. It came through thinking about it very carefully, writing it out, and then writing it out some more. I had a very clear strategy. To ensure my success, each night before I went to sleep I wrote out a list of what needed to be accomplished on the project the next day. It wasn't a long list, so it didn't overwhelm me. I knew what I was realistically capable of getting done every day given that I also had a job, two teenagers, a husband, a house to care for, and a social life I needed to keep up for balance in my life. I didn't give myself more than I was capable of accomplishing, only enough to challenge myself.

I also looked at my patience and concentration levels. I assigned myself a set number of hours every day—at the same time each day—to work on the items on my list and stuck to them no matter what else tempted me, including Reese's Peanut Butter Cups. I also gave myself a deadline to finish each chapter, then the book itself. It felt great to cross off the items on my list every day.

In retrospect, I didn't give myself a chance to fail. Because of my strategy—and also because I was smart enough to align myself with good people who could help me achieve my dreams, such as an agent and editors—I was never shocked at what I had accomplished. It was actually the result of a carefully designed plan. The "luck" my friends often spoke of was really the end product of an often monotonous and lonely strategy that I worked on daily with a great deal of commitment and passion. We all make our own "luck."

PLANNING FOR SUCCESS

At this point, I'll bet I wouldn't know any kind of success if it walked up to me, shook my hand, and introduced itself.

— BERNICE, 68

So, what does that long and ego-gratifying story about me have to do with you? Lots. Because unknowingly I was following a direct and time-honored plan used by life strategist Dr. Phil McGraw, to get what you want from your life: Be, Do, and Have.

- *Be* committed to a goal.
- *Do* whatever it takes to achieve that goal, and then you will:
- *Have* what you want.

Most often, when our lives or our plans fail, we conveniently skip the middle step, as that is the hardest one. So, what will you have to do to achieve your goal?

- Will you have to go back to school?

- Get more training?

- Request information brochures?

- Work late?

- Make childcare arrangements?

- Deal with your own fears or guilt?

- Make a lengthy apprenticeship with a mentor who does the job you would like?

- Examine the difficulties in your life?

Get honest with yourself about why you haven't been important enough until this moment. In his book, *Life Strategies*, Dr. Phil McGraw discusses a seven-step process for achieving goals. I think this is incredibly wise advice (the steps are his, the parentheses are mine):

1. Describe your goal in terms of an event or behavior (not a feeling you'd like to have).

2. It must be measurable (losing ten pounds, for example).

3. Your goal must have a timeline (not just "someday").

4. It has to be controllable (unlike my lottery idea).

5. You must be able to plan and program a strategy that will get you to your goal.

6. Create steps to your goal (such as making a daily list).

7. Create accountability toward your goal (tell someone about it).

Get clear about it, and then do whatever research it takes to achieve what you want.

Are you actually willing to do whatever it takes to achieve your goal? If you can honestly say that you are not, that's fine. Perhaps this is not the perfect time in your life to make such an enormous effort. Maybe a year from now would be better. Maybe when your kids are out of diapers. When they leave home to be on their own might be the perfect moment to begin your life with passion.

Just remember that life will continue to roll by day after day whether or not you decide to do something different with it. The rest of us will not wait for you, or your perfect moment, to take action. Unless you do something differently, all of your tomorrows will be exactly the same as they are today. If that's good enough for you, then that's more than good enough for me.

I believe, however, that you've already experienced that sameness in your life when you spent time with your abusers. You just kept waiting for the perfect time for them to change, come to their senses, see you differently, and understand what you were saying. It wasn't actually until you took action and disassociated yourself with them that your situation changed.

What is it that you risk by not doing anything? By not making change? By not being committed to your success?

ACTIVITY
What's the Worst That Can Happen?

I know that you are afraid and I truly appreciate that fear. To achieve success, you must confront your fears and disable them. Here is an exercise to help you with your fear of risk and change.

Ask yourself, "What is the worst thing that can happen to me and my family if I take a risk?" In other words, what is your worst-case scenario? Is it your death or the death of your children? If so, when you are approaching a new way of life, a risk, or a decision and you feel paralyzed by fear, ask yourself, "If this doesn't work out, will one of us die?"

I am asking you to play your fears out to the nth degree. Fear can only live in the dark. Once it's exposed, it dies. Sometimes, we just feel frightened but don't really know why. So, I am asking you to see the worst thing that can happen in Technicolor vision and then work out a way of handling it.

For example, if you start a business that you've always dreamed of and by some quirk of the universe it fails, will you be homeless? Is that your biggest fear? Then think about what you would do if you were suddenly homeless. Who could you ask for temporary housing? Perhaps a non-abusive family member or friend? Are there low-cost housing grants you could apply for? Are there homeless shelters in your area? I know the latter sounds dramatic, but if your fear is that you and your children will be living out of a cardboard freezer box under a bridge in the winter, a shelter is a better alternative, wouldn't you say?

To get what you want, you will need to examine the veracity of your abusers' messages to you. Will you really never amount to anything? Are you actually too stupid or lazy to do anything right? No, I don't think so. You are the only one who controls what you do from now on, not them. When their words come into your head to distract you or dissuade you from taking steps toward your success, say "Stop it," right out loud. I don't care where you are. If you are concerned that you will be taken away to a locked ward at a hospital, you could instead put your hand up in a stop position.

I am asking you to confront your fear of success and prepare for it. I would like you to say the following out loud right now:

"I know that taking risks in my life may be terrifying for a while. I know that it will be uncomfortable because it is a new skill. But I am worth it. I will not allow _____ (abuser's name) to control me anymore by disallowing myself a chance for success and a happy life!"

ACTIVITY
What Will My New Life Look Like?

Now, before you complete this chapter of your life, I want to make sure you have a very clear picture of your goal. I'd like you to determine the answers to these questions and write them in your journal.

If you woke up tomorrow and your life was exactly the way you wanted it to be, how would you explain it to me?

- Where would you be living?

- What kind of job would you have?

- What would you look like (no exaggerations here, please!)?

- What would your atmosphere smell like?

- What would you be wearing?

- What would you eat for dinner that night?

Imagine your goal at the end of a long, straight road in the countryside. Do you see it clearly? Good. Now visualize little country lanes intersecting your road. They are small streets that feed into your long road. If you want to get to your goal, you will need to be disciplined enough not to take all those lovely little detours on the side roads. There may be antique shops, fresh produce stands, or a charming little cafe on those roads. If you do take them then you'll probably still get to your goal eventually, but it will take longer than taking the direct route. You may give up due to exhaustion. So, whenever you are tempted not to "stay the course" and use distraction, fears, etc., you can ask yourself, "How will taking this route get me closer to my goal at the end of the road? Is it actually taking me further away? Will I have to backtrack in order to move forward?"

You've visualized your goals and taken action steps in preparation for personal success. Now is the time to get in gear and get moving!

Dealing with Your Abusers in the Real World

The fact is: I still have to deal with my parents who treat me so badly. Since I left my husband, the kids and I are living with them. I thought I could go home to them and they even said they would welcome us, but now they criticize my whole life, analyze the mistakes they think I made with him, and tell me how to parent my kids. I don't have anywhere else to go and even if I did, I don't have the money to do it. I wake up with a headache and go to sleep with a stomachache just worrying about how they're going to slam me. I don't know what to do.

— JANA, 29

MANY WOMEN ARE IN THE POSITION of having to deal with their abusers day in and day out. Perhaps your abusive situation is at work and until you can find another place of employment, you have to manage your anger and anxiety each day. If you live with your abusers—your spouse and/or children—you are intimately involved on a daily basis since you share your life with them. Abusive friends pose another problem. If one friend is destructive, you could drop her, but you fear what she's said about you to others in your friend network. If all of your friends are destructive, you face the possibility of being totally without friends and feeling alone should you sever these relationships. Abusive parents, of course, have contributed to a whole variety of feelings that you may still confront regularly. These probably developed over many years of unkind treatment. If you are in contact with your parents, that emotional sabotage may be ongoing.

In this chapter, I will speak to you about ways to manage these types of abusive relationships and some alternatives you have to cope with them. Each situation is unique and they often require different approaches.

WHAT DO THEY WANT FROM YOU?

As we've discussed, all abuse is about power and control. Your abusers, regardless of the relationships they have with you, want power over you, stemming from their own feelings of shame and powerlessness. All abuse is intentional and planned. They know what they are doing to you and the way they are making you feel. They don't want to have a mutual and equal relationship. They want to make you feel small, afraid, and insecure. They like it.

What women in abusive relationships don't seem to understand is that given the knowledge stated above, they actually have a tremendous amount of power. Really, the ball is in their court. Does that sound ridiculous? Let me explain.

Let's say you have a young child who is throwing a temper tantrum. You didn't let her have the ice cream bar she asked for ten minutes before dinner so now she's flailing on the floor, telling you what a mean mom you are and how much she hates you. "Suzie's mommy lets her eat ice cream whenever she wants. She gets to go to bed at ten o'clock and color on the walls. You're just bad and I wish I had another mommy!"

While your first instinct may be to say, "Then put a want ad in the paper and get one," or, "For this I had to go through 26 hours of labor and live with stretch marks for the rest of my life?" you know you can't do that. Why? Because you understand that what you are dealing with is a frustrated child who wants what she wants and her tirade isn't about you. It's about a little girl who can't control a situation.

Now, let's put this into the context of adult abusers. It's the same dynamic. The ball is in your court because you are actually dealing with children who want what they want and need to control a situation. It's never about you. If you can understand this, you can keep a certain amount of emotional distance. When you stop believing what your abusers say about you and stop reacting (because you have 100 percent control of your own behavior), you begin making better decisions about your relationships with them.

ACTIVITY
How You Can Choose to React Differently

Despite the relationship between you and your abuser, there are certain rules for everyone who comes into contact with you. Consider these questions:

- What do you deserve? Only you can decide the answer to this question. Do you deserve to be treated with respect? It's a trick question because the only correct answer is "yes." Do you deserve to feel peaceful and happy?

Another trick question because there is only one answer. Do you deserve to associate yourself with people who honor you or malign you? I won't repeat myself here. Now, think about your destructive relationships. Are you getting what you deserve? Unless you demand it, no one can know that you want it because that is passive communication.

- Can you express the way that you feel? Many women tell me, "If I tell him how I feel, he'll get mad at me." So? You can't control his reactions, only yours. If you disagree with your abuser or tell him how you feel, perhaps he will be mad at you. If you are fearful of expressing yourself, try to think of what the actual reaction will be. Not what you imagine it will be. Will he yell? Okay, no one ever withered away from yelling. Will he walk out, slam the door, and come back when he's cooled off? That's actually a good response to anger (minus the slamming door). That fear addresses your fear of abandonment. Will he call you names? You can silently repeat the phrase from your childhood that says, "Bounces off me and sticks to you," since you know that his rude comments are probably projections of the way he feels about himself.

  Do you remember the worst-case scenario exercise we did in the last chapter? Use it again here. If the worst that can happen is that your abuser won't think you're a "good girl" because you actually express yourself, maybe you need to reassess why an abusive person's opinion of you is more important than expressing your authentic self while showing your children a good role model.

- Are you allowed to have boundaries? Is it necessary for you to fuse with your abusers in order to gain their acceptance? Are you able to protect your time, feelings, space, and health? Do you need to spin around an abuser's maypole? Do you know where your thoughts and feelings end and your abusers' begin?

  You can practice setting boundaries today by assertively telling others what you want and need. You can tell them when they are invading your personal space both physically and emotionally. For example, earlier in the book, I talked about parents who demand to know every thought their child is having. If that is your case, you can practice setting boundaries with your parents by saying, "I appreciate your interest. I really do, but right now I'm just having private thoughts that I don't want to share with anyone." There is no need to feel like a terrible daughter for asking your parents to respect what is yours. Would it be all right with you if they came into your home and took all your dishes, clothing, and books out with them? Wouldn't that feel unfair and invasive? Are your thoughts any less precious?

DEALING WITH AN ABUSIVE EX

When your abuser is your children's father, the day-to-day maneuvering of a relationship you'd rather have out of your life can be very difficult. When you have an abusive boss or coworker, you can choose to leave the company. When you have an abusive friend, you can end the relationship. But when your abuser is the father of your children, you are joined at the parenthood hip for many years.

Do you revert back to the woman you were in the relationship when you have to interact with him? Let me give you a common example that I often see. Dad has visitation on Wednesdays and every other weekend, so Mom makes plans for herself on those days and also arranges play dates for the children, sports teams, etc. for the days when he isn't visiting. However, next week Dad has been invited to go on a weekend trip during his visitation time, so he won't be able to see the kids. A couple of weeks later, it's not convenient for him to pick them up on Wednesday for dinner because he's very tired. Then, he shows up unexpectedly on Monday morning as you're trying to get the kids ready for school and decides that is the perfect time to see them for a bit.

- Are you constantly whirling around in your partner's tornado?

- Do you have to adjust your—and your children's—schedules to meet his last minute wants and plans?

- Are you afraid not to do so because otherwise he might think you're not nice or cooperative?

- He might throw a fit and call you names just like he did when you were with him?

- It is just easier?

- Do you have a meek, little voice when he is around?

- Do these types of situations cause you
  extreme stress?

If so, you are reverting back to the woman you were and accepting the behaviors that caused you to break up with him.

You left this man for many good reasons. Remember what they were. Did he bully you? Did he try to make you feel crazy? Did he call you names? Did he dishonor your feelings or opinions? Did he cheat and lie?

Understand that when a man—or woman—is abusive to you, he doesn't become an angel when you leave. In other words, expect the same behaviors when you are apart that you experienced when you were together. Most women are completely shocked that their ex is behaving in a reprehensible way after they are separated. "I can't believe he's doing this to me," they cry. Why not? Aren't those all the reasons you parted? Did you think he'd "learned his lesson" when you separated and now he was going to be a great dad and wonderful co-parent?

It is very important for you to stay true to your own course when dealing with an abusive ex. If you feel like changing the visitation schedule on an occasional basis in a way that fits your needs as well, then feel free to do so. But most women don't do that. They forget all the empowerment skills they've learned, and all the ideals they know they deserve fly out the window when he begins making demands. The dynamic of the old relationship is back in full swing. That is often the reason why women who have left domestic violence situations feel that they aren't moving forward in their lives. They feel like they take one step forward and two steps back. Strangely, the backward steps seem to be just after they've had contact with their ex.

If your ex rattles your chain as well as your nerves, limit contact with him to brief discussions about necessary items pertaining to the kids. Johnny needs to get a tooth filled. Janey stayed home from school because she had the flu. I'm paying the childcare provider on Tuesday and you haven't mailed me your half of the payment yet. I'd appreciate your getting it to me by tomorrow at the latest (and then don't accept his whining about having so much to do that he can't get there and why do you have to be such a "hard bitch." He has a commitment to pay half of the bill, he knows that, he knows when it's due, and since he's chosen not to comply with the rules, it is his obligation to get the check to you). Robyn has a choir recital next Thursday at six o'clock at the school gym. Don't give him the opportunity to break your spirit.

One of my patients has an ex-husband who can't seem to resist throwing jabs at her after his pretense of wanting to discuss a situation pertaining to the children. "I can't believe how great sex is with other women. How did I put up with you for so long?" "I'm so much happier without you. All my friends say that I should have dumped you a long time ago. I only stayed because I felt sorry for you since you're so pathetic," or, "The last time I dropped the kids off, it looked like you had gained ten pounds since the week before." Just the sound of his voice sends shivers up her spine. It makes her feel terrible afterwards, and of course, that was his plan.

I advised her to communicate with him only via fax and let him know that she's keeping copies of all of his faxes. That way, he won't write anything inappropriate— not knowing who will read them—and she doesn't have to listen to his voice. The plan is working very well and she is able to move toward healing much more quickly.

DEALING WITH ABUSIVE PARENTS AND SIBLINGS

Destructive parents and siblings pose special problems. We grow up with the idea that we ought to love our parents and respect everything they say. We are told that we need to have good relationships with our brothers and sisters because they will be the only family we have after our parents are gone. This is all true when you have parents and siblings who treat you with kindness. But, what if you don't? You can't just fire them, as you would an employee, or leave the company as you would in an abusive work situation. Or can you?

Notice that the Fifth Commandment states that you must honor your mother and father. It doesn't say anything about love. To my mind, that means that you can honor the fact that they are your parents and that they gave you life. It doesn't mean that you are obligated to be their scapegoat for whatever is missing in their lives. It doesn't mean that you have to sit by and let your siblings disrespect you with cruelty.

You are allowed to limit your interactions with your family if you feel abused by them. You are also allowed to speak up in an assertive manner and tell them to stop treating you in a disrespectful way.

I have found a very effective way of doing this with my family of origin as well as anyone else who I feel is treating me unkindly: I call their attention to it and ask them to explain it. On one occasion, my older brother looked through my refrigerator and said, "Oh my God, don't you ever go to the market? There's nothing in here to eat," to which I replied, "That was a cruel comment. Why did you feel like you had to say that to me?" He was a little shocked and then said, "Because it's true." Not backing down, I tossed back, "Just because something is true doesn't mean you have to hurt someone with it or even mention it. You're a higher life form than a caterpillar. You can think things without expressing them. Did you think that by saying that, it was going to make the food you like appear in my fridge? What was your real intent when you said that? It seems like it was purely to hurt and embarrass me, right?"

The other family members in the room started fading away left and right. My brother had to stop his verbally abusive behavior. Even though there was no guarantee that he would begin contemplating his actions, I was pretty certain he wasn't going to do that to me again once he had been called on the carpet and found out that I wasn't just going to lie down for his cruelty any longer.

Another time, my mother kept pushing my daughter's bangs off her face and finally said, "Jennifer, you look terrible with your hair in your face." My daughter was very hurt, although she felt it would be disrespectful to tell her grandma to buzz off. So, I asked my mom, "What did you get out of saying that?" My mother was stunned and didn't say anything. So, I pushed the point and said, "You just hurt my daughter's feelings. You had to have known that would happen, so I'm asking you to tell me what you got out of hurting my daughter." She was backed into a corner and changed the subject, so I told her, "You can change the subject because you feel uncomfortable, but I want you to know that you can't speak to my daughter like that and if you love her, you'll consider the power your words have before you say something like that."

Now, I understand that you may feel that that exchange was disrespectful, however I would ask you, "Disrespectful to whom?" My main obligation is to protect my children from harm and also to provide good role models for them, beginning with me. I could have told my daughter, "Oh, you know how Grandma is. She just says things. I'm sure she didn't mean it." But that would have been wrong for several reasons:

1. I wouldn't be validating her hurt feelings.

2. I would be telling her that she's wrong to feel hurt by unkind comments.

3. I would be choosing my mother's decision to say cruel things over my daughter's right not to have them said to her.

4. I would be showing her by my actions that it's all right for people to treat you unkindly just because "that's the way they are."

5. I would be perpetuating a generational cycle of emotional and verbal cruelty in my family with the full knowledge that she would probably pass it on to her children.

6. I would be showing her a poor role model in how you relate to others.

7. I wouldn't be showing her that love is a behavior.

It is all right to say, "Stop it," to anyone who is treating you or your loved ones unkindly. They don't have more rights than you do. Their right to be abusive doesn't override your right to kindness and respect. Think about it.

DEALING WITH ABUSIVE FRIENDS

To me, this territory is a no-brainer. You dump 'em. The very definition of "friend" is erased when a person treats you abusively. But, here's the conundrum many women face: "If I get rid of all my abusive friends, I won't have any friends left." So, what you're saying is that you'd rather be treated like slime and have the pretense of having friendships than to go out and find new, respectful people to hang out with. Are you really so desperate for any kind of contact—even make-believe friends—that you are willing to suffer any kind of indignity to avoid not having a gal pal to shop with?

Remember, you attract others who are pretty much like you. When you have many abusive people in your life, it usually means that you don't think much of yourself and are willing to settle for anything. When you begin feeling better about yourself and asking for what you deserve, you attract others around you who think a lot of you as well. Funny how that works.

DEALING WITH AN ABUSIVE WORK ENVIRONMENT

This is a touchy relationship area. If you need to have a job and/or this is a job that provides great financial benefits, or it is a stepping-stone to bigger and better jobs, it may be difficult to jump up and quit. It may not even be advisable for your long-term career growth or security.

"But, Dr. Jill," I hear you saying, "you've been telling me to stand up for myself and rid my life of all abusers."

That is absolutely true in the grand scheme of things. However, let's not be shortsighted and act impulsively when there may be options. Yes, certainly, if you are in a low wage job in which you know you could be earning more elsewhere and you have the opportunity to find other good employment, by all means get away from your abusive boss or coworkers. You deserve better. That's a whole different kettle of fish. And, yes, I did tell you earlier that if worst came to worse, you could possibly make other arrangements if your finances were completely depleted.

But let's talk about the first situation. Your boss is demanding and treats you like dirt. Or, you have a coworker who spreads gossip about you around the office or steals your ideas and passes them off as her own. You don't have to take that kind of treatment, and, as I previously mentioned, you have the right—and the obligation—to make a report to your company's Human Resources Manager.

Aside from that, I recommend that if your job is important to you and you are not prepared to leave it at this time, you adjust your reactions to your abusers. Remember, you have 100 percent control over your reactions. I am not suggesting that you acquiesce and knuckle under their pressure. What I am saying is that you give yourself a little self-talk such as, "I am not going to take any of this to heart because I know it's not really about me. It is about their insecurities and fears in their own lives. I can choose not to believe what others say about me because I feel secure about who I am. All I have to do is be who I am and rise above this and others will either see the truth or not. I don't have any control over what they think, or how they react or behave. I am staying in this job for now because it is to my benefit. I will do what I need to do for myself, but will refuse to be vulnerable to others at my job. I will not socialize with them or allow them into my thoughts. When the time is right in my life, I will leave here with my head held high and move onto better things."

That is taking care of your own life and future success without allowing abusers to bring you down with them.

DEALING WITH ABUSIVE CHILDREN

It is not my job to tell you how to parent your children. I can't tell you what to say to them when they are unkind to you. You are their mom and know better than I. You can make the decision about the way they treat you and what your expectations for their behavior are. Just be aware that you are the most important female role model your kids have for a long time. They learn from you.

So, if you are willing to be disrespected, that goes quite a way in letting them know how they can treat other women. It also lets them know that they don't need to respect authority, and that later translates to teachers, police officers, bosses, etc.

I have a patient whose kids treat her obnoxiously. I was conducting a telephone therapy session with her one day because she couldn't make it to my office. Her four-year-old daughter decided that she wanted to call her daddy at work, so she picked up a phone in another room and began pushing the buttons. No problem with that. But, when Mommy told her to hang up, the girl began throwing a fit. She came to her mother with the cordless phone and began hitting her with it.

Mom's reaction was to say, "Sweetie pie, Mommy is on the phone right now and when I'm done with this little conversation, you can call Daddy." The girl continued terrorizing her mother by screaming and hitting her with the phone. "No, you can just hang up right now because I'm calling Daddy," the little one yelled. Mommy then said, "Now, pussycat, I can understand that you are frustrated and missing Daddy right now. It must be very hard for you. But I need to talk for just a couple more minutes. Can you let me do that?"

It was all I could do not to jump through the phone and grab her. (By "her," I'm not sure if I'm referring to the mother or daughter. Either one would do.) How do I begin listing the atrocities of this short situation, which, by the way, ended after that because the mother gave in to allowing her daughter to call her dad?

1. She allowed the daughter to hit her and did nothing about it.

2. She talked too much, rather than taking action.

3. She spoke in a soothing namby-pamby voice instead of a no-nonsense voice that told the little girl she meant business.

4. She asked a four-year-old's permission to talk on the phone.

5. She ultimately gave in to the atrocious tantrum, thereby telling her that the child rules the roost.

6. She let the little one know that her sense of entitlement is more important than any business the mother needs to conduct.

7. She also showed her—by her behavior—that bullying someone is the way to get what you want and you also don't need to take other people's words or feelings into consideration.

As I said, I'm not Dr. Spock or T. Berry Brazelton, but I do advise reading their books, as well as other childcare books, if you want some input on ways to deal with difficult situations with your children. You might also want to join a Mommy-and-Me group in order to investigate the ways that other moms handle their kids in similar situations.

Your children are not allowed to use and abuse you. Make that clear and give them a good example. As I said earlier in this book, your job is to be their parent, not their pal. It is really all right if they hate you for ten minutes. They'll pout and stamp their feet, and then they'll get over it. Eventually, they will have to learn a new way of interacting with you because they get too much grief over the old, familiar way. And you will be doing them an incredible favor.

So, I will restate my opening opinion: The ball is in your court. You have the power to decide what you deserve, how much you'll take, and what you want to do about it. I suggest you take that ball and run with it.

CHAPTER
FIFTEEN

Can Abusers Ever Change?

I told him over and over that he was hurting my feelings. I'd talk until I was blue in the face. Each time, he told me that he was sorry and that it would never happen again. I believed that he would change until I just couldn't believe it anymore.

— CASSANDRA, 40

I T IS THE CRY OF EVERY WOMAN in an abusive relationship: "He promised he'd change and now things will be different," or, "If I just understand him better, I know I can help change him," or, "He said he'd go to counseling for me, so don't you think that means he wants to change?" or, "My love can change him," or, "I've talked to him so many times. I know that this time he really heard me." I could go on and on, but I won't.

If you have a history of abusive relationships, you've heard the stories more often than I have and you could write this chapter. It doesn't matter who your abusers are and what relationships you have with them, the hope and desire for change is what keeps you going and stuck. If you have a stake in the relationship, you also have an optimistic outlook and want it to turn out well. You have a vested interest in the power of change.

If I didn't believe in the power of change in every individual, I couldn't be a therapist. My work is based on every person's ability to look at the difficulties in their lives, assess what behaviors they are exhibiting that are detrimental, pointing out new options and ways of dealing with those difficulties, and helping to put the idea of change into action. Everyone who seeks therapy comes in with the desire to change personally, change her partner, or change her situation—which requires personal change. As a matter of fact, on the intake paperwork each new patient in my office receives, I ask, "On a scale of one to ten, how motivated are you to make the changes that you feel are necessary?" Each patient has always marked "ten."

Yes, I believe abusers can change. I have led groups of court-mandated batterers and seen at least superficial change. I haven't followed their progress after the one year of classes required by the court, so I cannot tell you if those changes were permanent, only that they lasted for the time that they remained in class. It is also possible that they were such good actors that they convinced me that they had at least made some change intermittently. Nonetheless, I believe change is possible under certain conditions.

Remember that none of us does anything without getting a payoff. We have already discussed the idea that abusers get lots of payoffs for their behavior. Would you change your behavior if everything were going your way? Neither would I. I'd think: What I am doing gets me all the goodies I want. I feel like a complete success in my life. Why would I want to change even one thing that I'm doing? Just because "she" tells me I should? Who is she to tell me what to do? She feels miserable most of the time.

An abuser can change his behavior if the following six steps are taken:

1. He understands that his behavior is inappropriate and abusive.

2. He doesn't cast blame for his behavior onto his girlfriend, parents, boss, etc.

3. He takes full responsibility for his abusive behavior.

4. He has a desire to change. He's not just doing it to stay out of trouble with the law, at work, or because his mate nagged him to do so.

5. He follows up his stated desire to change with concrete actions. Love is a behavior!

6. His new actions are continuous, not just for the moment. Most abusers apologize for their bad behavior, and tell their partners it will never happen again. But often, they are contrite for only a few days.

That's a long list, but it can be done if the abuser is self-motivated. It takes tremendous effort because it is not just a matter of changing a bad habit. If you wanted to stop biting your nails, you could tell yourself not to bite them each time you had the urge. You could put that horrible tasting polish on your nails that is designed for this purpose. If you wanted to, you could also insure that you wouldn't revert to biting your nails later by understanding that it is a response to anxiety and figure out what you are anxious about. Then, you would have changed your bad habit of biting your nails. Not very difficult.

However, if you are an abuser, there is a great deal of work to be done in order to provide lasting change. Abusing another person isn't just a bad habit. It is intentional cruelty designed to achieve power and control over another person. As you can imagine, abusers must uncover what their need for power and control is about, where it started, why it began, process family of origin dynamics, what they get out of it, and then learn an entirely new way of relating to others. Changing abusive behavior is a long effort, with emphasis on the word effort.

"BUT I'VE TOLD HIM OVER AND OVER THE WAY HIS ABUSIVE BEHAVIOR FEELS TO ME"

Most women in abusive situations sing that same refrain. This is most often true in close family relationships with a spouse or boyfriend, parent, sibling, or child. They have a fundamental misunderstanding about what motivates change and are unwilling to face the reality of what they must do if their abusers are resistant to change.

> I used to tell him, "You are destroying our family. You can't talk to me that way. How do you think the kids feel when they hear you do that? It hurts my feelings and makes me feel like nothing." Depending on his mood, he'd either shrug and mumble, "Sorry," or he'd say something like, "Oh, stop being such a drama queen. I didn't do anything wrong. Everything hurts your feelings." Sometimes, he'd change his ways for a couple of days and the kids and I would be so happy. The house was so calm. Just when I'd let my guard down, he'd go back to his old behavior.
>
> — LINDA, 38

Linda made the mistake most women do: They tell their abusers time and time again the way they feel, expecting them to feel sorry and then change. Do you remember the philosophy I stated earlier in this book? If something's working, do more of it and if it's not working, do something else. Obviously, Linda's something wasn't working.

As women, we communicate through words. We are verbal and feeling oriented. We are usually in touch with the way we feel and can express it. We are heavily invested in our relationships and will do most anything to make them work. And we expect that everyone with whom we come in contact feel as we do, but that's often not true. Even if they are women as well.

When women tell me, "I've told my mother (husband, son, girlfriend, etc.) over and over that what she is doing is hurting my feelings," I often reply, "Does your mother speak fluent Japanese (or Malaysian, Greek, and so on)?" My patient is usually confused by my question and replies, "No," to which I ask her, "Then why do you keep speaking Japanese to her? You are speaking in a language she doesn't understand."

When women look at the way they speak to their abusers with this idea in mind, it changes their view of the way in which they've been reacting. Usually, when abusers are unkind, the abusee's reaction is to talk with them from a feeling base and beg for change. Some therapists believe that this is the correct way to address the situation, as abusers don't understand the effect their behavior is having on their partners. But I disagree. I have found that abuse is intentional and the desired effect is to have power and control, I am fairly certain that abusers fully comprehend—and enjoy—how abuse makes their partners feel. When women explain it again and again, it just reinforces the joy in their abusers' hearts!

Since you now recognize that the only person you can change is yourself that is the angle from which you need to work on the problem. All of the activities in this book up to this point have led you to be aware of the changes you must make in yourself:

- Understanding what abuse is.

- Knowing the place your family had in the process.

- Getting a clear picture of who your abusers are.

- Raising your level of self-esteem.

- Getting a grip on your fears.

- Dealing with your feelings of shame and guilt.

- Learning new ways of expressing yourself in an assertive manner.

- Understanding the power you have over your own life.

Know that before you approach your abuser as the new, changed you, you will have to make one crucial decision: Are you prepared for this person to exit your life? It is very important for you to make this decision, because inherent in every abusive situation that involves one person who has self-respect (you) is the possibility that the abuser won't want to change. There are very few choices, then, for the woman with high self-esteem.

The first option: I won't allow myself to be treated that way, and therefore if he doesn't change his behaviors, I cannot live with him, work with him, be friends with him, or interact with him.

The other choice is: I know who I am and won't allow what she does or says to have any effect on me.

The second choice is not the better alternative. When you have become a person with a positive self-concept, you understand both what you do and do not deserve and you won't choose to have anyone in your life that doesn't respect those desires.

Of course, I am mindful that you can't tell your young children, "I won't allow you to treat me that way, and so if you can't behave respectfully, I'll have to ask you to leave." A six-year-old doesn't take well to that and neither does the social services system. The alternative in such a case is to impose consequences for behavior or whatever new parenting decisions you choose.

ACTIVITY
What You Can Say to Your Abuser

How many times have you been in a difficult situation in which you felt tongue-tied? After you think about it for a while, you then come up with five snappy replies. Or you tell a friend about the situation and she says, "Why didn't you say . . .," to which you think: Why didn't I think of that? She always has such good comebacks.

When you are in an emotionally volatile situation and your feelings are taking over your logical brain, it's difficult to think. Adrenaline is racing, and you are feeling angry and threatened. So, why don't you take a few minutes now—while you're calm—to imagine yourself with your abuser, what he might say or how he might behave, and how you would respond. (You may want to write the answer in your journal for privacy.)

When _____ (name of abuser) says/does _____ (words or actions), I will _____ (your words or actions).

Let's look at some ways of answering this exercise:

- When my husband shuts me out and ignores me, I will not talk with him at that point, and will either go for a walk, read a book, or call a friend. When we are both calm, I will explain what the consequences of his continued behavior will mean to our marriage and I am prepared to follow through on whatever I state.

- When my boss humiliates me in front of the staff, I will quietly talk with her later when I am calm and ask her why she did that. I will ask her to talk to me privately if she has an issue with me. I understand that I may need to file a complaint with my company's Human Resource's Manager if the behavior continues.

- When my mother criticizes the way I parent, I will tell her that she had her turn when I was small, but now it's my turn and I'm doing the best I can.

- When my friend gossips about me, I will tell her that she has hurt my feelings and I now understand that I cannot trust her, which severely damages our relationship.

- When my sister accuses me once again of being Dad's favorite child and blames me for everything that has gone wrong in her life, I will tell her that I didn't have any control over how our father treated her when we were kids, but she has control over her choices as an adult and those are not my fault.

- When my son tells me that he won't clean up his room as I've requested, I'll tell him that if I have to clean up his room, it won't give us any time to go to the ice cream store as I'd planned. If he still chooses not to clean his room, I will explain what the consequences are and follow through on them.

- When my coworker steals my ideas, I will tell her that since we both know that they are my ideas, she can either go into the boss' office with me now and fess up or I will go in there alone with the evidence.

- When my boyfriend begins to say unkind words to me, I will say, "Stop it right now. I will not tolerate being spoken to that way anymore. Either you change the way you act or you will have to leave."

I could give you more examples, but I know you understand the idea. The basis for all of your statements comes from a place of self-respect and stating assertively what you—or they can—expect. Try practicing your statements out loud. Your new voice may sound unfamiliar to you and the words may sound strange, but if you continue to practice this exercise, you will become more comfortable with speaking like this. Don't expect your abusers to appreciate being spoken to in this way. You will be showing them by your behavior that they do not have power and control over you any longer.

Understanding that you cannot change your abusers' behavior, you can only change your reaction to it, gives you a great feeling of calm and composure. If you have spent many years frantically doing whatever you think is necessary either to change their way of treating you, or adjusting your true self to fit into the mold of what they want, your life has just gotten 100 percent easier.

A very nice side benefit of living your life in this way is that you begin attracting healthy people into your circle. These folks also have high self-esteem and because of that can truly understand the Golden Rule: Do unto others, as you would have them do unto you. Because they would not want to be treated unfairly, it is not within them to treat you unfairly. You will find that they have a real appreciation for your gifts and are secure enough to compliment you on them. They consider your feelings and value your opinions. Health attracts health. When you are comfortable with your new non-abusive life, you will wonder how you could have allowed all your abusers to stick around as long as they did and treat you so unkindly.

CHAPTER
SIXTEEN

Who Do You Want
Your Children to Become?

My son and daughter have seen me in two abusive marriages. They have also seen the way my parents and brother treat me. They heard me cry when I got home from work with a boss who was so verbally abusive I didn't know how I would get through each day. They are now six and nine. What are they thinking? What kind of terrible role model have I been for them? Is abuse just normal behavior to them? Are they going to grow up to be abusers or be abused themselves? I have so much guilt about all of that and what I've put them through and so much worry about their futures, that I can't sleep and just find myself apologizing to them all the time.

— KARI, 31

KARI'S FEARS AND WORRIES are very common among women who have experienced abuse at any level. Her concerns are also very legitimate. There is no doubt whatsoever that a mother's abusive relationships have detrimental psychological effects on her children. The kids do not have to be the direct recipient of the abuse themselves. It is true that in more than 50 percent of domestic violence cases in which the father physically batters the mother, he also abuses his kids as well. Additionally, most studies do not take into account the impact of being a child witness to emotional or verbal abuse.

It is also true that Kari's fear that her children would grow up to be abusers or be abused is founded in evidence. 91 percent of men in prison came from domestic violence households and girls who have experienced abuse in their childhood homes—either directly or indirectly—are four times more likely to experience abusive relationships as women.

HOW DOES WITNESSING DOMESTIC VIOLENCE AFFECT CHILDREN?

While all children are affected by abuse, signs of stress may be varied in different kids because of how they: a) decode and interpret the experience; b) have learned to survive in stressful situations; and c) use support systems or coping mechanisms.

Emotional Effects

- *Guilt*—feels responsible for violence

- *Shame*—believes it doesn't happen anywhere but his home

- *Fear*—of expressing feelings (for instance, anger), of divorce or separation, of the unknown, of injury, of a hostile world

- *Confusion*—conflicted loyalties (love/hate relationship with Mom or Dad)

- *Anger*—about violence, abuse, chaos, not having a "normal life"

- *Depression/Helplessness/Powerlessness*—to change things (this is especially true in children who have appointed themselves the caretakers of Mom and the other children in the household)

- *Grief*—of the losses he's experienced

- *Burdened*—by inappropriate roles as caretaker or parent

Behavioral Effects

- Acting out vs. withdrawal

- Overachiever vs. underachiever

- Refusing to go to school

- Care taking—filling/assuming adult roles

- Aggressive bullying or passive doormats

- Rigid defenses—aloof, sarcastic, rigid, blaming, defensive

- Attention-seeking behaviors

- Bed-wetting, nightmares

Physical Effects

- Somatic complaints (headaches, stomach aches, asthma, etc.)

- Nervous attention—short attention span, sudden diagnosis as Attention Deficit Hyperactivity Disorder (ADHD or ADD)

- Tired, sick, lethargic
- Often sick with colds or flu
- Neglecting personal hygiene
- Regressive behaviors
- No reaction, at times, to physical pain

Social Effects

- Isolated—no friends or distant in relationships
- Relationships with friends may start intensely or end abruptly
- Difficulty trusting others
- Poor conflict resolution skills
- May be excessively socially involved (wants to stay away from home)

Cognitive Effects

- Feels responsible for violence or abuse
- Blames others for his behavior (to not act responsibly)
- Feels that it is alright to hit or verbally abuse others you care about to: a) get what you want; b) express anger; c) feel powerful
- Low self-concept (cannot succeed in changing violence/abuse)
- Doesn't ask for what he needs
- Doesn't trust (promises for change, etc.)

- Being a boy means . . . Being a girl means . . . Being a man/woman means . . . (often uses abuser or abusee as examples)

(Adapted from the Domestic Violence site on America Online)

It is important for you to understand that feelings that flow through you also flow through your children. You are the most consistent and important person in their lives, so when you experience stress, anger, fear, depression, or uncertainty, you will see signs of stress, anger, fear, depression, and uncertainty in your children. Children often do not exhibit these signs in the same way that adults do. They are too emotionally and verbally immature and may not understand what they are feeling, just that they are feeling "bad."

Below is another list for you to consider. These are warning signs that your child may be experiencing distress as a result of direct or indirect exposure to an abusive relationship:

Ages 0-2

- Demands a lot of attention

- Easily startled

- Cries or screams excessively

- Sleep disturbances, nightmares, hard to get to sleep

- Frequent health problems

- Feeding/eating problems

- Excessive separation anxiety

Preschool

- Has many temper tantrums in a single day or several lasting more than 15 minutes, and often cannot be calmed by parents, family members, or other caregivers

- Has many aggressive outbursts, often for no reason

- Is extremely active, impulsive, and fearless

- Consistently refuses to follow directions and listen to adults

- Does not seem attached to parents; for example, does not touch, look for, or return to parents in strange places

- Frequently watches violence on television, engages in play that has violent themes, or is cruel toward other children

School-aged

- Has trouble paying attention and concentrating

- Often disrupts classroom activities

- Does poorly in school

- Frequently gets into fights with other children in school

- Reacts to disappointments, criticism, or teasing with extreme and intense anger, blame, or revenge

- Watches many violent television shows and movies or plays a lot of violent video games

- Has few friends and is often rejected by other children because of his or her behavior

- Makes friends with other children known to be unruly or aggressive

- Consistently does not listen to adults

- Is not sensitive to the feelings of others

- Is cruel or violent toward pets or other animals

- Is easily frustrated

Preteen or Teenaged

- Consistently does not listen to authority figures

- Pays no attention to the feelings or rights of others

- Mistreats people and seems to rely on physical violence or threats of violence to solve problems

- Often expresses the feeling that life has treated him or her unfairly

- Does poorly in school and often skips class

- Misses school frequently for no identifiable reason

- Gets suspended from or drops out of school

- Joins a gang and/or gets involved in fighting, stealing, or destroying property

- Drinks alcohol and/or uses inhalants or drugs

(Adapted from the pamphlet "Raising Children to Resist Violence" by the American Psychological Association and the American Academy of Pediatrics)

As you can see, children often exhibit signs of stress and depression in very different ways than adults. When I see children in my office who have been labeled "hyperactive," I begin my assessment by getting as much information about their levels of difficulty in other areas and their feelings about it. Does the child feel frightened? Overwhelmed? Sad? Angry? Not important? Is something going on at home or school?

While ADHD is a true diagnosis, I feel that the label is attached far too often without consideration of the child's outside stresses and the activity as a symptom of those stresses. Giving a child Ritalin or Aderall is an easy out, but may not be the solution to the problem.

WHAT DOES YOUR CHILD DESERVE?

We all want the very best for our children. This is especially true if you were raised in a home in which you didn't feel important or cherished. How many times did you think to yourself, when I have kids, I'll never treat them like that. So, perhaps you have not been abusive to your children but may have unwittingly exposed them to abusive people. If so, you may now feel guilty and ashamed. That can be fixed, both for yourself and your children.

You may have constructed a whole list of "shoulds" for yourself that has not only held you back, but your kids as well. For example:

1. The children should have a father in the home.

2. I should be able to provide financially for my children . . . at all costs.

3. I should stay home with my kids, so I
   need a man to support us.

4. I should always be strong and never let my
   children see me upset.

5. I should always be emotionally available
   to my kids.

6. I should provide them with the perfect life
   I never had as a child.

7. I should give my children loving grandparents,
   aunts, uncles, and cousins.

When you put that much pressure on yourself to be
the perfect mother, you are only doomed to failure. Can
anyone really attain perfection all the time?

Let's look at a few of the "shoulds" on the list above:

- *The children should have a father in the house:*
  While it is true that a two parent, happy,
  respectful and loving household is optimal for
  a child, it is highly destructive for a child to be
  exposed to abuse, either directly or indirectly.
  Many women feel most guilty when trying to
  make a decision about leaving their abusers if
  they have children. A woman may feel they
  are entitled to a father in the home and she is
  being selfish to deny them of his presence. If
  they are being emotionally or physically
  injured, she may also feel that if she remains
  with him, at least she can protect them from
  his wrath, thinking that if they are divorced
  he will have partial custody or visitation without
  her present to supervise.

This is well intentioned but faulty thinking. Consider the model they are seeing at home, the model in which the man has power over the woman and children and is free to do whatever he likes. The woman and children just have to take it. It is also untrue that she can protect her children if he remains in the home. How has that logic worked so far? Are the children continuing to witness abuse or be abused themselves? No one can protect children 24 hours a day when there is an abuser in the home. That's because the abuse isn't about the children or woman, it's about the abuser and so he will always find reasons and opportunities to do so. If he is in the home, it will just be that much easier for him.

Your children are entitled to a safe home in which they are not fearful. They are entitled to a home in which they are made to feel important by the parent's behaviors as well as by receiving affection and security. You can provide that for them by yourself. Then, hire yourself the best lawyer you can afford to make sure your children's rights and well-being are protected if and when they are with their father.

• *I should be able to provide for my children . . . at all costs:* Not if the cost is your emotional and physical health. If you work for an abusive boss or with abusive coworkers, you are undoubtedly upset and exhausted when you arrive home. You are not able to be emotionally available to them, which is "should" number five. While it is not possible to offer your children full time availability—and they don't need it—you do

284

owe it to them to show them a mom who can go out in the world without fear and also knows that when you've given your all to make a bad situation work, you have enough self-respect to walk away and find something better.

Being strong in the face of destructive behaviors ("should" number four) actually means being a good role model for your kids and showing them that strength isn't always the person with the loudest voice or biggest fist. Strength is often the person who looks at the whole picture and understands that she has options. You don't want your children to feel helpless and powerless as adults. You want them to use their critical thinking skills to logic out alternatives when times are rough. That's strength.

- *I should stay home with my kids, so I need a man to support us:* When you hold to that philosophy, you put yourself in a helpless position. You are giving the man the upper hand and power over you. If you are in a relationship with a partner who feels likewise about your being a stay at home mom and sees that as a valuable job, then your unspoken arrangement is: We are equals in this partnership; we just have different jobs. The man's job is to work outside the home and earn the income that the family lives on, while the woman's job is to work inside the home and care for the children, house, and so on. One of us does not perform more important work than the other. We both realize the equal importance of our jobs.

If you don't have a partner like that, or one who thinks that you aren't working when you care for children, or that you sit around and eat Bon-Bons all day, he will have a sense of entitlement in the relationship. It may mean that he feels entitled to have the power and control in the family, rather than sharing it equally. You may feel that you are providing your kids with "should" number six, but in fact you may not.

- I *should give my children loving grandparents, aunts, uncles, and cousins:* This is not for you to provide because you haven't any control over the way they act towards you and your children. Yes, it would be wonderful if all of you could be a terrific extended family. It's great for kids to have that kind of love and support. However, if you have an abusive family of origin, you cannot count on that. While it is true that oftentimes a woman's abusive parents give her children the love and affection she never had, it is also equally important that they treat you in the same manner in front of your children, and that they don't disparage you to the children.

Remember that the word "family" means whatever you choose it to mean. Grandparents, aunts, uncles, and cousins can be family, of course, but so can loving friends and associates. When you are a child, you have no choice about who your family is. When you are an adult, you have the opportunity to create whatever "family" you choose. Don't make the mistake of keeping the narrow focus of "blood" as family only.

In the end, what your children truly deserve is the very best you can do for them and yourself. Take a critical look at your life and the model you are showing your children. It is far too easy to spit out the words, "I'm doing the best I can." I'm confident that you are doing the best you can in any situation over which you have control.

Remember that you don't have control over the way an abuser treats you, but you do have control over the ways in which you react to the abuse. Do you stay and take it out of some type of fear? Do you speak up and demand that the abuse stop? Do you take active measures to rectify the situation if the abuse continues?

As I said previously, your children deserve to feel safe, loved, secure, and have their emotional and physical needs met. They deserve to know that their feelings and concerns are important to you. They deserve to be heard and for you to validate their reality. That cannot happen when you are involved in abusive relationships.

ACTIVITY
What I Want for My Children

Knowing that you are the most important role model your children have, it is time to ask yourself a few questions about the future you are asking them to expect for themselves. Answer these questions as honestly as you can.

1. If my children grow up to make the same choices I have made, would I generally feel proud or guilty?

2. If my children told me that they were working in the same type of environment I am, what advice would I give them?

3. If my daughter brought home a boyfriend who had the same personality and behaviors as my husband or partner, would I feel like it was the best she could do?

4. If my son grew up to have the same personality and behaviors as my husband or partner, would I feel that I had done the very best job as a mom that I could have? Would I have preferred to make different choices in my son's exposure to him?

5. If my children tell me, "You're just like Grandma or Grandpa," will that make me happy?

6. If my children have friends who treat them the same way my friends treat me, what advice should I give them? Should they keep those friends? Would I tell them, "They couldn't really be your friends if they act that way"?

7. If I could turn back the clock and make a new decision about getting involved with their father (taking into account that you would still have them as your children), would I make the same choice?

8. If they raise their children in the same way I raised them, will I be a proud grandma?

I think that this exercise is self-evident in what it is attempting to convey. It is never too late to make different choices in your life. You cannot erase what has already happened, but you can begin today to create a more positive future for you and your children.

CHAPTER SEVENTEEN

Building New and Healthy Relationships

You want me to start dating again? What, are you kidding? I'd rather spend the rest of my life in a convent!

— ASTRID, 36

ARE YOU READY to make clear and conscious choices in your relationships? Are you ready to be in control of all of your relationships instead of just letting them happen? Are you ready to get what you truly deserve from your parents, siblings, mate, children, friends, boss, and coworkers? Of course you are, otherwise you wouldn't have done all the gut wrenching work in this book up to this point. So, how do you begin?

SETTING GOOD BOUNDARIES

Do you recall that earlier in this book, we discussed what your life looks like when you give up your boundaries in a relationship? Well, I think a good place to start, then, is to focus on establishing good boundaries with every-one who comes into contact with you. It's true that first impressions are lasting, so make the first impression another person has of you one of self-respect, intelligence, success, and purpose!

When you have good boundaries in a relationship, you:

1. Have clear preferences and act upon them.

2. Know when you are happy or unhappy.

3. Live actively rather than reactively.

4. Create your own reality rather than letting another person tell you what reality is.

5. Extend yourself to others only when they are appreciative.

6. Trust your own intuition.

7. Are encouraged by sincere, ongoing change in others (not promises of change).

8. Have your own interests and hobbies that excite you.

9. Have a personal standard of conduct that applies to everyone and demands accountability.

10. Know the difference between well-intentioned feedback and manipulation or control.

11. Relate to others only when they show respect for your feelings and opinions.

12. Look at another person's behavior, rather than your feelings.

13. Don't need another person to make you feel "complete."

14. Insist that others' boundaries are as safe as yours . . . and respect them.

15. Feel secure, focused, and clear-headed most of the time.

16. Are always aware of your choices.

17. Understand that you create your own future and don't depend on others to do so for you.

18. Decide how, to what extent, and for what length of time you will be committed in a romantic relationship.

19. Know that you have a right to privacy and protect it.

20. Don't use denial as a coping mechanism, but see things as they are even if they are painful.

That's a long list, isn't it? Hopefully, at this point in your journey it doesn't appear overwhelming or impossible to achieve. Rather, it seems like a common sense way to live and one that can be easily followed.

HOW CAN YOU BUILD HEALTHY RELATIONSHIPS WHEN ALL YOU HAVE ARE TOXIC RELATIONSHIPS?

I can't think of one person in my life that doesn't treat me badly on some level. Am I supposed to get rid of everyone in my life all at once?

— SAMMY, 27

Okay, that's a legitimate question. When you have had a longstanding pattern of destructive relationships what you may find is that all of them are unhealthy. Yikes! What do you do now, other than to join Astrid in the convent? The answer to that is similar to the advice given to substance abusers leaving rehab: Don't hang out in the same places or with the same friends. Otherwise relapse is almost a certainty.

So, think about this idea for a moment. Knowing what you now understand about your pattern of abusive relationships, and your phenomenal effort at change, why would any of those creeps look good to you now? You know how they treat you and why. You know you aren't going to change them. So, why would you want them as your pals, mates, work buddies, or confidantes? No, you can't choose your parents or your kids, but by now you understand how to deal with them.

Do you remember the quote I referred to earlier from psychotherapist Virginia Satir? "Most people prefer the certainty of misery to the misery of uncertainty." Sit with that thought for a moment. Getting out of your destructive relationship rut requires risk and perhaps a bit of time on your own. You won't die from it! You will quickly see that health attracts health and new, exciting, healthy people will soon fill your life.

Let's go over the warning signs of a toxic person so that you can be absolutely certain when beginning new relationships that you don't latch onto one of these losers. An important concept to keep in mind: These warning signs are true of any type of toxic relationship, not just those that are romantic. If you have toxic friends or family members, relate them to this list as well:

- *No boundaries:* Take a look at the list of
  healthy boundaries in a relationship and
  turn it on its head. When you are involved
  with a person who doesn't understand the

concept of boundaries—and ignores yours—
what he is really trying to do is blur the lines
between you and he so that you no longer exist
separately. He doesn't know where he ends and
you begin.

- *It's all your fault:* You are the problem, the
beginning and end of all the difficulties in his
life. He doesn't take responsibility for any
problems he's created and doesn't accept the
consequences. It's all about you, you, you!

- *He's a control freak:* He wants to tell you how
you should wear your hair, what kind of
clothes look good on you, how much makeup
to use, who your friends should be, what time
you need to eat, etc. Be very aware that female
"pals" do this constantly to each other. Unless
you really understand that your friend has
only the most benevolent of feelings for you,
don't take another person shopping with you.
If she is a control or jealousy freak, you will
walk out of the store thinking that you are the
most repulsive person ever put on the earth.

- *Criminal behavior:* This may seem obvious to
you, but I can't tell you how many women
I've counseled that hook up with a partner,
friend, or boss who has had previous "experience" with the law. They've had charges of
theft, drug possession or dealing, violence,
weapons, etc. in the past. You may now say,
"That happened when she was young and
stupid. She learned her lesson and would never
do that again." Okay, maybe not, but is she
really the only person on Earth you can find
to establish a friendship, business, or romantic

relationship with? The best predictor of future behavior is past behavior. Move on to someone with an established history of honesty.

- *Addictions:* When you are involved with a person who has an addiction, that person's relationship is with the addiction, not you. They will always choose their addiction over you. You don't even come close. If he is addicted, he has many problems that he doesn't want to address. Get out now, while you can.

- *Sexually cheating:* You don't have to be in a romantic relationship with someone in order for this to matter. Cheaters are cheaters. If they feel they can get away with cheating on their mates, why would you expect them to be honest in any way with you? I know women who are actually accomplices to their friend's sexual cheating. They offer their home or are the alibi for their female pal when she has her liaison. "Her husband is such a jerk. She deserves to have a good time and a loving relationship," they will defend. Sure, right, so then she should do the honest thing and dump the clown she's married to and have a legitimate relationship with her paramour. If she doesn't leave him because he provides her a good income (with which she can then buy lingerie for her lover and rent a motel room), then understand that she's a user and a liar. Is this really the best you can do?

- *Black and white thinking:* Do you remember when we discussed your all or nothing thinking? It was harmful to you, wasn't it? Being in a relationship of any sort with a person who can't think in shades of gray means you don't have room to make mistakes or have a differing opinion. You are just wrong!

- *When we put each other down, we're just kidding:* Don't bet on it. If you are in a relationship with someone who just loves to call you little insulting names or make fun of you and then says, "You know I was only kidding," ask yourself why he can't kid around in another way, like telling knock-knock jokes.

- *Double binds:* This is a situation in which, no matter what you do, you're wrong. Sometimes we do this to our friend or partner when we ask the question, "Do I look fat in this dress?" If she says yes, she's hurt your feelings and if she says no, you call her a liar. She can't win! If you're in a relationship in which double binds are the name of the game a good bit of the time, understand that it is that person's way of keeping you off balance and insecure.

- *Yeah, but:* But is an eraser word. It erases everything the person said before it. So, he sounds like he's agreeing with you, although actually he's not. So, if you accuse him of hurting your feelings and his answer is, "Yeah, but . . .," be assured that what he's saying is that he had a darned good reason for making you feel badly and it was your fault anyway.

- *Liar, liar, pants on fire:* If you are in a relationship with someone who lies habitually, how can you trust her? How do you know when she's telling you the truth? Even if she lies a little more than occasionally, she's a person who has a difficult time confronting difficulties and taking responsibility for her actions. You don't need her on your team.

(The list above was adapted from the book *How to Recognize Emotional Unavailability and Make Healthier Relationship Choices* by Dr. Bryn Collins)

When I see women in my practice who desire new friendships or romantic relationships, I ask them what qualities they would expect in that person. Surprisingly, most are unable to tell me. "I'll know it when I see it," they say. Actually, that idea couldn't be further from the truth. Dr. Phil McGraw says, "You have to name it before you claim it," and that's absolutely correct thinking. Unless you know what you're looking for, how would you know if you found it? If you were driving to a new, unfamiliar place in an out of state city, would you just think to yourself, I don't need a map or any kind of directions whatsoever. I'll just know how to get there instinctively. I don't really know what signs I'm looking for, but I'll know them when I see 'em? Of course not. So, why wouldn't you want a complete roadmap when making some of the most important decisions in your life?

ACTIVITY
What Characteristics Are You Seeking in a Friend/Mate, etc?

Get out your journal again and make a list of every possible quality you can think of that you would find desirable in a person you'd spend time with. You may want to make separate lists for friend, mate, coworkers, children, parents, boss. Don't hold back; make it a big ol' list. The lists belong only to you so you can be as frivolous as you like.

Once you are finished with that list, pare it down to ten non-negotiables. These are ten qualities on which you absolutely will not compromise. If you meet someone who seems interesting and they possess eight of the ten qualities, they simply aren't good enough for you.

When you finish your second list, take a long, hard look at the items you have on it. Now, take a long, hard look at yourself in relation to the list. Are there qualities on that list that you don't possess? Ah ha! Now, you see what work you need to do on yourself. Here's why: As women we often look to others to fill in the spaces in our lives. We don't feel confident, but want the people in our lives to have oodles of confidence. We are fairly needy, but want those with whom we spend the most time to be outgoing, and independent. We don't make much money, yet are looking for a man who makes a six-figure income so that he can take care of us. Many women not only look for their partner to complete them, but their friends as well. They look to their girlfriends to understand them totally, while not understanding themselves. They expect these friends to have all the answers as to how they should live their lives or to take away loneliness or pain. That's your job, my friend, not theirs.

The problem with those ideas is that it immediately puts you in an inferior position in the relationship. You feel "less than" and so the other person has more power by default. You look to that person for answers you think you don't have. They seem smarter, funnier, and more confident than you are. They "complete" you.

Did you see the movie, *Jerry Maguire*? The worst line in cinematic history was in that movie. Tom Cruise gets Renee Zellwegger back by telling her, "You complete me." All the women in the theater swooned while I nearly choked on my popcorn. I found it offensive that women would think it was great to be incomplete before they got into a serious relationship and that only he had the power to make her feel whole. Yuck!

The idea with this list, ladies, is to be your own perfect friend or partner first. You need to possess all the qualities you are looking for. If you want your parents to treat you in a certain way, ask yourself whether you treat your own kids like that or others around you. If you want your children to treat you with respect, for instance, ask yourself whether you are respectful of them and yourself.

If you aren't the complete package on the list of qualities you are looking for in others, here is your opportunity to create that within yourself. You will be amazed at the results.

HOW DO I STOP BEING THE OLD ME IN A NEW RELATIONSHIP?

I got out of a bad marriage and brushed off a couple of friends who were flakes. I was so proud of myself. Then a year later, I found that I was in a similar relationship with a man and had new disgusting friends. Am I just hopeless?

— GINGER, 38

Ginger's fear may be one of yours as well, but I can assure you that it won't happen. You have done too much work on your self-esteem and feelings of guilt and shame. You have uncovered the secrets you were keeping and understand what a bad relationship looks like, as well as identified what you deserve in all of your relationships. Can you imagine going back to that old life again? The one in which you were used and abused, and thought of as a doormat and dumping ground? Where your feelings and opinions didn't matter? The one where you just lived reactively and in a state of constant fear, anxiety, and depression?

Below is a simple wheel to quickly and easily show you what a good relationship really looks like. You need to give and receive every item in every piece of pie on this wheel in order to identify it as a healthy relationship, whether it be a romantic relationship, family, or friends. While some may only apply to a romantic partner, use your imagination and configure it so that it fits your other relationships as well.

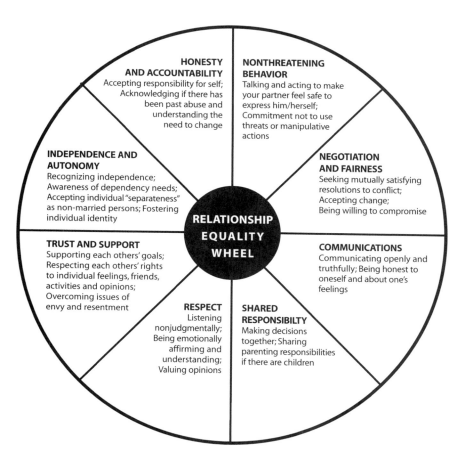

When you become involved in new relationships, proceed slowly and with caution. Remember, you are trying out a new experience. Every step of the way, you can ask yourself, "Would I consider this loving behavior?" By loving, I don't necessarily mean romantic love, but also the type of love parents, children, and siblings have for each other, the type of love friends share with each other, and the type of respectful relationship those in your work environment should share with you.

Look at your actions as well and ask yourself, "Would I consider this loving behavior toward myself?" If you have regressed back to old, self-destructive behaviors or are allowing others to disrespect you, that isn't loving behavior toward yourself.

THE STAGES OF ROMANTIC LOVE

If you have been in one or several destructive romantic relationships you may feel as ill informed as a young teenager when making decisions of the heart. And therein lies one of the big problems: When you are making romantic choices, don't use your heart as a compass. Do you remember hearing the phrase, "Listen to your heart? Your heart will never lead you astray"? Well, that's just nonsense! Your heart will always lead you astray because your heart's job is to pump blood throughout your body, not make decisions for you. It's your brain's job to make decisions. Listen to your brain. Your brain will never lead you astray.

While we're debunking myths here, let me tell you about the old "love at first sight" fairy tale. Love is not an out of control feeling that makes no sense. Love is a choice. The reason there can't be love at first sight is that love takes time to create. You need to see your partner in all sorts of situations, especially crises and disappointments. How does he cope? Does he rage and blame others? Does he use substances, gamble, or have sex to get rid of the bad feelings. Does he intellectualize and not really feel his feelings? How does he treat his mother and sisters and his other female friends? These are all crucial things to understand about your partner before you become involved and allow yourself to become vulnerable to another person.

So, there is no love at first sight, but there is lust at first sight. And lust is great, too, if the recipient deserves it. Don't mistake sexual desire for love or caring. They can intermingle in a committed relationship, but sex is not a replacement nor does it create love and caring in a man.

There are three stages of love. We all go through the first one—infatuation—to some degree no matter how old we are. Then, if you've chosen wisely and both you and your partner are complete and separate people, you move into the mature love stage. However, if you are incomplete, it is very easy to cycle into an addictive love pattern—after the infatuation stage—which you may have already experienced. Let me outline them for you.

Signs of Infatuation

- Usually occurs at the beginning of a relationship

- Physical and sexual attraction is central

- Characterized by urgency, intensity, sexual desire, and anxiety

- Driven by the excitement of being involved with a person whose character is not fully known

- Involves nagging doubts and unanswered questions; the partner remains unexamined so as not to spoil the dream

- Is based on fantasy

- Is consuming, and often exhausting

- Entails discomfort with individual differences

- Relationship not enduring because it lacks a firm foundation

Signs of Mature Love

- Develops gradually through learning about each other

- Sexual attraction is present, but warm affection/friendship is central

- Characterized by calm, peacefulness, empathy, support, trust, confidence, and tolerance of each other; no feelings of being threatened

- Driven by deep attachment; based on extensive knowledge of both positive and negative qualities in the other person; mature acceptance of imperfections

- Partners want to be together but are not obsessed with the relationship

- Is based on empathy

- Is energizing in a healthy way

- Partners have high self-esteem; each has a sense of self-worth with or without the partner and feels complete even without the relationship

- Individuality is accepted

- Each brings out the best in the other; relationship is nurturing

- Partners are patient; feel no need to rush the events of the relationship; there is a sense of security and no fear of losing the partner

- Each encourages the other's growth

- Is enduring and sustaining because it is based on a strong foundation of friendship

Signs of an Addictive Love Relationship

- A feeling of not being able to live without the partner

- Insecurity, distrust, lack of confidence, feeling threatened

- Low self-esteem; looking to partner for validation and affirmation of self-worth

- Fewer happy times together; more time spent on apologies, fear, guilt, and broken promises

- Needing the other in order to feel complete

- Feeling worse about oneself as the relationship progresses

- Loss of self-control

- Making fewer decisions or plans; waiting for the partner to tell you what to do

- Discomfort with individual differences

- Tearing down or criticizing the other

- Feeling as though one is "killing time" until with the partner again

- Rushing things, like sex or marriage, so as not to lose the partner

- Breaking promises to oneself or others because of the relationship

- Being threatened by the other partner's growth

- Constant insecurity and jealousy

- Using drugs or alcohol as coping mechanisms

- Friends or family report that the person is "different" from the way she used to be

How did you fare on these lists? Can you identify your involvement in past romantic relationships and where you want to be today? Remember, I have outlined these lists so that if you choose to become involved romantically, you can make better choices. There is no law that I am aware of that demands each and every women to have a mate. As women, we are programmed since childhood that we should get married and that staying single is something undesirable. That creates a kind of desperation and hysteria about getting attached to a man, almost at any cost. As an adult woman, you are now free to choose how you want to live. You're strong. You get to choose what is right for your life.

Remember, you are the only role model your children have for the relationships they can expect for themselves in the future. If they see an unhealthy relationship, you can certainly expect that they will have a similar relationship when they are teens or adults. Why wouldn't they? If it were enough for you, why wouldn't it be okay enough for them?

If you decide that you would like to become involved in a romantic relationship, think long and hard about those ideas on the lists above before you become involved in a new romance, and certainly before you introduce your children to your new partner. Children become very insecure and view relationships as purely temporary when a cattle call of men wanders in and out of your life and their lives. That is probably not the image you want to create for them.

A FINAL THOUGHT TO ALL MY STRONG AND WONDERFUL "SISTERS"

So, you have done significant work on yourself and have begun to look at all of your relationships—as well as yourself—differently.

Remember that you don't have to "settle" in any part of your life. You don't have to settle for unhealthy, destructive relationships with your parents, friends, partner, children, or in your work environment. You always have choices. You don't have control over the way in which you are treated by abusive people, however you do have 100 percent choice in the decisions you make about your level of contact with those people and the ways in which you allow—or disallow—them to affect your self-concept and success in life.

Visualize a plan for your life and take active steps to follow it. Remember that when you feel helpless, powerless, out of control, anxious, and depressed, the very best cure I know of is positive action on your own behalf. In that way, you do not have to live reactively to other people's plans and ideas for you while you just go along for the ride—even though you don't like where it's taking you. You pick the destination and you make the roadmap. It is your one-and-only life. "Life is not a dress rehearsal," as Dr. Toni Grant, the radio psychologist likes to say. It is opening night and you are the star in the spotlight. What would you like the reviews to say about your performance?

If you remember nothing else from this book, please promise me that you will remember this: *Love is a behavior.*

If you can recall that phrase when interacting with anyone in your life, you will never go astray. Merely by looking at another's behaviors, you will acquire all the information you need about them and be able to make wise decisions about your level of involvement.

I hope this book has been helpful in exploring new ideas for you. In the Resources section, you will find many books, Websites, and telephone numbers that can further your growth.

Take good care of yourself. You deserve it.

Resources

THROUGHOUT THIS BOOK, you have seen what destructive relationships look like, their causes, the impact they have had on your life, and finally, clear steps you can take to extricate yourself from these unhealthy relationships and take control of your future success. The following books and Websites can lead you on the rest of your journey.

I have not included referrals for services that offer psychological counseling because the choice of a therapist is very personal. However, please be assured that there is counseling available to those in every income bracket. Refer to your yellow pages for low-cost counseling centers in your area.

Additional counseling services may be available to you through your place of worship and usually incorporate a spiritual component. Your local YWCA may also be a good resource for therapeutic services and referrals in your area.

Finally, consult the front of your telephone directory for a listing of community services in your area in all categories listed below.

DOMESTIC VIOLENCE

BOOKS

Anderson, Vera. *A Woman Like You: The Face of Domestic Violence.* Seattle, WA: Seal Press, 1997.

Berry, Dawn Bradley. *The Domestic Violence Sourcebook.* New York: McGraw Hill, 2000.

Betancourt, Marian. *What to Do When Love Turns Violent: A Practical Resource for Women in Abusive Relationships.* NY: HarperPerennial Library, 1997.

Dugan, Meg Kennedy and Roger Hock. *It's My Life Now: Starting Over After an Abusive Relationship or Domestic Violence.* NY: Routledge, 2000.

Evans, Patricia. *Verbal Abuse Survivors Speak Out on Relationship and Recovery.* Holbrook, MA: Bob Adams Inc., 1993.

Deaton, Wendy and Michael Hertica. *Growing Free: A Manual for Survivors of Domestic Violence.* Binghamton, NY: Haworth Press, 2001.

Geffner, Robert, Ph.D. and Peter Jaffe, Ph.D. *Children Exposed to Domestic Violence: Current Issues in Research, Intervention, Prevention, and Policy Development.* Binghamton, NY: Haworth Press, 2000.

Mareck, Mary et al. *Breaking Free from Partner Abuse: Voices of Battered Women Caught in the Cycle of Domestic Violence.* Buena Park, CA: Morning Glory Press, 1999.

Mariani, Cliff and Patricia Sokolich. *Domestic Violence Survival Guide.* Fresh Meadows, NY: Looseleaf Law Publishing Corp., 1996.

McDill, Linda and S. Rutherford McDill. *Dangerous Marriage: Breaking the Cycle of Domestic Violence.* NY: Spire Books, 1998.

Murphy-Milano, Susan. *Defending Our Lives: Getting Away from Domestic Violence and Staying Safe.* NY: Anchor Books, 1996.

Murray, Dr. Jill. *But I Love Him: Protecting Your Teen Daughter from Controlling, Abusive Dating Relationships.* NY: ReganBooks, 2000.

Nelson, Noelle. *Dangerous Relationships: How to Stop Domestic Violence Before it Stops You.* Cambridge, MA: Perseus Press, 1997.

NiCarthy, Ginny, M.S.W. *Getting Free: You Can End Abuse and Take Back Your Life*. Seattle, WA: Seal Press, 1997.

O'Leary, Daniel, Ph.D. and Roland D. Mauiro. *Psychological Abuse in Violent Relationships*. NY: Springer Publications, 2001.

Renzetta, Claire and Charles Harvey Miley. *Violence in Gay and Lesbian Domestic Partnerships*. Binghamton, NY: Haworth Press, 1996.

Wilson, Karen. *When Violence Begins at Home: A Comprehensive Guide to Understanding and Ending Domestic Violence*. Alameda, CA: Hunter House, 1997.

WEBSITES

Keyword: Domestic Violence. There are 183,396 sites, so there will be many links to information, support groups, books, and organizations specializing in domestic violence.

ORGANIZATIONS

National Domestic Violence Hotline: 800-799-SAFE. A 24-hour referral service for domestic violence shelters and therapists specializing in the treatment of abusive relationships.

CHILDHOOD TRAUMA AND ABUSIVE FAMILIES

BOOKS

Bass, Ellen and Laura Davis. *The Courage to Heal: A Guide for Women Survivors of Child Sexual Abuse*. NY: HarperPerennial, 1994.

Bass, Ellen and Louise Thornton. *I Never Told Anyone: Writings by Women Survivors of Child Sexual Abuse*. NY: HarperCollins, 1991.

Cameron, Grant. *What About Me? A Guide for Men Helping Female Partners Deal with Childhood Sexual Abuse.* NY: Creative Bound, 1994.

Farmer, Steven. *Adult Children of Abusive Parents: A Healing Program for Those Who Have Been Physically, Sexually, or Emotionally Abused.* NY: Ballantine Books, 1990.

Forward, Susan. *Toxic Parents: Overcoming their Hurtful Legacy and Reclaiming Your Life.* NY: Bantam Books, 1990.

Gil, Eliana. *Outgrowing the Pain: A Book for and About Adults Abused as Children.* NY: DTP, 1998.

McCarthy, Barry and Emily McCarthy. *Confronting the Victim Role: Healing from an Abusive Childhood.* NY: Carroll and Graff, 1993.

Napier, Nancy. *Getting Through the Day: Strategies for Adults Hurt as Children.* NY: W.W. Norton and Co., 1994.

Neuharth, Dan. *If You Had Controlling Parents: How to Make Peace with Your Past and Take Your Place in the World.* NY: Cliff Street Books, 1999.

Wisechild, Louise. *The Mother I Carry: A Memoir of Healing from Emotional Abuse.* Seattle, WA, 1993.

WEBSITES

Keywords: Sexual abuse, Childhood abuse. There are many links to information, support groups, books, and organizations specializing in recovery of childhood abuse.

www.ksu.edu/ucs/dysfunc.html. A Website containing books and support groups dealing with dysfunctional families.

www.boxplanet.com. A Website dedicated to information about rejecting and neglectful parents.

ORGANIZATIONS

Adults Molested as Children (AMAC). Phone numbers are different in each city. Look in the community services guide in the front of your telephone directory.

{}

American Psychological Association: (800) 374-2721 or visit their Website at **www.apa.org.**
American Academy of Pediatrics: (847) 434-4000 or visit their Website at **www.aap.org.**

SELF-ESTEEM, SHAME AND GUILT, AND EMOTIONAL WELL-BEING

BOOKS

Aron, Elaine. *The Highly Sensitive Person: How to Thrive When the World Overwhelms You.* NY: Broadway Books, 1999.

Bach, George R and Herb Goldberg. *Creative Aggression: The Art of Assertive Living.* Gretna, LA: Wellness Institute Books, 1974.

Branden, Nathaniel. *Honoring the Self: The Psychology of Confidence and Respect.* NY: Bantam Books, 1985.

Branden, Nathaniel. *How to Raise Your Self-Esteem.* NY: Bantam Books, 1988.

Branden, Nathaniel. *The Six Pillars of Self-Esteem.* NY: Bantam Books, 1995.

Bradshaw, John. *Healing the Shame that Binds You.* Deerfield Beach, FL: Health Communications, Inc., 1988.

Burns, David, M.D. *The Feeling Good Handbook.* NY: Penguin Books, 1990.

Burns, David, M.D. *Ten Days to Self-Esteem.* San Francisco: Quill Books, 1999.

Carter, Steven. *Men Like Women Who Like Themselves (and Other Secrets that the Smartest Women Know).* NY: DTP, 1997.

Matthews, Andrew. *Being Happy: A Handbook to Greater Confidence and Security.* NY: Price Stern Sloan, 1990.

Mellody, Pia. *Facing Codependence.* NY: HarperCollins, 1989.

Middleton-Moz, Jane. *Shame and Guilt: Masters of Disguise.* Deerfield Beach, FL: Health Communications Inc., 1990.

Potter, Ronald and Patricia Potter-Efron. *Letting Go of Shame.* Center City, MN: Hazelden Information Education, 1996.

Sanford, Linda and Mary Ellen Donovan. *Women and Self-Esteem.* NY: Viking Press, 1985.

Steinem, Gloria. *Revolution from Within: A Book of Self-Esteem*. NY: Little, Brown and Co., 1993.

Vanzant, Iyanla. *Faith in the Valley: Lessons for Women on the Journey Toward Peace*. NY: Simon & Schuster, 1996.

Vanzant, Iyanla. *In the Meantime: Finding Yourself and the Love You Want*. NY: Simon & Schuster, 1998.

Vanzant, Iyanla and Awo Osun Kunle Erindele. *Yesterday, I Cried: Celebrating the Lessons of Living and Loving*. NY: Fireside Books, 2000.

WEBSITES

www.theselfesteeminstitute.com. A Website dealing with issues of self-esteem.

www.breakingthechain.com. A Website dedicated to issues of self-esteem, social anxiety, and anger.

www.aolwomen.com. This Website has many good articles and resources dealing with all aspects of women's emotional and physical health and well-being.

www.ivillage.com. A Website dealing with many aspects of women's emotional health and well-being as well as physical health articles and chat rooms.

PERSONAL POWER

BOOKS

Capacchione, Lucia. *Visioning: Ten Steps to Designing the Life of Your Dreams*. NY: JP Tarcher, 2000.

Covey, Stephen. *The Seven Habits of Highly Effective People*. NY: Fireside Books, 1990.

De Becker, Gavin. *The Gift of Fear: Survival Signals that Protect Us From Violence*. NY: Dell Books, 1998.

Ellis, David. *Creating Your Future*. Boston, MA: Houghton Mifflin, 1999.

Godwin, Malcolm. *Who Are You? 101 Ways of Seeing Yourself.* NY: Penguin Books, 2000.

Jeffers, Susan. *Feel the Fear and Do It Anyway.* NY: Fawcett Books, 1992.

Markova, Dawna. *I Will Not Die an Unlived Life: Reclaiming Purpose and Passion.* Berkeley, CA: Conari Press, 2000.

McGraw, Phillip, Ph.D. *Life Strategies: Doing What Works, Doing What Matters.* NY: Hyperion, 1999.

McMeekin, Carl. *The Twelve Steps of Highly Creative Women: A Portable Mentor.* Berkeley, CA: Conari Press, 2000.

Myss, Caroline. *Anatomy of the Spirit: The Seven Stages of Power and Healing.* NY: Random House, 1997.

Nepo, Mark. *The Book of Awakening: Having the Life You Want By Being Present to the Life You Have.* Berkeley, CA: Conari Press, 2000.

Prather, Hugh and Gerald Jampolsky. *The Little Book of Letting Go: A Revolutionary 30-Day Program to Cleanse Your Mind, Lift Your Spirit, and Replenish Your Soul.* Berkeley, CA: Conari Press, 2000.

Richardson, Cheryl. *Life Makeovers.* NY: Broadway Books, 2000.

Richardson, Cheryl. *Take Time for Your Life: A Personal Coach's Seven-Step Program for Creating the Life You Want.* NY: Broadway Books, 1999.

Robbins, Anthony and Frederick L. CoVan. *Awaken the Giant Within: How to Take Immediate Control of Your Mental, Emotional, Physical, and Financial Destiny.* NY: Fireside Books, 1993.

Robbins, Anthony et al. *Unlimited Power: The New Science of Personal Achievement.* NY: Fireside Books, 1997.

Zukav, Gary. *The Seat of the Soul.* NY: Fireside Books, 1990.

WORKPLACE ABUSE
AND SEXUAL HARASSMENT

BOOKS

Callender, Dale. *Sexual Harassment Claims Step-By-Step*. Hauppauge, NY: Barrons Educational Series, 1998.

Demars, Nan. *You Want Me to Do What? When, Where, and How to Draw the Line at Work*. NY: Fireside Books, 1998.

Lemoncheck, Linda and James Sterba. *Sexual Harassment: Issues and Answers*. NY: Oxford University Press, 2001.

Neville, Kathleen. *Internal Affairs: The Abuse of Power, Sexual Harassment, and Hypocrisy in the Workplace*. E-book: McGraw-Hill.

Petrocelli, William and Barbara Repa. *Sexual Harassment on the Job: What It Is and How to Stop It*. Berkeley, CA: Nolo Press, 1998.

Weiss, Donald H. *Fair, Square, and Legal: Safe Hiring, Managing & Firing Practices to Keep You & Your Company Out of Court*. NY: Amacom Books, 1999.

WEBSITES

www.law.com. A Website dedicated to articles on all aspects of the law, including workplace abuse and sexual harassment.

ORGANIZATIONS

Equal Employment Opportunity Commission (EEOC): For information about local field offices, call (800) 669-4000. You can also visit their Website at **www.eeoc.gov.**

NEW RELATIONSHIPS ... OR NOT

BOOKS

Anders, Dana et al. *Single and Content*. Nashville, TN: W. Publishing, 1999.

Clements, Marcelle. *The Improvised Woman: Single Women Reinventing Single Life*. NY: WW Norton and Co., 1999.

Collins, Bryn, Ph.D. *How to Recognize Emotional Unavailability and Make Healthier Relationship Choices*. NY: MFJ Books, 1997.

Cowan, Connell and Melvyn Kinder. *Smart Women/Foolish Choices: Finding the Right Men, Avoiding the Wrong Ones*. NY: New American Library, 1991.

Forward, Susan and Joan Torres. *Men Who Hate Women and the Women Who Love Them*. NY: Bantam Books, 1987.

Norwood, Robin. *Women Who Love Too Much: Why You Keep Wishing and Hoping He'll Change*. NY: Pocket Books, 1991.

Widder, Wendy. *Living Whole Without a Better Half*. Grand Rapids, MI: Kregel Publications, 2000.

Zobel, Allia. *The Joy of Being Single*. NY: Workman Publications, 1992.

WEBSITES

www.ivillage.com. Again, this Website deals with relationship issues and has chat rooms so that women can compare stories and offer each other advice.

ORGANIZATIONS

There are many organizations that are essentially match-making services and are listed in your local magazines. Parents Without Partners is a national organization. Your local chapter can be found in the community services section of your telephone directory.

CAREER COUNSELING AND JOB TRAINING

BOOKS

Bollis, Richard. *What Color is Your Parachute? A Practical Manual for Job-Hunters and Career-Changers*. Berkeley, CA: Ten Speed Press, 2000.

Finney, Martha and Deborah Dasch. *Find Your Calling, Love Your Life: Paths to Your Truest Self in Life*. NY: Simon and Schuster, 1998.

Isaacson, Lee. *Career Information, Career Counseling, and Career Development*. Boston, MA: Allyn and Bacon, 1999.

Kancher, Carol, Ph.D. *Dare to Change Your Job and Your Life*. Indianapolis, IN: Jist Works, 2000.

Ruge, Kenneth. *Where Do I Go From Here? An Inspirational Guide to Making Authentic Career and Life Choices*. NY: McGraw-Hill Professional Publications, 1998.

Tieger, Paul and Barbara Tieger. *Do What You Are: Discover the Perfect Career for You Through the Secrets of Personality Type*. NY: Little Brown, 2001.

WEBSITES

www.101careers.com Career testing and counseling services

www.Kforce.com. Career counseling services

www.careerdoctor.com. Career counseling services

www.yourpassion.com. Career advice and counseling services

www.career-counseling.com. Just as the name implies.

www.centerfornewdirections.com. Career testing and counseling services.

www.monster.com. Jobs posted in all fields.

www.headhunter.com. Services that will help you find a job.

ORGANIZATIONS

Learning Annex is a national organization that offers evening and weekend classes in all area of interest.

About Dr. Jill Murray

DR. JILL MURRAY is a licensed psychotherapist with a private practice in Laguna Niguel, California. She speaks to thousands of young people and adults around the country each year on topics of abusive relationships, domestic violence, and child abuse. Dr. Murray is the leading authority in America on teen abusive dating relationships, and is one of only a handful of experts who have responded to the immediate crisis in this under-examined area of adolescent life and behavior.

Dr. Murray is already familiar to millions who have seen and heard her on such shows as *Oprah, Montel, Leeza*, and numerous radio call-in shows like *Dr. Laura*, talking about her first book, for teenage girls, *But I Love Him*. This new book comes to us with updated information and tools geared toward negative behaviors in adult relationships and how to change them.

An associate professor of psychology at the American Behavioral Studies Institute, Dr. Jill Murray teaches graduate level courses on "Treatment of Victims of Violent Crimes" and "Teen Couples and the Cycle of Violence." Additionally, she has taught several courses at the community education program, Learning Tree University, on the topics of self-esteem, parenting, "Breaking Free of Abusive Relationships," "Healthy Dating Relationships," and often lectures to members of charitable organizations. Dr. Jill is also on the Board of Directors of Laura's House Domestic Violence Shelter, where she has worked as a therapist for several years.

We hope this JODERE GROUP book has benefited you
in your quest for personal, intellectual,
and spiritual growth.

JODERE GROUP is passionate about bringing new
and exciting books, such as *Destructive Relationships*,
to readers worldwide. Our company was created as a
unique publishing and multimedia avenue for individuals
whose mission it is to positively impact the lives of others.
We recognize the strength of an original thought,
a kind word and a selfless act—and the power of the
individuals who possess them. We are committed
to providing the support, passion, and creativity
necessary for these individuals to achieve
their goals and dreams.

JODERE GROUP is comprised of a dedicated and creative group
of people who strive to provide the highest quality
of books, audio programs, online services, and live
events to people who pursue life-long learning.
It is our personal and professional commitment
to embrace our authors, speakers, and readers
with helpfulness, respect, and enthusiasm.

For more information about
our products, authors, or live events,
please call (800) 569-1002
or visit us on the Web at
www.jodere.com